Contents

Course	Integrative Strategic Experience
Course Number	**BA 466**
	Oregon State University

http://create.mheducation.com

ISBN-10: 1121958451   ISBN-13: 9781121958456

Credits

chapter 1

WHAT IS STRATEGY AND WHY IS IT IMPORTANT?

LEARNING OBJECTIVES

LO1   Understand why every company needs a sound strategy to compete successfully, manage its business operations, and strengthen its prospects for long-term success.

LO2   Develop an awareness of the five most dependable strategic approaches for setting a company apart from rivals and winning a sustainable competitive advantage.

LO3   Understand that a company's strategy tends to evolve over time because of changing circumstances and ongoing management efforts to improve the strategy.

LO4   Learn why it is important for a company to have a viable business model that outlines the company's customer value proposition and its profit formula.

LO5   Learn the three tests of a winning strategy.

Managers in all types of businesses face three central questions. *Where are we now? Where do we want to go from here? How are we going to get there?* Arriving at a thoughtful and probing answer to the question, *"Where are we now?"* prompts managers to examine the company's current financial performance and market standing, its competitively valuable resources and capabilities, its competitive weaknesses, and changing industry conditions that might affect the company. The question *"Where do we want to go from here?"* pushes managers to consider what emerging buyer needs to try to satisfy, which growth opportunities to emphasize, and how the company should change its business makeup. The question *"How are we going to get there?"* challenges managers to craft a series of competitive moves and business approaches—what henceforth will be referred to as the company's **strategy**—for moving the company in the intended direction, staking out a market position, attracting customers, and achieving targeted financial and market performance.

The role of this chapter is to define the concepts of strategy and competitive advantage, the relationship between a company's strategy and its business model, why strategies are partly proactive and partly reactive, and why company strategies evolve over time. Particular attention will be paid to what sets a winning strategy apart from a ho-hum or flawed strategy and why the caliber of a company's strategy determines whether it will enjoy a competitive advantage or be burdened by competitive disadvantage. By the end of this chapter, you will have a clear idea of why the tasks of crafting and executing strategy are core management functions and why excellent execution of an excellent strategy is the most reliable recipe for turning a company into a standout performer.

WHAT DO WE MEAN BY *STRATEGY?*

▶ LO1

Understand why every company needs a sound strategy to compete successfully, manage its business operations, and strengthen its prospects for long-term success.

Developing clear answers to the question *"How are we going to get there?"* is the essence of managing strategically. Rather than rely on the status quo as a road map and dealing with new opportunities and threats as they emerge, managing strategically involves developing a full-blown game plan that spells out the particular competitive moves and operating approaches that will be employed to move the company in the intended direction, strengthen its market position and competitiveness, and meet or beat performance objectives. Thus, a company's strategy is all about *how:*

- *How* to attract and please customers.
- *How* to compete against rivals.
- *How* to position the company in the marketplace and capitalize on attractive opportunities to grow the business.
- *How* best to respond to changing economic and market conditions.
- *How* to manage each functional piece of the business (e.g., R&D, supply chain activities, production, sales and marketing, distribution, finance, and human resources).
- *How* to achieve the company's performance targets.

Of course, a company's strategy includes planning for topics not included in the list above. The important thing to recognize is that every activity involved in

Elements of a Company's Strategy

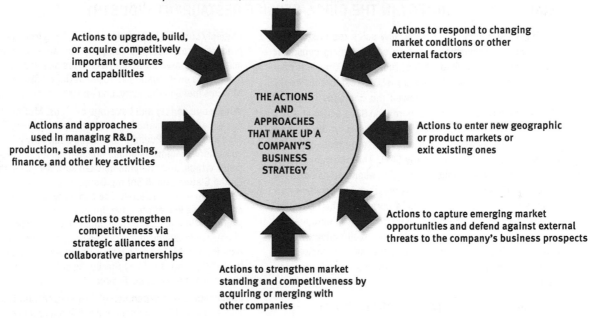

delivering a business's product or service should be guided by strategic thinking. There's really no single activity, process, department, or functional area that should be left to chance. Figure 1.1 presents a diagram showing actions and approaches that make up a company's strategy. Concepts & Connections 1.1 describes the various elements of McDonald's strategy in the quick-service restaurant industry. The capsule makes it clear how the strategy includes actions related to such wide-ranging issues as menu selection, supplier relationships, advertising expenditures, expansion into foreign markets, restaurant operating policies and practices, and responses to changing economic and market conditions.

CORE CONCEPT

A company's **strategy** consists of the competitive moves and business approaches management has developed to attract and please customers, compete successfully, capitalize on opportunities to grow the business, respond to changing market conditions, conduct operations, and achieve performance objectives.

STRATEGY AND THE QUEST FOR COMPETITIVE ADVANTAGE

The heart and soul of any strategy is the actions and moves in the marketplace that managers are taking to gain a competitive edge over rivals.[1] In Concepts & Connections 1.1, it's evident that McDonald's has gained a competitive advantage over rivals through its efforts to minimize costs, ensure a high level

▶**LO2**

Develop an awareness of the five most dependable strategic approaches for setting a company apart from rivals and winning a sustainable competitive advantage.

CONCEPTS & CONNECTIONS 1.1

MCDONALD'S STRATEGY IN THE QUICK-SERVICE RESTAURANT INDUSTRY

In 2011, McDonald's was setting new sales records despite a widespread economic slowdown and declining consumer confidence in the United States. More than 60 million customers visited one of McDonald's 32,000 restaurants in 117 countries each day, which allowed the company to record 2010 revenues and earnings of more than $24.1 billion and $4.9 billion, respectively. McDonald's performance in the marketplace allowed its share price to increase by more than 150 percent between 2005 and early 2011. The company's sales were holding up well amid the ongoing economic uncertainty in early 2011, with global sales as measured in constant currencies increasing by more than 4 percent in the first quarter. Its earnings per share had risen to nearly 30 percent. The company's success was a result of its well-conceived and executed Plan-to-Win strategy that focused on "being better, not just bigger." Key initiatives of the Plan-to-Win strategy included:

- **Improved restaurant operations.** McDonald's global restaurant operations improvement process involved employee training programs ranging from on-the-job training for new crew members to college-level management courses offered at the company's Hamburger University. The company also sent nearly 200 high-potential employees annually to its McDonald's Leadership Institute to build the leadership skills needed by its next generation of senior managers. McDonald's commitment to employee development earned the company a place on *Fortune's* list of Top 25 Global Companies for Leaders in 2010. The company also trained its store managers to closely monitor labor, food, and utility costs.

- **Affordable pricing.** In addition to tackling operating costs in each of its restaurants, McDonald's kept its prices low by scrutinizing administrative costs and other corporate expenses. McDonald's saw the poor economy in the United States as opportunity to renegotiate its advertising contracts with newspapers and television networks. The company also began to replace its company-owned vehicles with more fuel-efficient models when gasoline prices escalated dramatically in the United States. However, McDonald's did not choose to sacrifice product quality in order to offer lower prices. The company implemented extensive supplier monitoring programs to ensure that its suppliers did not change product specifications to lower costs. For example, the company's chicken breasts were routinely checked for weight when arriving from suppliers' production facilities. The company's broad approach to minimizing non-value-adding expenses allowed it to offer more items on its Dollar Menu in the United States, its Ein Mal Eins menu in Germany, and its 100 Yen menu in Japan.

- **Wide menu variety and beverage choices.** McDonald's has expanded its menu beyond the popular-selling Big Mac and Quarter Pounder to include such new healthy quick-service items as grilled chicken salads, chicken snack wraps, and premium chicken sandwiches in the United States, Lemon Shrimp Burgers in Germany, and Ebi shrimp wraps in Japan. The company has also added an extensive line of premium coffees that included espressos, cappuccinos, and lattes sold in its McCafe restaurant locations in the United States, Europe, and Asia/Pacific. McDonald's latte was judged "as good or better" than lattes sold by Starbucks or Dunkin' Donuts in a review by the *Chicago Tribune*.

- **Convenience and expansion of dining opportunities.** The addition of McCafes helped McDonald's increase same-store sales by extending traditional dining hours. Customers wanting a mid-morning coffee or an afternoon snack helped keep store traffic high after McDonald's had sold it last Egg McMuffin, McGriddle, or chicken biscuit and before the lunch crowd arrived to order Big Macs, Quarter Pounders, chicken sandwiches, or salads. The company also extended its drive-thru hours to 24 hours in more than 25,000 locations in cities around the world where consumers tended to eat at all hours of the day. At many high-traffic locations in the United States, double drive-thru lanes were added to get customers served more quickly.

- **Ongoing restaurant reinvestment and international expansion.** With more than 14,000 restaurants in the United States, the focus of McDonald's expansion of units was in rapidly growing emerging markets such as China. McDonald's planned to have nearly 2,000 restaurants in China by 2013. The company also intended to refurbish 90 percent of the interiors and 50 percent of the exteriors of its restaurants by the end of 2012 to make its restaurants a pleasant place for both customers to dine and employees to work.

Sources: Janet Adamy, "McDonald's Seeks Way to Keep Sizzling," *The Wall Street Journal Online,* March 10, 2009; various annual reports; various company press releases.

of food quality, add innovative new menu items, and keep its prices low. A creative, distinctive strategy such as that used by McDonald's is a company's most reliable ticket for developing a sustainable competitive advantage and earning above-average profits. A **sustainable competitive advantage** allows a company to attract sufficiently large numbers of buyers who have a lasting preference for its products or services over those offered by rivals, despite the efforts of competitors to offset that appeal and overcome the company's advantage. The bigger and more durable the competitive advantage, the better a company's prospects for winning in the marketplace and earning superior long-term profits relative to rivals.

> **CORE CONCEPT**
> A company achieves **sustainable competitive advantage** when an attractively large number of buyers develop a durable preference for its products or services over the offerings of competitors, despite the efforts of competitors to overcome or erode its advantage.

In most industries companies have considerable freedom in choosing among marketplace moves and business approaches designed to produce a competitive edge over rivals. For example, a company can compete against rivals by striving to keep costs low and selling its products at attractively low prices. Or it can aim at offering buyers more features or better performance or more personalized customer service. But whatever the strategic approach taken, it stands a better chance of succeeding when aimed at (1) appealing to buyers in ways that *set a company apart from its rivals* and (2) staking out a market position that is not crowded with strong competitors. Indeed, the essence of good strategy making is about choosing to compete differently—doing what rivals don't do or can't do—and thereby delivering value to buyers that proves to be superior and unique to what is offered by rivals.

> Mimicking the strategies of successful industry rivals—with either copycat product offerings or efforts to stake out the same market position—rarely works. A creative, distinctive strategy that sets a company apart from rivals and yields a competitive advantage is a company's most reliable ticket for earning above-average profits.

Five of the most frequently used and dependable strategic approaches to setting a company apart from rivals and winning a sustainable competitive advantage are:

1. *A low-cost provider strategy*—achieving a cost-based advantage over rivals. Walmart and Southwest Airlines have earned strong market positions because of the low-cost advantages they have achieved over their rivals and their consequent ability to underprice competitors. Low-cost provider strategies can produce a durable competitive edge when rivals find it hard to match the low-cost leader's approach to driving costs out of the business.

2. *A broad differentiation strategy*—seeking to differentiate the company's product or service from rivals' in ways that will appeal to a broad spectrum of buyers. Successful adopters of broad differentiation strategies include Johnson & Johnson in baby products (product reliability) and Apple (innovative products). Differentiation strategies can be powerful so long as a company is sufficiently innovative to thwart rivals' attempts to copy or closely imitate its product offering.

3. *A focused low-cost strategy*—concentrating on a narrow buyer segment (or market niche) and outcompeting rivals by having lower costs than rivals and thus being able to serve niche members at a lower price. Private-label manufacturers of food, health and beauty products, and nutritional supplements use their low-cost advantage to offer supermarket buyers lower prices than those demanded by producers of branded products.

4. *A focused differentiation strategy*—concentrating on a narrow buyer segment (or market niche) and outcompeting rivals by offering niche members customized attributes that meet their tastes and requirements better than rivals' products. Chanel and Rolex have sustained their advantage in the luxury goods industry through a focus on affluent consumers demanding luxury and prestige.

5. *A best-cost provider strategy*—giving customers more value for the money by satisfying buyers' expectations on key quality/features/performance/service attributes, while beating their price expectations. This approach is a hybrid strategy that blends elements of low-cost provider and differentiation strategies; the aim is to have the lowest (best) costs and prices among sellers offering products with comparable differentiating attributes. Target's best-cost advantage allows it to give discount store shoppers more value for the money by offering an attractive product lineup and an appealing shopping ambience at low prices.

WHY A COMPANY'S STRATEGY EVOLVES OVER TIME

LO3

Understand that a company's strategy tends to evolve over time because of changing circumstances and ongoing management efforts to improve the strategy.

The appeal of a strategy that yields a sustainable competitive advantage is that it offers the potential for an enduring edge over rivals. However, managers of every company must be willing and ready to modify the strategy in response to the unexpected moves of competitors, shifting buyer needs and preferences, emerging market opportunities, new ideas for improving the strategy, and mounting evidence that the strategy is not working well. Most of the time, a company's strategy evolves incrementally as management fine-tunes various pieces of the strategy and adjusts the strategy to respond to unfolding events. However, on occasion, major strategy shifts are called for, such as when the strategy is clearly failing or when industry conditions change in dramatic ways.

Regardless of whether a company's strategy changes gradually or swiftly, the important point is that the task of crafting strategy is not a onetime event, but is always a work in progress.[2] The evolving nature of a company's strategy means the typical company strategy is a blend of (1) *proactive* moves to improve the company's financial performance and secure a competitive edge and (2) *adaptive* reactions to unanticipated developments and fresh market conditions—see Figure 1.2.[3] The biggest portion of a company's current strategy flows from ongoing actions that have proven themselves in the marketplace and newly launched initiatives aimed at building a larger lead over rivals

> Changing circumstances and ongoing management efforts to improve the strategy cause a company's strategy to evolve over time—a condition that makes the task of crafting a strategy a work in progress, not a onetime event.

▶FIGURE 1.2 **A Company's Strategy Is a Blend of Planned Initiatives and Unplanned Reactive Adjustments**

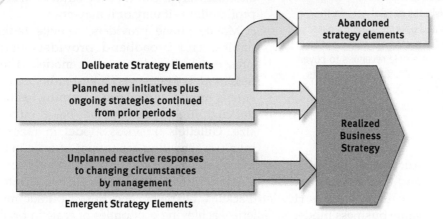

and further boosting financial performance. This part of management's action plan for running the company is its proactive, **deliberate strategy.**

At times, certain components of a company's deliberate strategy will fail in the marketplace and become **abandoned strategy elements.** Also, managers must always be willing to supplement or modify planned, deliberate strategy elements with as-needed reactions to unanticipated developments. Inevitably, there will be occasions when market and competitive conditions take unexpected turns that call for some kind of strategic reaction. Novel strategic moves on the part of rival firms, unexpected shifts in customer preferences, fast-changing technological developments, and new market opportunities call for unplanned, reactive adjustments that form the company's **emergent strategy.** As shown in Figure 1.2, a company's **realized strategy** tends to be a *combination* of deliberate planned elements and unplanned, emergent elements.

THE RELATIONSHIP BETWEEN A COMPANY'S STRATEGY AND ITS BUSINESS MODEL

Closely related to the concept of strategy is the concept of a company's **business model.** A company's business model is management's blueprint for delivering a valuable product or service to customers in a manner that will generate revenues sufficient to cover costs and yield an attractive profit.[4] The two elements of a company's business model are (1) its *customer value proposition* and (2) its *profit formula.* The customer value proposition lays out the company's approach to satisfying buyer wants and needs at a price customers will consider a good value. The greater the value provided and the lower the price, the more attractive the value proposition is to customers. The profit formula describes the company's approach to determining a cost structure that will allow for acceptable profits given the pricing tied to its customer value proposition. The lower the costs given the customer value proposition, the greater the ability of the business model to be a moneymaker. The nitty-gritty issue surrounding a company's business model is whether it can execute its customer value proposition profitably. Just because company managers have crafted a strategy

▶**LO4**

Learn why it is important for a company to have a viable business model that outlines the company's customer value proposition and its profit formula.

> **CORE CONCEPT**
>
> A company's **business model** sets forth how its strategy and operating approaches will create value for customers, while at the same time generate ample revenues to cover costs and realize a profit. The two elements of a company's business model are its (1) customer value proposition and (2) its profit formula.

for competing and running the business does not automatically mean that the strategy will lead to profitability—it may or it may not.[5]

Mobile phone providers, satellite radio companies, and broadband providers employ a subscription-based business model. The business model of network TV and radio broadcasters entails providing free programming to audiences but charging advertising fees based on audience size. Gillette's business model in razor blades involves achieving economies of scale in the production of its shaving products, selling razors at an attractively low price, and then making money on repeat purchases of razor blades. Printer manufacturers such as Hewlett-Packard, Lexmark, and Epson pursue much the same business model as Gillette—achieving economies of scale in production and selling printers at a low (virtually break-even) price and making large profit margins on the repeat purchases of printer supplies, especially ink cartridges. Concepts & Connections 1.2 discusses the contrasting business models of Netflix and Redbox in the movie rental industry.

THE THREE TESTS OF A WINNING STRATEGY

LO5

Learn the three tests of a winning strategy.

Three questions can be used to distinguish a winning strategy from a so-so or flawed strategy:

1. *How well does the strategy fit the company's situation?* To qualify as a winner, a strategy has to be well matched to the company's external and internal situations. The strategy must fit competitive conditions in the industry and other aspects of the enterprise's external environment. At the same time, it should be tailored to the company's collection of competitively important resources and capabilities. It's unwise to build a strategy upon the company's weaknesses or pursue a strategic approach that requires resources that are deficient in the company. Unless a strategy exhibits tight fit with both the external and internal aspects of a company's overall situation, it is unlikely to produce respectable first-rate business results.

> A winning strategy must fit the company's external and internal situation, build sustainable competitive advantage, and improve company performance.

2. *Is the strategy helping the company achieve a sustainable competitive advantage?* Strategies that fail to achieve a durable competitive advantage over rivals are unlikely to produce superior performance for more than a brief period of time. Winning strategies enable a company to achieve a competitive advantage over key rivals that is long lasting. The bigger and more durable the competitive edge that the strategy helps build, the more powerful it is.

3. *Is the strategy producing good company performance?* The mark of a winning strategy is strong company performance. Two kinds of performance improvements tell the most about the caliber of a company's strategy: (1) gains in profitability and financial strength and (2) advances in the company's competitive strength and market standing.

CONCEPTS & CONNECTIONS 1.2

NETFLIX AND REDBOX: TWO CONTRASTING BUSINESS MODELS

The strategies of rival companies are often predicated on strikingly different business models. Consider, for example, the business models of Redbox and Netflix in the movie rental industry.

The business models of movie rental companies Netflix and Redbox have both proven to be moneymakers even though they differ significantly. Netflix's subscription-based business model allows subscribers paying a flat monthly fee to receive movies delivered to their homes by mail and stream movies and TV episodes over the Internet. In 2011, Netflix had more than 23 million subscribers in the United States and Canada and had generated revenues of more than $2.1 billion in fiscal 2010. The company's net income in 2010 exceeded $160 million. The business model employed by

Redbox entailed the deployment of more 30,000 DVD rental vending machines in high-traffic retail locations such as discount stores, drugstores, convenience stores, and quick-service restaurants. Redbox charged customers $1 per day to rent movies from its vending machine kiosks and allowed customers to return the movie to the same location or any other Redbox kiosk location. Customers were able to browse each machine's inventory of available movies while using the machine's touch screen or could reserve a movie online or from a smartphone. Customers could also purchase movies from a Redbox kiosk for $7. Redbox's annual revenues and operating income in 2010 were approximately $1.2 billion and $193 million, respectively.

	NETFLIX	**REDBOX**
Customer Value Proposition	Convenient delivery of movies to customers' mailboxes or streamed to their PCs, Macs, or TVs. Eight subscription plans ranging from $4.99 to $47.99 allowed customers to choose from limited or unlimited video streaming and receive limited or unlimited DVDs. Netflix's subscription plan pricing allowed customers to have as few as one DVD out at a time and as many as 8 movies out at a given time.	Economical 24-hour movie rentals and purchases that could be picked up at conveniently located DVD kiosks. DVDs could be returned to any kiosk location. DVDs could also be reserved online or from a smartphone.
Profit Formula	*Revenue Generation:* Monthly subscription fees started at $4.99 for up to two hours of video streaming to a PC or Mac and two DVDs per month. The company's $8.99 plan allowed unlimited DVDs per month with one title out at a time, plus unlimited video streaming to a PC, Mac, or to a TV via a Netflix-ready device. The company's $47.99 plan allowed eight titles out at a time and unlimited streaming. Netflix had more than 23 million subscribers to the various plans in 2011. *Cost Structure:* Fixed and variable costs associated with DVD acquisitions, licensing fees and revenue sharing agreements, development of movie selection software, website operation and maintenance, Internet streaming capabilities, distribution center operations, and administrative activities. *Profit Margin:* Netflix's profitability was dependent on attracting a sufficiently large number of subscribers to cover its costs and provide for attractive profits.	*Revenue Generation:* Customers could rent DVDs for $1 per day and purchase DVDs for $7 from any of Redbox's 30,000 + DVD vending machine kiosks. *Cost Structure:* Fixed and variable costs associated with the kiosk purchases and deployment, DVD acquisitions, licensing fees and revenue sharing agreements, website operation and maintenance, kiosk stocking, and administrative activities. *Profit Margin:* Redbox's profitability was dependent on generating sufficient revenues from DVD rentals and sales to cover costs and provide for a healthy bottom line.

Source: Company documents, 10-Ks, and information posted on their websites.

Strategies that come up short on one or more of the above tests are plainly less appealing than strategies passing all three tests with flying colors. Managers should use the same questions when evaluating either proposed or existing strategies. New initiatives that don't seem to match the company's internal and external situation should be scrapped before they come to fruition, while existing strategies must be scrutinized on a regular basis to ensure they have good fit, offer a competitive advantage, and have contributed to above-average performance or performance improvements.

THE ROAD AHEAD

Throughout the chapters to come and the accompanying case collection, the spotlight is trained on the foremost question in running a business enterprise: *What must managers do, and do well, to make a company a winner in the marketplace?* The answer that emerges is that doing a good job of managing inherently requires good strategic thinking and good management of the strategy-making, strategy-executing process.

The mission of this book is to provide a solid overview of what every business student and aspiring manager needs to know about crafting and executing strategy. We will explore what good strategic thinking entails, describe the core concepts and tools of strategic analysis, and examine the ins and outs of crafting and executing strategy. The accompanying cases will help build your skills in both diagnosing how well the strategy-making, strategy-executing task is being performed and prescribing actions for how the strategy in question or its execution can be improved. The strategic management course that you are enrolled in may also include a strategy simulation exercise where you will run a company in head-to-head competition with companies run by your classmates. Your mastery of the strategic management concepts presented in the following chapters will put you in a strong position to craft a winning strategy for your company and figure out how to execute it in a cost-effective and profitable manner. As you progress through the chapters of the text and the activities assigned during the term, we hope to convince you that first-rate capabilities in crafting and executing strategy are essential to good management.

KEY POINTS

1. A company's strategy is management's game plan to grow the business, attract and please customers, compete successfully, conduct operations, and achieve targeted levels of performance.

2. The central thrust of a company's strategy is undertaking moves to build and strengthen the company's long-term competitive position and financial performance. Ideally, this results in a competitive advantage over rivals that then becomes the company's ticket to above-average profitability.

3. A company's strategy typically evolves over time, arising from a blend of (1) proactive and deliberate actions on the part of company managers and (2) adaptive emergent responses to unanticipated developments and fresh market conditions.

4. Closely related to the concept of strategy is the concept of a company's business model. A company's business model is management's blueprint for delivering a valuable product or service to customers in a manner that will generate revenues sufficient to cover costs and yield an attractive profit. The two elements of a company's business model are its (1) customer value proposition and (2) its profit formula.

5. A winning strategy fits the circumstances of a company's external and internal situations, builds competitive advantage, and boosts company performance.

ASSURANCE OF LEARNING EXERCISES

1. Based on what you know about the quick-service restaurant industry, does McDonald's strategy as described in Concepts & Connections 1.1 seem to be well matched to industry and competitive conditions? Does the strategy seem to be keyed to a cost-based advantage, differentiating features, serving the unique needs of a niche, or some combination of these? What is there about McDonald's strategy that can lead to sustainable competitive advantage?

LO1, LO2

www.mcgrawhillconnect.com

2. Elements of Walmart's strategy have evolved in meaningful ways since the company's founding in 1962. Prepare a one- to two-page report that discusses how its strategy has evolved after reviewing all of the links at Walmart's About Us page, which can be found at walmartstores.com/AboutUs/. Your report should also assess how well Walmart's strategy passes the three tests of a winning strategy.

LO3, LO5

www.mcgrawhillconnect.com

3. Go to www.nytco.com/investors and check whether *The New York Times'* recent financial reports indicate that its business model is working. Does the company's business model remain sound as more consumers go to the Internet to find general information and stay abreast of current events and news stories? Is its revenue stream from advertisements growing or declining? Are its subscription fees and circulation increasing or declining?

LO4

EXERCISES FOR SIMULATION PARTICIPANTS

This chapter discusses three questions that must be answered by managers of organizations of all sizes:

- Where are we now?
- Where do we want to go from here?
- How are we going to get there?

After you have read the Participant's Guide or Player's Manual for the strategy simulation exercise that you will participate in this academic term, you and your co-managers should come up with brief one- or two-paragraph answers to these three questions *before* entering your first set of decisions. While your answers to the first of the three questions can be developed from your reading of the manual, the second and third questions will require a collaborative discussion among the members of your company's management team about how you intend to manage the company you have been assigned to run.

LO1, LO2   1.   What is our company's current situation? A substantive answer to this question should cover the following issues:
- Is your company in a good, average, or weak competitive position vis-à-vis rival companies?
- Does your company appear to be in sound financial condition?
- What problems does your company have that need to be addressed?

LO3, LO5   2.   Where do we want to take the company during the time we are in charge? A complete answer to this question should say something about each of the following:
- What goals or aspirations do you have for your company?
- What do you want the company to be known for?
- What market share would you like your company to have after the first five decision rounds?
- By what amount or percentage would you like to increase total profits of the company by the end of the final decision round?
- What kinds of performance outcomes will signal that you and your co-managers are managing the company in a successful manner?

LO3, LO4   3.   How are we going to get there? Your answer should cover these issues:
- Which of the basic strategic and competitive approaches discussed in this chapter do you think makes the most sense to pursue?
- What kind of competitive advantage over rivals will you try to achieve?
- How would you describe the company's business model?
- What kind of actions will support these objectives?

ENDNOTES

1.   Michael E. Porter, "What Is Strategy?" *Harvard Business Review* 74, no. 6 (November–December 1996).

2.   Cynthia A. Montgomery, "Putting Leadership Back Into Strategy," *Harvard Business Review* 86, no. 1 (January 2008).

3.   Henry Mintzberg and Joseph Lampel, "Reflecting on the Strategy Process, *Sloan Management Review* 40, no. 3 (Spring 1999); Henry Mintzberg and J. A. Waters, "Of Strategies, Deliberate and Emergent," *Strategic Management Journal* 6 (1985); Costas Markides, "Strategy as Balance: From 'Either-Or' to 'And,'" *Business Strategy Review* 12, no. 3 (September 2001); Henry Mintzberg, Bruce Ahlstrand, and Joseph Lampel, *Strategy Safari: A Guided Tour through the Wilds of Strategic Management* (New York: Free Press, 1998); and C. K. Prahalad and Gary Hamel, "The Core Competence of the Corporation," *Harvard Business Review* 70, no. 3 (May–June 1990).

4.   Mark W. Johnson, Clayton M. Christensen, and Henning Kagermann, "Reinventing Your Business Model," *Harvard Business Review* 86, no. 12 (December 2008); and Joan Magretta, "Why Business Models Matter," *Harvard Business Review* 80, no. 5 (May 2002).

5.   W. Chan Kim and Renée Mauborgne, "How Strategy Shapes Structure," *Harvard Business Review* 87, no. 9 (September 2009).

chapter 2

CHARTING A COMPANY'S DIRECTION: VISION AND MISSION, OBJECTIVES, AND STRATEGY

LEARNING OBJECTIVES

LO1   Grasp why it is critical for company managers to have a clear strategic vision of where a company needs to head and why.

LO2   Understand the importance of setting both strategic and financial objectives.

LO3   Understand why the strategic initiatives taken at various organizational levels must be tightly coordinated to achieve companywide performance targets.

LO4   Become aware of what a company must do to achieve operating excellence and to execute its strategy proficiently.

LO5   Become aware of the role and responsibility of a company's board of directors in overseeing the strategic management process.

Crafting and executing strategy are the heart and soul of managing a business enterprise. But exactly what is involved in developing a strategy and executing it proficiently? What are the various components of the strategy-making, strategy-executing process and to what extent are company personnel—aside from senior management—involved in the process? This chapter presents an overview of the ins and outs of crafting and executing company strategies. Special attention will be given to management's direction-setting responsibilities—charting a strategic course, setting performance targets, and choosing a strategy capable of producing the desired outcomes. We will also explain why strategy making is a task for a company's entire management team and discuss which kinds of strategic decisions tend to be made at which levels of management. The chapter concludes with a look at the roles and responsibilities of a company's board of directors and how good corporate governance protects shareholder interests and promotes good management.

WHAT DOES THE STRATEGY-MAKING, STRATEGY-EXECUTING PROCESS ENTAIL?

The managerial process of crafting and executing a company's strategy consists of five integrated stages:

1. *Developing a strategic vision* that charts the company's long-term direction, a *mission statement* that describes the company's business, and a set of *core values* to guide the pursuit of the strategic vision and mission.

2. *Setting objectives* for measuring the company's performance and tracking its progress in moving in the intended long-term direction.

3. *Crafting a strategy* for advancing the company along the path to management's envisioned future and achieving its performance objectives.

4. *Implementing and executing the chosen strategy* efficiently and effectively.

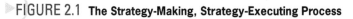

▶FIGURE 2.1 **The Strategy-Making, Strategy-Executing Process**

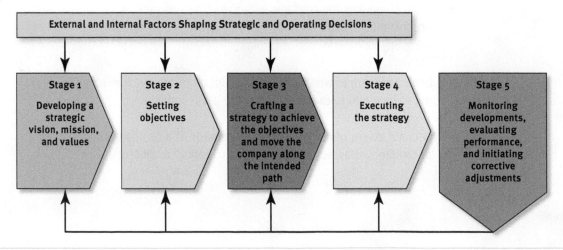

5. *Monitoring developments, evaluating performance, and initiating corrective adjustments* that are needed in the company's long-term direction, objectives, strategy, or approach to strategy execution.

Figure 2.1 displays this five-stage process. The model illustrates the need for management to evaluate a number of external and internal factors in deciding upon a strategic direction, appropriate objectives, and approaches to crafting and executing strategy (see Table 2.1). Management's decisions that are made in the strategic management process must be shaped by the prevailing economic conditions and competitive environment and the company's own internal resources and competitive capabilities. These strategy-shaping conditions will be the focus of Chapters 3 and 4.

The model shown in Figure 2.1 also illustrates the need for management to evaluate the company's performance on an ongoing basis. Any indication that the company is failing to achieve its objectives calls for corrective adjustments in one of the first four stages of the process. The company's implementation efforts might have fallen short and new tactics must be devised to fully exploit the potential of the company's strategy. If management determines that the company's execution efforts are sufficient, it should challenge the assumptions underlying the company's business strategy and alter the strategy to better fit competitive conditions and the company's internal capabilities. If the company's strategic approach to competition is rated as sound, then perhaps management set overly ambitious targets for the company's performance.

▶ TABLE 2.1

Factors Shaping Decisions in the Strategy-Making, Strategy-Executing Process	
External Considerations	**Internal Considerations**
• Does sticking with the company's present strategic course present attractive opportunities for growth and profitability?	• Does the company have an appealing customer value proposition?
• What kind of competitive forces are industry members facing and are they acting to enhance or weaken the company's prospects for growth and profitability?	• What are the company's competitively important resources and capabilities and are they potent enough to produce a sustainable competitive advantage?
• What factors are driving industry change and what impact on the company's prospects will they have?	• Does the company have sufficient business and competitive strength to seize market opportunities and nullify external threats?
• How are industry rivals positioned and what strategic moves are they likely to make next?	• Are the company's prices and costs competitive with those of key rivals?
• What are the key factors of future competitive success and does the industry offer good prospects for attractive profits for companies possessing those capabilities?	• Is the company competitively stronger or weaker than key rivals?

The evaluation stage of the strategic management process shown in Figure 2.1 also allows for a change in the company's vision, but this should be necessary only when it becomes evident to management that the industry has changed in a significant way that renders its vision obsolete. Such occasions can be referred to as **strategic inflection points.** When a company reaches a strategic inflection point, management has tough decisions to make about the company's direction because abandoning an established course carries considerable risk. However, responding to unfolding changes in the marketplace in a timely fashion lessens a company's chances of becoming trapped in a stagnant or declining business or letting attractive new growth opportunities slip away.

> A company's **strategic plan** lays out its future direction, performance targets, and strategy.

The first three stages of the strategic management process make up a strategic plan. A **strategic plan** maps out where a company is headed, establishes strategic and financial targets, and outlines the competitive moves and approaches to be used in achieving the desired business results.[1]

STAGE 1: DEVELOPING A STRATEGIC VISION, A MISSION, AND CORE VALUES

▶**LO1**

Grasp why it is critical for company managers to have a clear strategic vision of where a company needs to head and why.

At the outset of the strategy-making process, a company's senior managers must wrestle with the issue of what directional path the company should take and whether its market positioning and future performance prospects could be improved by changing the company's product offerings and/or the markets in which it participates and/or the customers it caters to and/or the technologies it employs. Top management's views about the company's direction and future product-customer-market-technology focus constitute a **strategic vision** for the company. A clearly articulated strategic vision communicates management's aspirations to stakeholders about "where we are going" and helps steer the energies of company personnel in a common direction. For instance, Henry Ford's vision of a car in every garage had power because it captured the imagination of others, aided internal efforts to mobilize the Ford Motor Company's resources, and served as a reference point for gauging the merits of the company's strategic actions.

> **CORE CONCEPT**
>
> A **strategic vision** describes "where we are going"—the course and direction management has charted and the company's future product-customer-market-technology focus.

Well-conceived visions are *distinctive* and *specific* to a particular organization; they avoid generic, feel-good statements like "We will become a global leader and the first choice of customers in every market we choose to serve"—which could apply to any of hundreds of organizations.[2] And they are not the product of a committee charged with coming up with an innocuous but well-meaning one-sentence vision that wins consensus approval from various stakeholders. Nicely worded vision statements with no specifics about the company's product-market-customer-technology focus fall well short of what it takes for a vision to measure up.

For a strategic vision to function as a valuable managerial tool, it must provide understanding of what management wants its business to look like and provide managers with a reference point in making strategic decisions. It must say something definitive about how the company's leaders intend to position the company beyond where it is today. Table 2.2 lists some characteristics of effective vision statements.

A surprising number of the vision statements found on company websites and in annual reports are vague and unrevealing, saying very little about the company's future product-market-customer-technology focus. Some could apply to most any company in any industry. Many read like a public relations statement—lofty words that someone came up with because it is fashionable for companies to have an official vision statement.[3] Table 2.3 provides a list of

▶ TABLE 2.2

Characteristics of Effectively Worded Vision Statements

Graphic—Paints a picture of the kind of company that management is trying to create and the market position(s) the company is striving to stake out.

Directional—Is forward looking; describes the strategic course that management has charted and the kinds of product-market-customer-technology changes that will help the company prepare for the future.

Focused—Is specific enough to provide managers with guidance in making decisions and allocating resources.

Flexible—Is not so focused that it makes it difficult for management to adjust to changing circumstances in markets, customer preferences, or technology.

Feasible—Is within the realm of what the company can reasonably expect to achieve.

Desirable—Indicates why the directional path makes good business sense.

Easy to communicate—Is explainable in 5 to 10 minutes and, ideally, can be reduced to a simple, memorable "slogan" (like Henry Ford's famous vision of "a car in every garage").

Source: Based partly on John P. Kotter, *Leading Change* (Boston: Harvard Business School Press, 1996), p. 72.

▶ TABLE 2.3

Common Shortcomings in Company Vision Statements

Vague or incomplete—Short on specifics about where the company is headed or what the company is doing to prepare for the future.

Not forward looking—Doesn't indicate whether or how management intends to alter the company's current product-market-customer-technology focus.

Too broad—So all-inclusive that the company could head in most any direction, pursue most any opportunity, or enter most any business.

Bland or uninspiring—Lacks the power to motivate company personnel or inspire shareholder confidence about the company's direction.

Not distinctive—Provides no unique company identity; could apply to companies in any of several industries (including rivals operating in the same market arena).

Too reliant on superlatives—Doesn't say anything specific about the company's strategic course beyond the pursuit of such distinctions as being a recognized leader, a global or worldwide leader, or the first choice of customers.

Sources: Based on information in Hugh Davidson, *The Committed Enterprise* (Oxford: Butterworth Heinemann, 2002), chap. 2; and Michel Robert, *Strategy Pure and Simple II* (New York: McGraw-Hill, 1998), chaps. 2, 3, and 6.

CONCEPTS & CONNECTIONS 2.1

EXAMPLES OF STRATEGIC VISIONS—HOW WELL DO THEY MEASURE UP?

VISION STATEMENT	EFFECTIVE ELEMENTS	SHORTCOMINGS
Coca-Cola Our vision serves as the framework for our roadmap and guides every aspect of our business by describing what we need to accomplish in order to continue achieving sustainable, quality growth.	• Focused • Flexible • Feasible • Desirable	• Long • Not forward-looking

- People: Be a great place to work where people are inspired to be the best they can be.
- Portfolio: Bring to the world a portfolio of quality beverage brands that anticipate and satisfy people's desires and needs.
- Partners: Nurture a winning network of customers and suppliers, together we create mutual, enduring value.
- Planet: Be a responsible citizen that makes a difference by helping build and support sustainable communities.
- Profit: Maximize long-term return to shareowners while being mindful of our overall responsibilities.
- Productivity: Be a highly effective, lean and fast-moving organization.

VISION STATEMENT	EFFECTIVE ELEMENTS	SHORTCOMINGS
UBS We are determined to be the best global financial services company. We focus on wealth and asset management, and on investment banking and securities businesses. We continually earn recognition and trust from clients, shareholders, and staff through our ability to anticipate, learn and shape our future. We share a common ambition to succeed by delivering quality in what we do. Our purpose is to help our clients make financial decisions with confidence. We use our resources to develop effective solutions and services for our clients. We foster a distinctive, meritocratic culture of ambition, performance and learning as this attracts, retains and develops the best talent for our company. By growing both our client and our talent franchises, we add sustainable value for our shareholders.	• Focused • Feasible • Desirable	• Not forward-looking • Bland or uninspiring
Walmart Saving People Money So They Can Live Better	• Focused • Easy to communicate • Feasible • Flexible • Desirable	• Not forward-looking

Sources: Company documents and websites.

the most common shortcomings in company vision statements. Like any tool, vision statements can be used properly or improperly, either clearly conveying a company's strategic course or not. Concepts & Connections 2.1 provides a critique of the strategic visions of several prominent companies.

The Importance of Communicating the Strategic Vision

A strategic vision has little value to the organization unless it's effectively communicated down the line to lower-level managers and employees. It would be difficult for a vision statement to provide direction to decision makers and energize employees toward achieving long-term strategic intent unless they know of the vision and observe management's commitment to that vision. Communicating the vision to organization members nearly always means putting "where we are going and why" in writing, distributing the statement organizationwide, and having executives personally explain the vision and its rationale to as many people as feasible. Ideally, executives should present their vision for the company in a manner that reaches out and grabs people's attention. An engaging and convincing strategic vision has enormous motivational value—for the same reason that a stonemason is inspired by building a great cathedral for the ages. Therefore, an executive's ability to paint a convincing and inspiring picture of a company's journey to a future destination is an important element of effective strategic leadership.[4]

Expressing the Essence of the Vision in a Slogan   The task of effectively conveying the vision to company personnel is assisted when management can capture the vision of where to head in a catchy or easily remembered slogan. A number of organizations have summed up their vision in a brief phrase. Nike's vision slogan is "To bring innovation and inspiration to every athlete in the world." The Mayo Clinic's vision is to provide "The best care to every patient every day," while Greenpeace's envisioned future is "To halt environmental abuse and promote environmental solutions." Creating a short slogan to illuminate an organization's direction and then using it repeatedly as a reminder of "where we are headed and why" helps rally organization members to hurdle whatever obstacles lie in the company's path and maintain their focus.

> An effectively communicated vision is a valuable management tool for enlisting the commitment of company personnel to engage in actions that move the company in the intended direction.

Why a Sound, Well-Communicated Strategic Vision Matters   A well-thought-out, forcefully communicated strategic vision pays off in several respects: (1) it crystallizes senior executives' own views about the firm's long-term direction; (2) it reduces the risk of rudderless decision making by management at all levels; (3) it is a tool for winning the support of employees to help make the vision a reality; (4) it provides a beacon for lower-level managers in forming departmental missions; and (5) it helps an organization prepare for the future.

Developing a Company Mission Statement

The defining characteristic of a well-conceived **strategic vision** is what it says about the company's *future strategic course—"where we are headed and what our future product-customer-market-technology focus will be."* The **mission statements** of most companies say much more about the enterprise's *present* business scope and purpose—"who we are, what we do, and why we are here." Very few mission statements are forward looking in content or emphasis. Consider, for example, the mission statement of Trader Joe's (a specialty grocery chain):

> The distinction between a **strategic vision** and a mission statement is fairly clear-cut: A strategic vision portrays a company's *future business scope* ("where we are going") whereas a company's **mission** typically describes its *present business and purpose* ("who we are, what we do, and why we are here").

> The mission of Trader Joe's is to give our customers the best food and beverage values that they can find anywhere and to provide them with the information required for informed buying decisions. We provide these with a dedication to the highest quality of customer satisfaction delivered with a sense of warmth, friendliness, fun, individual pride, and company spirit.

Note that Trader Joe's mission statement does a good job of conveying "who we are, what we do, and why we are here," but it provides no sense of "where we are headed."

An example of a well-stated mission statement with ample specifics about what the organization does is that of the Occupational Safety and Health Administration (OSHA): "to assure the safety and health of America's workers by setting and enforcing standards; providing training, outreach, and education; establishing partnerships; and encouraging continual improvement in workplace safety and health." Google's mission statement, while short, still captures the essence of what the company is about: "to organize the world's information and make it universally accessible and useful." An example of a not-so-revealing mission statement is that of Microsoft. "To help people and businesses throughout the world realize their full potential" says nothing about its products or business makeup and could apply to many companies in many different industries. A well-conceived mission statement should employ language specific enough to give the company its own identity. A mission statement that provides scant indication of "who we are and what we do" has no apparent value.

> **CORE CONCEPT**
> A well-conceived **mission statement** conveys a company's purpose in language specific enough to give the company its own identity.

Ideally, a company mission statement is sufficiently descriptive to:

- Identify the company's products or services.
- Specify the buyer needs it seeks to satisfy.
- Specify the customer groups or markets it is endeavoring to serve.
- Specify its approach to pleasing customers.
- Give the company its own identity.

Occasionally, companies state that their mission is to simply earn a profit. This is misguided. Profit is more correctly an *objective* and a *result* of what a company does. Moreover, earning a profit is the obvious intent of every commercial enterprise. Such companies as BMW, Netflix, Shell Oil, Procter & Gamble, Google, and McDonald's are each striving to earn a profit for shareholders, but the fundamentals of their businesses are substantially different when it comes to "who we are and what we do."

Linking the Strategic Vision and Mission with Company Values

Many companies have developed a statement of **values** (sometimes called *core values*) to guide the actions and behavior of company personnel in conducting the company's business and pursuing its strategic vision and mission. These values are the designated beliefs and desired ways of doing things at the company and frequently relate to such things as fair treatment, honor and integrity, ethical behavior, innovativeness, teamwork, a passion for excellence, social responsibility, and community citizenship.

> **CORE CONCEPT**
>
> A company's **values** are the beliefs, traits, and behavioral norms that company personnel are expected to display in conducting the company's business and pursuing its strategic vision and mission.

Most companies normally have four to eight core values. At Kodak, the core values are respect for the dignity of the individual, uncompromising integrity, unquestioned trust, constant credibility, continual improvement and personal renewal, and open celebration of individual and team achievements. Home Depot embraces eight values—entrepreneurial spirit, excellent customer service, giving back to the community, respect for all people, doing the right thing, taking care of people, building strong relationships, and creating shareholder value—in its quest to be the world's leading home improvement retailer.[5]

Do companies practice what they preach when it comes to their professed values? Sometimes no, sometimes yes—it runs the gamut. At one extreme are companies with window-dressing values; the professed values are given lip service by top executives but have little discernible impact on either how company personnel behave or how the company operates. At the other extreme are companies whose executives are committed to grounding company operations on sound values and principled ways of doing business. Executives at these companies deliberately seek to ingrain the designated core values into the corporate culture—the core values thus become an integral part of the company's DNA and what makes it tick. At such values-driven companies, executives "walk the talk" and company personnel are held accountable for displaying the stated values. Concepts & Connections 2.2 describes how core values drive the company's mission at Zappos, a widely known and quite successful online shoe and apparel retailer.

STAGE 2: SETTING OBJECTIVES

The managerial purpose of setting **objectives** is to convert the strategic vision into specific performance targets. Objectives reflect management's aspirations for company performance in light of the industry's prevailing economic and competitive conditions and the company's internal capabilities. Well-stated objectives are *quantifiable*, or *measurable*, and contain a *deadline for achievement*. Concrete, measurable objectives are managerially valuable

▶**LO2**

Understand the importance of setting both strategic and financial objectives.

CONCEPTS & CONNECTIONS 2.2

ZAPPOS MISSION AND CORE VALUES

We've been asked by a lot of people how we've grown so quickly, and the answer is actually really simple.... We've aligned the entire organization around one mission: *to provide* *the best customer service possible.* Internally, we call this our **WOW** philosophy.

These are the 10 core values that we live by:

Deliver Wow through Service. At Zappos, anything worth doing is worth doing with WOW. WOW is such a short, simple word, but it really encompasses a lot of things. To WOW, you must differentiate yourself, which means doing something a little unconventional and innovative. You must do something that's above and beyond what's expected. And whatever you do must have an emotional impact on the receiver. We are not an average company, our service is not average, and we don't want our people to be average. We expect every employee to deliver WOW.

Embrace and Drive Change. Part of being in a growing company is that change is constant. For some people, especially those who come from bigger companies, the constant change can be somewhat unsettling at first. If you are not prepared to deal with constant change, then you probably are not a good fit for the company.

Create Fun and a Little Weirdness. At Zappos, We're Always Creating Fun and A Little Weirdness! One of the things that makes Zappos different from a lot of other companies is that we value being fun and being a little weird. We don't want to become one of those big companies that feels corporate and boring. We want to be able to laugh at ourselves. We look for both fun and humor in our daily work.

Be Adventurous, Creative, and Open Minded. At Zappos, we think it's important for people and the company as a whole to be bold and daring (but not reckless). We do not want people to be afraid to take risks and make mistakes. We believe if people aren't making mistakes, then that means they're not taking enough risks. Over time, we want everyone to develop his/her gut about business decisions. We want people to develop and improve their decision-making skills. We encourage people to make mistakes as long as they learn from them.

Pursue Growth and Learning. At Zappos, we think it's important for employees to grow both personally and professionally. It's important to constantly challenge and stretch yourself and not be stuck in a job where you don't feel like you are growing or learning.

Build Open and Honest Relationships with Communication. Fundamentally, we believe that openness and honesty make for the best relationships because that leads to trust and faith. We value strong relationships in all areas: with managers, direct reports, customers (internal and external), vendors, business partners, team members, and co-workers.

Build a Positive Team and Family Spirit. At Zappos, we place a lot of emphasis on our culture because we are both a team and a family. We want to create an environment that is friendly, warm, and exciting. We encourage diversity in ideas, opinions, and points of view.

Do More with Less. Zappos has always been about being able to do more with less. While we may be casual in our interactions with each other, we are focused and serious about the operations of our business. We believe in working hard and putting in the extra effort to get things done.

Be Passionate and Determined. Passion is the fuel that drives us and our company forward. We value passion, determination, perseverance, and the sense of urgency. We are inspired because we believe in what we are doing and where we are going. We don't take "no" or "that'll never work" for an answer because if we had, then Zappos would have never started in the first place.

Be Humble. While we have grown quickly in the past, we recognize that there are always challenges ahead to tackle. We believe that no matter what happens we should always be respectful of everyone.

Source: Information posted at www.zappos.com, accessed June 6, 2010.

because they serve as yardsticks for tracking a company's performance and progress toward its vision. Vague targets such as "maximize profits," "reduce costs," "become more efficient," or "increase sales," which specify neither how much nor when, offer little value as a management tool to improve company performance. Ideally, managers should develop *challenging,* yet *achievable* objectives that *stretch an organization to perform at its full potential.* As Mitchell Leibovitz, former CEO of the auto parts and service retailer Pep Boys, once said, "If you want to have ho-hum results, have ho-hum objectives."

> **CORE CONCEPT**
>
> **Objectives** are an organization's performance targets—the results management wants to achieve.

What Kinds of Objectives to Set

Two very distinct types of performance yardsticks are required: those relating to financial performance and those relating to strategic performance. **Financial objectives** communicate management's targets for financial performance. Common financial objectives relate to revenue growth, profitability, and return on investment. **Strategic objectives** are related to a company's marketing standing and competitive vitality. The importance of attaining financial objectives is intuitive. Without adequate profitability and financial strength, a company's long-term health and ultimate survival is jeopardized. Furthermore, subpar earnings and a weak balance sheet alarm shareholders and creditors and put the jobs of senior executives at risk. However, good financial performance, by itself, is not enough.

> **CORE CONCEPT**
>
> **Financial objectives** relate to the financial performance targets management has established for the organization to achieve. **Strategic objectives** relate to target outcomes that indicate a company is strengthening its market standing, competitive vitality, and future business prospects.

A company's financial objectives are really *lagging indicators* that reflect the results of past decisions and organizational activities.[6] The results of past decisions and organizational activities are not reliable indicators of a company's future prospects. Companies that have been poor financial performers are sometimes able to turn things around, and good financial performers on occasion fall upon hard times. Hence, the best and most reliable predictors of a company's success in the marketplace and future financial performance are strategic objectives. Strategic outcomes are *leading indicators* of a company's future financial performance and business prospects. The accomplishment of strategic objectives signals the company is well positioned to sustain or improve its performance. For instance, if a company is achieving ambitious strategic objectives, then there's reason to expect that its *future* financial performance will be better than its current or past performance. If a company begins to lose competitive strength and fails to achieve important strategic objectives, then its ability to maintain its present profitability is highly suspect.

Consequently, utilizing a performance measurement system that strikes a *balance* between financial objectives and strategic objectives is optimal.[7] Just tracking a company's financial performance overlooks the fact that what ultimately enables a company to deliver better financial results is the achievement of strategic objectives that improve its competitiveness and market

TABLE 2.4

The Balanced Scorecard Approach to Performance Measurement		
FINANCIAL OBJECTIVES	**STRATEGIC OBJECTIVES**	
• An x percent increase in annual revenues • Annual increases in earnings per share of x percent • An x percent return on capital employed (ROCE) or shareholder investment (ROE) • Bond and credit ratings of x • Internal cash flows of x to fund new capital investment	• Win an x percent market share • Achieve customer satisfaction rates of x percent • Achieve a customer retention rate of x percent • Acquire x number of new customers • Introduce x number of new products in the next three years • Reduce product development times to x months	• Increase percentage of sales coming from new products to x percent • Improve information systems capabilities to give frontline managers defect information in x minutes • Improve teamwork by increasing the number of projects involving more than one business unit to x

strength. Representative examples of financial and strategic objectives that companies often include in a **balanced scorecard** approach to measuring their performance are displayed in Table 2.4.[8]

In 2010, nearly 50 percent of global companies used a balanced scorecard approach to measuring strategic and financial performance.[9] Examples of organizations that have adopted a balanced scorecard approach to setting objectives and measuring performance include SAS Institute, UPS, Ann Taylor Stores, Fort Bragg Army Garrison, Caterpillar, Daimler AG, Hilton Hotels, Susan G. Komen for the Cure, and Siemens AG.[10] Concepts & Connections 2.3 provides selected strategic and financial objectives of three prominent companies.

 CORE CONCEPT

The **balanced scorecard** is a widely used method for combining the use of both strategic and financial objectives, tracking their achievement, and giving management a more complete and balanced view of how well an organization is performing.

Short-Term and Long-Term Objectives A company's set of financial and strategic objectives should include both near-term and long-term performance targets. Short-term objectives focus attention on delivering performance improvements in the current period, while long-term targets force the organization to consider how actions currently under way will affect the company at a later date. Specifically, long-term objectives stand as a barrier to an undue focus on short-term results by nearsighted management. When trade-offs have to be made between achieving long-run and short-run objectives, long-run objectives should take precedence (unless the achievement of one or more short-run performance targets has unique importance).

The Need for Objectives at All Organizational Levels Objective setting should not stop with the establishment of companywide performance targets. Company objectives need to be broken into performance targets for each of the organization's separate businesses, product lines, functional

---

 ## CONCEPTS & CONNECTIONS 2.3

EXAMPLES OF COMPANY OBJECTIVES

PEPSICO

Accelerate top-line growth; build and expand our better-for-your snacks and beverages and nutrition businesses; improve our water use efficiency by 20 percent per unit of production by 2015; reduce packaging weight by 350 million pounds by 2012; improve our electricity use efficiency by 20 percent per unit of production by 2015; maintain appropriate financial flexibility with ready access to global capital and credit markets at favorable interest rates.

GOODYEAR

Increase operating income from $917 million in 2010 to $1.6 billion in 2013; increase operating income from international tire division from $899 million in 2010 to $1,150 million in 2013; increase operating income from North American division from $18 million in 2010 to $450 million in 2013; reduce the percentage of non-branded replacement tires sold from 16 percent in 2010 to 9 percent in 2013; improve brand awareness in Mexico; increase number of retail outlets in China from 735 in 2010 to 1,555 in 2015; increase fuel efficiency of automobile and truck tires; improve braking distance on new tire designs; improve tread-life on new tire designs; collaborate with regulatory agencies in the U.S. and Europe to develop tire labeling standards by 2013.

YUM! BRANDS (KFC, PIZZA HUT, TACO BELL, LONG JOHN SILVER'S)

Increase operating profit derived from international operations from 65 percent in 2010 to 75 percent in 2010; increase operating profit derived from operations in emerging markets from 48 percent in 2010 to 60 percent in 2015; increase number of KFC units in Africa from 655 in 2010 to 2,100 in 2020; increase KFC revenues in Africa from $865 million in 2010 to $1.94 billion in 2014; increase number of KFC units in India from 101 in 2010 to 1,250 in 2020; increase number of KFC units in Vietnam from 87 in 2010 to 500 in 2020; increase number of KFC units in Russia from 150 in 2010 to 500 in 2020; open 100+ new Taco Bell units in international markets in 2015; increase annual cash flows from operations from $1.5 billion in 2010 to $2 + billion in 2015.

Source: Information posted on company websites, accessed May 27, 2011.

---

departments, and individual work units. Employees within various functional areas and operating levels will be guided much better by narrow objectives relating directly to their departmental activities than broad organizational level goals. Objective setting is thus a top-down process that must extend to the lowest organizational levels. And it means that each organizational unit must take care to set performance targets that support—rather than conflict with or negate—the achievement of companywide strategic and financial objectives.

STAGE 3: CRAFTING A STRATEGY

As indicated earlier, the task of stitching a strategy together entails addressing a series of *hows: how* to attract and please customers, *how* to compete against rivals, *how* to position the company in the marketplace and capitalize on attractive opportunities to grow the business, *how* best to respond to changing economic and market conditions, *how* to manage each functional piece of the business, and *how* to achieve the company's performance targets. It also means choosing among the various strategic alternatives and proactively searching for opportunities to do new things or to do existing things in new or better ways.[11]

 LO3

Understand why the strategic initiatives taken at various organizational levels must be tightly coordinated to achieve companywide performance targets.

Strategy Making Involves Managers at All Organizational Levels

In some enterprises, the CEO or owner functions as strategic visionary and chief architect of the strategy, personally deciding what the key elements of the company's strategy will be, although the CEO may seek the advice of key subordinates in fashioning an overall strategy and deciding on important strategic moves. However, it is a mistake to view strategy making as a *top* management function—the exclusive province of owner-entrepreneurs, CEOs, high-ranking executives, and board members. The more a company's operations cut across different products, industries, and geographical areas, the more that headquarters executives have little option but to delegate considerable strategy-making authority to down-the-line managers. On-the-scene managers who oversee specific operating units are likely to have a more detailed command of the strategic issues and choices for the particular operating unit under their supervision—knowing the prevailing market and competitive conditions, customer requirements and expectations, and all the other relevant aspects affecting the several strategic options available.

> In most companies, crafting strategy is a *collaborative team effort* that includes managers in various positions and at various organizational levels. Crafting strategy is rarely something only high-level executives do.

A Company's Strategy-Making Hierarchy

The larger and more diverse the operations of an enterprise, the more points of strategic initiative it will have and the more managers at different organizational levels will have a relevant strategy-making role. In diversified companies, where multiple and sometimes strikingly different businesses have to be managed, crafting a full-fledged strategy involves four distinct types of strategic actions and initiatives, each undertaken at different levels of the organization and partially or wholly crafted by managers at different organizational levels, as shown in Figure 2.2. A company's overall strategy is therefore *a collection of strategic initiatives and actions* devised by managers up and down the whole organizational hierarchy. Ideally, the pieces of a company's strategy up and down the strategy hierarchy should be cohesive and mutually reinforcing, fitting together like a jigsaw puzzle.

> **Corporate strategy** establishes an overall game plan for managing a *set of businesses* in a diversified, multibusiness company. **Business strategy** is primarily concerned with strengthening the company's market position and building competitive advantage in a single business company or a single business unit of a diversified multibusiness corporation.

As shown in Figure 2.2, **corporate strategy** is orchestrated by the CEO and other senior executives and establishes an overall game plan for managing a *set of businesses* in a diversified, multibusiness company. Corporate strategy addresses the questions of how to capture cross-business synergies, what businesses to hold or divest, which new markets to enter, and how to best enter new markets—by acquisition, creation of a strategic alliance, or through internal development. Corporate strategy and business diversification are the subject of Chapter 8, where they are discussed in detail.

Business strategy is primarily concerned with building competitive advantage in a single business unit of a diversified company or strengthening the

▶ FIGURE 2.2 **A Company's Strategy-Making Hierarchy**

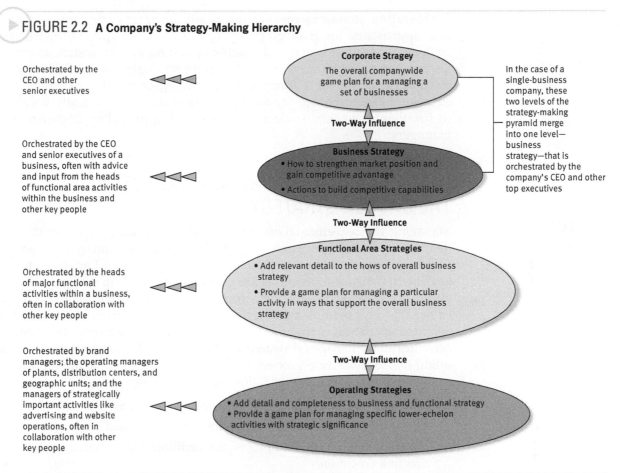

market position of a nondiversified single business company. Business strategy is also the responsibility of the CEO and other senior executives, but key business-unit heads may also be influential, especially in strategic decisions affecting the businesses they lead. *In single-business companies, the corporate and business levels of the strategy-making hierarchy merge into a single level—business strategy—*because the strategy for the entire enterprise involves only one distinct business. So, a single-business company has three levels of strategy: business strategy, functional-area strategies, and operating strategies.

Functional-area strategies concern the actions related to particular functions or processes within a business. A company's product development strategy, for example, represents the managerial game plan for creating new products that are in tune with what buyers are looking for. Lead responsibility for functional strategies within a business is normally delegated to the heads of the respective functions, with the general manager of the business having final approval over functional strategies. For the overall business strategy to have maximum impact, a company's marketing strategy, production strategy, finance strategy, customer service strategy, product development strategy, and human resources strategy should be compatible and mutually reinforcing rather than each serving its own narrower purpose.

Operating strategies concern the relatively narrow strategic initiatives and approaches for managing key operating units (plants, distribution centers, geographic units) and specific operating activities such as materials purchasing or Internet sales. Operating strategies are limited in scope, but add further detail to functional-area strategies and the overall business strategy. Lead responsibility for operating strategies is usually delegated to frontline managers, subject to review and approval by higher-ranking managers.

STAGE 4: IMPLEMENTING AND EXECUTING THE CHOSEN STRATEGY

LO4

Become aware of what a company must do to achieve operating excellence and to execute its strategy proficiently.

Managing the implementation and execution of strategy is easily the most demanding and time-consuming part of the strategic management process. Good strategy execution entails that managers pay careful attention to how key internal business processes are performed and see to it that employees' efforts are directed toward the accomplishment of desired operational outcomes. The task of implementing and executing the strategy also necessitates an ongoing analysis of the efficiency and effectiveness of a company's internal activities and a managerial awareness of new technological developments that might improve business processes. In most situations, managing the strategy execution process includes the following principal aspects:

- Staffing the organization to provide needed skills and expertise.
- Allocating ample resources to activities critical to good strategy execution.
- Ensuring that policies and procedures facilitate rather than impede effective execution.
- Installing information and operating systems that enable company personnel to perform essential activities.
- Pushing for continuous improvement in how value chain activities are performed.
- Tying rewards and incentives directly to the achievement of performance objectives.
- Creating a company culture and work climate conducive to successful strategy execution.
- Exerting the internal leadership needed to propel implementation forward.

STAGE 5: EVALUATING PERFORMANCE AND INITIATING CORRECTIVE ADJUSTMENTS

The fifth stage of the strategy management process—monitoring new external developments, evaluating the company's progress, and making corrective adjustments—is the trigger point for deciding whether to continue or change the company's vision, objectives, strategy, and/or strategy execution methods.

So long as the company's direction and strategy seem well matched to industry and competitive conditions and performance targets are being met, company executives may well decide to stay the course. Simply fine-tuning the strategic plan and continuing with efforts to improve strategy execution are sufficient.

But whenever a company encounters disruptive changes in its environment, questions need to be raised about the appropriateness of its direction and strategy. If a company experiences a downturn in its market position or persistent shortfalls in performance, then company managers are obligated to ferret out the causes—do they relate to poor strategy, poor strategy execution, or both?—and take timely corrective action. A company's direction, objectives, and strategy have to be revisited any time external or internal conditions warrant.

> A company's vision, objectives, strategy, and approach to strategy execution are never final; managing strategy is an ongoing process, not an every-now-and-then task.

Also, it is not unusual for a company to find that one or more aspects of its strategy implementation and execution are not going as well as intended. Proficient strategy execution is always the product of much organizational learning. It is achieved unevenly—coming quickly in some areas and proving nettlesome in others. Successful strategy execution entails vigilantly searching for ways to improve and then making corrective adjustments whenever and wherever it is useful to do so.

CORPORATE GOVERNANCE: THE ROLE OF THE BOARD OF DIRECTORS IN THE STRATEGY-MAKING, STRATEGY-EXECUTING PROCESS

Although senior managers have *lead responsibility* for crafting and executing a company's strategy, it is the duty of the board of directors to exercise strong oversight and see that the five tasks of strategic management are done in a manner that benefits shareholders (in the case of investor-owned enterprises) or stakeholders (in the case of not-for-profit organizations). In watching over management's strategy-making, strategy-executing actions, a company's board of directors has four important corporate governance obligations to fulfill:

▶ **LO5**

Become aware of the role and responsibility of a company's board of directors in overseeing the strategic management process.

1. *Oversee the company's financial accounting and financial reporting practices.* While top management, particularly the company's CEO and CFO (chief financial officer), is primarily responsible for seeing that the company's financial statements accurately report the results of the company's operations, board members have a fiduciary duty to protect shareholders by exercising oversight of the company's financial practices. In addition, corporate boards must ensure that generally acceptable accounting principles (GAAP) are properly used in preparing the company's financial statements and determine whether proper financial controls are in place to prevent fraud and misuse of funds. Virtually all boards of directors monitor the financial reporting activities by appointing an audit committee, always composed entirely of *outside directors* (*inside directors* hold management positions in the company and either directly or indirectly report to

the CEO). The members of the audit committee have lead responsibility for overseeing the decisions of the company's financial officers and consulting with both internal and external auditors to ensure that financial reports are accurate and adequate financial controls are in place. Faulty oversight of corporate accounting and financial reporting practices by audit committees and corporate boards during the early 2000s resulted in the federal investigation of more than 20 major corporations between 2000 and 2002. The investigations of such well-known companies as AOL Time Warner, Global Crossing, Enron, Qwest Communications, and WorldCom found that upper management had employed fraudulent or unsound accounting practices to artificially inflate revenues, overstate assets, and reduce expenses. The scandals resulted in the conviction of a number of corporate executives and the passage of the Sarbanes-Oxley Act of 2002, which tightened financial reporting standards and created additional compliance requirements for public boards.

2. *Diligently critique and oversee the company's direction, strategy, and business approaches.* Even though board members have a legal obligation to warrant the accuracy of the company's financial reports, directors must set aside time to guide management in choosing a strategic direction and to make independent judgments about the validity and wisdom of management's proposed strategic actions. Many boards have found that meeting agendas become consumed by compliance matters and little time is left to discuss matters of strategic importance. The board of directors and management at Philips Electronics hold annual two- to three-day retreats devoted to evaluating the company's long-term direction and various strategic proposals. The company's exit from the semiconductor business and its increased focus on medical technology and home health care resulted from management–board discussions during such retreats.[12]

3. *Evaluate the caliber of senior executives' strategy-making and strategy-executing skills.* The board is always responsible for determining whether the current CEO is doing a good job of strategic leadership and whether senior management is actively creating a pool of potential successors to the CEO and other top executives.[13] Evaluation of senior executives' strategy-making and strategy-executing skills is enhanced when outside directors go into the field to personally evaluate how well the strategy is being executed. Independent board members at GE visit operating executives at each major business unit once per year to assess the company's talent pool and stay abreast of emerging strategic and operating issues affecting the company's divisions. Home Depot board members visit a store once per quarter to determine the health of the company's operations.[14]

4. *Institute a compensation plan for top executives that rewards them for actions and results that serve shareholder interests.* A basic principle of corporate governance is that the owners of a corporation delegate operating authority and managerial control to top management in return for compensation. In their role as an *agent* of shareholders, top executives have a clear

CONCEPTS & CONNECTIONS 2.4

CORPORATE GOVERNANCE FAILURES AT FANNIE MAE AND FREDDIE MAC

Executive compensation in the financial services industry during the mid-2000s ranks high among examples of failed corporate governance. Corporate governance at the government-sponsored mortgage giants Fannie Mae and Freddie Mac was particularly weak. The politically appointed boards at both enterprises failed to understand the risks of the subprime loan strategies being employed, did not adequately monitor the decisions of the CEO, did not exercise effective oversight of the accounting principles being employed (which led to inflated earnings), and approved executive compensation systems that allowed management to manipulate earnings to receive lucrative performance bonuses. The audit and compensation committees at Fannie Mae were particularly ineffective in protecting shareholder interests, with the audit committee allowing the government-sponsored enterprise's financial officers to audit reports prepared under their direction and used to determine performance bonuses. Fannie Mae's audit committee also was aware of management's use of questionable accounting practices that reduced losses and recorded one-time gains to achieve EPS targets linked to bonuses. In addition, the audit committee failed to investigate formal charges of accounting improprieties filed by a manager in the Office of the Controller.

Fannie Mae's compensation committee was equally ineffective. The committee allowed the company's CEO, Franklin Raines, to select the consultant employed to design the mortgage firm's executive compensation plan and agreed to a tiered bonus plan that would permit Raines and other senior managers to receive maximum bonuses without great difficulty. The compensation plan allowed Raines to earn performance-based bonuses of $52 million and total compensation of $90 million between 1999 and 2004. Raines was forced to resign in December 2004 when the Office of Federal Housing Enterprise Oversight found that Fannie Mae executives had fraudulently inflated earnings to receive bonuses linked to financial

performance. Securities and Exchange Commission investigators also found evidence of improper accounting at Fannie Mae and required it to restate its earnings between 2002 and 2004 by $6.3 billion.

Poor governance at Freddie Mac allowed its CEO and senior management to manipulate financial data to receive performance-based compensation as well. Freddie Mac CEO Richard Syron received 2007 compensation of $19.8 million while the mortgage company's share price declined from a high of $70 in 2005 to $25 at year-end 2007. During Syron's tenure as CEO the company become embroiled in a multibillion-dollar accounting scandal, and Syron personally disregarded internal reports dating to 2004 that warned of an impending financial crisis at the company. Forewarnings within Freddie Mac and by federal regulators and outside industry observers proved to be correct, with loan underwriting policies at Freddie Mac and Fannie Mae leading to combined losses at the two firms in 2008 of more than $100 billion. The price of Freddie Mac's shares had fallen to below $1 by Syron's resignation in September 2008.

Both organizations were placed into a conservatorship under the direction of the U.S. government in September 2008 and were provided bailout funds of more than $150 billion by early 2011. The U.S. Federal Housing Finance Agency estimated the bailout of Fannie Mae and Freddie Mac would potentially reach $200 billion to $300 billion by 2013.

Sources: Chris Isidore, "Fannie, Freddie Bailout: $153 Billion . . . and Counting," *CNNMoney,* February 11, 2011; "Adding Up the Government's Total Bailout Tab," *The New York Times Online,* February 4, 2009; Eric Dash, "Fannie Mae to Restate Results by $6.3 Billion Because of Accounting," *The New York Times Online,* www.nytimes.com, December 7, 2006; Annys Shin, "Fannie Mae Sets Executive Salaries," *The Washington Post,* February 9, 2006, p. D4; and Scott DeCarlo, Eric Weiss, Mark Jickling, and James R. Cristie, *Fannie Mae and Freddie Mac: Scandal in U.S. Housing* (Nova Publishers, 2006), pp. 266–286.

and unequivocal duty to make decisions and operate the company in accord with shareholder interests (but this does not mean disregarding the interests of other stakeholders, particularly those of employees, with whom they also have an agency relationship). Most boards of directors have a compensation committee, composed entirely of directors from outside the company, to develop a salary and incentive compensation plan that rewards senior executives for boosting the company's *long-term* performance and growing the economic value of the enterprise on behalf of shareholders; the compensation committee's recommendations are presented to the full board for approval. But during the past 10 to 15 years, many boards of directors have done a poor job of ensuring that executive salary increases, bonuses, and stock option awards are tied tightly to performance measures that are truly in the long-term interests of shareholders. Rather, compensation packages at many companies have increasingly rewarded executives for short-term performance improvements—most notably, achieving quarterly and annual earnings targets and boosting the stock price by specified percentages. This has had the perverse effect of causing company managers to become preoccupied with actions to improve a company's near-term performance, often motivating them to take unwise business risks to boost short-term earnings by amounts sufficient to qualify for multimillion-dollar bonuses and stock option awards (that, in the view of many people, were obscenely large). The greater weight being placed on short-term performance improvements has worked against shareholders since, in many cases, the excessive risk-taking has proved damaging to long-term company performance—witness the huge loss of shareholder wealth that occurred at many financial institutions in 2008–2009 because of executive risk-taking in subprime loans, credit default swaps, and collateralized mortgage securities in 2006–2007. As a consequence, the need to overhaul and reform executive compensation has become a hot topic in both public circles and corporate boardrooms. Concepts & Connections 2.4 discusses how weak governance at Fannie Mae and Freddie Mac allowed opportunistic senior managers to secure exorbitant bonuses, while making decisions that imperiled the futures of the companies they managed.

Every corporation should have a strong, independent board of directors that (1) is well informed about the company's performance, (2) guides and judges the CEO and other top executives, (3) has the courage to curb management actions it believes are inappropriate or unduly risky, (4) certifies to shareholders that the CEO is doing what the board expects, (5) provides insight and advice to management, and (6) is intensely involved in debating the pros and cons of key decisions and actions.[15] Boards of directors that lack the backbone to challenge a strong-willed or "imperial" CEO or that rubber-stamp most anything the CEO recommends without probing inquiry and debate abandon their duty to represent and protect shareholder interests.

KEY POINTS

The strategic management process consists of five interrelated and integrated stages:

1. *Developing a strategic vision* of where the company needs to head and what its future product-customer-market-technology focus should be. This managerial step provides long-term direction, infuses the organization with a sense of purposeful action, and communicates to stakeholders management's aspirations for the company.

2. *Setting objectives* and using the targeted results as yardsticks for measuring the company's performance. Objectives need to spell out *how much* of *what kind* of performance *by when*. A *balanced scorecard* approach for measuring company performance entails setting both *financial objectives and strategic objectives.*

3. *Crafting a strategy to achieve the objectives* and move the company along the strategic course that management has charted. The total strategy that emerges is really a collection of strategic actions and business approaches initiated partly by senior company executives, partly by the heads of major business divisions, partly by functional-area managers, and partly by operating managers on the frontlines. A single business enterprise has three levels of strategy—business strategy for the company as a whole, functional-area strategies for each main area within the business, and operating strategies undertaken by lower-echelon managers. In diversified, multibusiness companies, the strategy-making task involves four distinct types or levels of strategy: corporate strategy for the company as a whole, business strategy (one for each business the company has diversified into), functional-area strategies within each business, and operating strategies. Typically, the strategy-making task is more top-down than bottom-up, with higher-level strategies serving as the guide for developing lower-level strategies.

4. *Implementing and executing the chosen strategy efficiently and effectively.* Managing the implementation and execution of strategy is an operations-oriented, make-things-happen activity aimed at shaping the performance of core business activities in a strategy supportive manner. Management's handling of the strategy implementation process can be considered successful if things go smoothly enough that the company meets or beats its strategic and financial performance targets and shows good progress in achieving management's strategic vision.

5. *Evaluating performance and initiating corrective adjustments* in vision, long-term direction, objectives, strategy, or execution in light of actual experience, changing conditions, new ideas, and new opportunities. This stage of the strategy management process is the trigger point for deciding whether to continue or change the company's vision, objectives, strategy, and/or strategy execution methods.

The sum of a company's strategic vision, objectives, and strategy constitutes a *strategic plan.*

Boards of directors have a duty to shareholders to play a vigilant role in overseeing management's handling of a company's strategy-making, strategy-executing process. A company's board is obligated to (1) ensure that the company issues accurate financial reports and has adequate financial controls, (2) critically appraise and ultimately approve strategic action plans, (3) evaluate the strategic leadership skills of the CEO, and (4) institute a compensation plan for top executives that rewards them for actions and results that serve stakeholder interests, most especially those of shareholders.

ASSURANCE OF LEARNING EXERCISES

LO1

1. Using the information in Tables 2.2 and 2.3, critique the adequacy and merit of the following vision statements, listing effective elements and shortcomings. Rank the vision statements from best to worst once you complete your evaluation.

VISION STATEMENT	EFFECTIVE ELEMENTS	SHORTCOMINGS

Wells Fargo

We want to satisfy all of our customers' financial needs, help them succeed financially, be the premier provider of financial services in every one of our markets, and be known as one of America's great companies.

www.mcgrawhillconnect.com

Hilton Hotels Corporation

Our vision is to be the first choice of the world's travelers. Hilton intends to build on the rich heritage and strength of our brands by:

- Consistently delighting our customers
- Investing in our team members
- Delivering innovative products and services
- Continuously improving performance
- Increasing shareholder value
- Creating a culture of pride
- Strengthening the loyalty of our constituents

H. J. Heinz Company

Be the world's premier food company, offering nutritious, superior tasting foods to people everywhere. Being the premier food company does not mean being the biggest but it does mean being the best in terms of consumer value, customer service, employee talent, and consistent and predictable growth.

BASF

We are "The Chemical Company" successfully operating in all major markets.

- Our customers view BASF as their partner of choice.
- Our innovative products, intelligent solutions and services make us the most competent worldwide supplier in the chemical industry.
- We generate a high return on assets.
- We strive for sustainable development.
- We welcome change as an opportunity.
- We, the employees of BASF, together ensure our success.

Source: Company websites and annual reports.

LO2

2. Go to the company investor relations websites for Home Depot (http://corporate.homedepot.com/wps/portal), Avon (www.avoncompany.com/), and Intel (www.intc.com) to find examples of strategic and financial objectives. List four objectives for each company and indicate which of these are strategic and which are financial.

LO3

3. The primary strategic initiatives of Ford Motor Company's restructuring plan executed between 2005 and 2010 involved accelerating the development of new cars that customers would value, improving its balance sheet, working with its union employees to improve manufacturing competitiveness, reducing product engineering costs, reducing production capacity by approximately 40 percent,

and reducing hourly head count by 40 to 50 percent. At the conclusion of the restructuring plan in 2010, Ford was ranked first among U.S. automobile manufacturers by J.D. Power in initial quality and had earned more than $5.4 billion in pre-tax profit on net revenues of $64.4 billion. Explain why its strategic initiatives taken at various organizational levels and functions were necessarily tightly coordinated to achieve its commendable results.

4. Go to the investor relations website for Walmart (http://investors.walmartstores .com) and review past presentations it has made during various investor conferences by clicking on the Events option in the navigation bar. Prepare a one- to two-page report that outlines what Walmart has said to investors about its approach to strategy execution. Specifically, what has management discussed concerning staffing, resource allocation, policies and procedures, information and operating systems, continuous improvement, rewards and incentives, corporate culture, and internal leadership at the company?

LO4

5. Based on the information provided in Concepts & Connections 2.4 on page 31, explain how corporate governance at Freddie Mac failed the enterprise's shareholders and other stakeholders. Which important obligations to shareholders were fulfilled by Fannie Mae's board of directors? What is your assessment of how well Fannie Mae's compensation committee handled executive compensation at the government-sponsored mortgage giant?

LO5

www.mcgrawhillconnect.com

→→→→ EXERCISES FOR SIMULATION PARTICIPANTS

1. Meet with your co-managers and prepare a strategic vision statement for your company. It should be at least one sentence long and no longer than a brief paragraph. When you are finished, check to see if your vision statement meets the conditions for an effectively worded strategic vision set forth in Table 2.2 and avoids the shortcomings set forth in Table 2.3. If not, then revise it accordingly. What would be a good slogan that captures the essence of your strategic vision and that could be used to help communicate the vision to company personnel, shareholders, and other stakeholders?

LO1

2. What are your company's financial objectives? What are your company's strategic objectives?

LO2

3. What are the three or four key elements of your company's strategy?

LO3

ENDNOTES

1. Gordon Shaw, Robert Brown, and Philip Bromiley, "Strategic Stories: How 3M Is Rewriting Business Planning," *Harvard Business Review* 76, no. 3 (May–June 1998); and David J. Collins and Michael G. Rukstad, "Can You Say What Your Strategy Is?" *Harvard Business Review* 86, no. 4 (April 2008).

2. Hugh Davidson, *The Committed Enterprise: How to Make Vision and Values Work* (Oxford: Butterworth Heinemann, 2002); W. Chan Kim and Renée Mauborgne, "Charting Your Company's Future," *Harvard Business Review* 80, no. 6 (June 2002); James C. Collins and Jerry I. Porras, "Building Your Company's Vision," *Harvard Business Review* 74, no. 5 (September–October 1996); Jim Collins and Jerry Porras, *Built to Last: Successful Habits of Visionary Companies* (New York: HarperCollins, 1994); Michel Robert, *Strategy Pure and Simple II: How Winning Companies Dominate Their Competitors* (New York: McGraw-Hill, 1998).

3. Hugh Davidson, *The Committed Enterprise* (Oxford: Butterworth Heinemann, 2002).

4. Ibid.

5. Jeffrey K. Liker, *The Toyota Way* (New York: McGraw-Hill, 2004); and Steve Hamm, "Taking a Page from Toyota's Playbook," *BusinessWeek,* August 22/29, 2005, p. 72.

6. Robert S. Kaplan and David P. Norton, *The Strategy-Focused Organization* (Boston: Harvard Business School Press, 2001).

7. Ibid. Also, see Robert S. Kaplan and David P. Norton, *The Balanced Scorecard: Translating Strategy into Action* (Boston: Harvard Business School Press, 1996); Kevin B. Hendricks, Larry Menor, and Christine Wiedman, "The Balanced Scorecard: To Adopt or Not to Adopt," *Ivey Business Journal* 69, no. 2 (November–December 2004); and Sandy Richardson, "The Key Elements of Balanced Scorecard Success," *Ivey Business Journal* 69, no. 2 (November–December 2004).

8. Kaplan and Norton, *The Balanced Scorecard: Translating Strategy into Action*, pp. 25–29. Kaplan and Norton classify strategic objectives under the categories of customer-related, business processes, and learning and growth. In practice, companies using the balanced scorecard may choose categories of strategic objectives that best reflect the organization's value-creating activities and processes.

9. Information posted on the website of Bain and Company, www.bain.com, accessed May 27, 2011.

10. Information posted on the website of Balanced Scorecard Institute, accessed May 27, 2011.

11. Henry Mintzberg, Bruce Ahlstrand, and Joseph Lampel, *Strategy Safari: A Guided Tour through the Wilds of Strategic Management* (New York: Free Press, 1998); Bruce Barringer and Allen C. Bluedorn, "The Relationship between Corporate Entrepreneurship and Strategic Management," *Strategic Management Journal* 20 (1999); Jeffrey G. Covin and Morgan P. Miles, "Corporate Entrepreneurship and the Pursuit of Competitive Advantage," *Entrepreneurship: Theory and Practice* 23, no. 3 (Spring 1999); and David A. Garvin and Lynned C. Levesque, "Meeting the Challenge of Corporate Entrepreneurship," *Harvard Business Review* 84, no. 10 (October 2006).

12. Jay W. Lorsch and Robert C. Clark, "Leading from the Boardroom," *Harvard Business Review* 86, no. 4 (April 2008).

13. Ibid., p. 110.

14. Stephen P. Kaufman, "Evaluating the CEO," *Harvard Business Review* 86, no. 10 (October 2008).

15. David A. Nadler, "Building Better Boards," *Harvard Business Review* 82, no. 5 (May 2004); Cynthia A. Montgomery and Rhonda Kaufman, "The Board's Missing Link," *Harvard Business Review* 81, no. 3 (March 2003); John Carver, "What Continues to Be Wrong with Corporate Governance and How to Fix It," *Ivey Business Journal* 68, no. 1 (September/October 2003); and Gordon Donaldson, "A New Tool for Boards: The Strategic Audit," *Harvard Business Review* 73, no. 4 (July–August 1995).

chapter **3**

EVALUATING A COMPANY'S EXTERNAL ENVIRONMENT

LEARNING OBJECTIVES

LO1   Gain command of the basic concepts and analytical tools widely used to diagnose a company's industry and competitive conditions.

LO2   Become adept at recognizing the factors that cause competition in an industry to be fierce, more or less normal, or relatively weak.

LO3   Learn how to determine whether an industry's outlook presents a company with sufficiently attractive opportunities for growth and profitability.

In Chapter 1, we learned that one of the three central questions that managers must address in evaluating their company's business prospects is *"Where are we now?"* Two facets of the company's situation are especially pertinent: (1) the industry and competitive environments in which the company operates—its external environment; and (2) the company's resources and organizational capabilities—its internal environment. Developing answers to the questions *"Where do we want to go from here?"* and *"How are we going to get there?"* without first gaining an understanding of the company's external and internal environments hamstrings attempts to build competitive advantage and boost company performance. Indeed, the first test of a winning strategy inquires, *"How well does the strategy fit the company's situation?"*

This chapter presents the concepts and analytical tools for zeroing in on a single-business company's external environment. Attention centers on the competitive arena in which the company operates, the drivers of market change, the market positions of rival companies, and the factors that determine competitive success. Chapter 4 explores the methods of evaluating a company's internal circumstances and competitiveness.

THE STRATEGICALLY RELEVANT COMPONENTS OF A COMPANY'S MACRO-ENVIRONMENT

▶ **LO1**

Gain command of the basic concepts and analytical tools widely used to diagnose a company's industry and competitive conditions.

The performance of all companies is affected by such external characteristics as general economic conditions and global factors; population demographics; societal values and lifestyles; political, regulatory, and legal factors; the natural environment; and technological factors. Strictly speaking, a company's "macro-environment" includes *all relevant factors and influences* outside the company's boundaries; by *relevant*, we mean these factors are important enough that they should shape management's decisions regarding the company's long-term direction, objectives, strategy, and business model. Figure 3.1 presents a depiction of macro-environmental factors with a high potential to affect a company's business situation. The impact of outer-ring factors on a company's choice of strategy can range from big to small. But even if the factors in the outer ring of the macro-environment change slowly or are likely to have a low impact on the company's business situation, they still merit a watchful eye. Motor vehicle companies must adapt their strategies to current customer concerns about carbon emissions and high gasoline prices. The demographics of an aging population and longer life expectancies will have a dramatic impact on the health care and prescription drug industries in the next few decades. As company managers scan the external environment, they must be alert for potentially important outer-ring developments, assess their impact and influence, and adapt the company's direction and strategy as needed.

However, the factors and forces in a company's macro-environment that have the *biggest* strategy-shaping impact typically pertain to the company's immediate industry and competitive environment—competitive pressures, the actions of rivals firms, buyer behavior, supplier-related considerations, and so on. Consequently, this chapter concentrates on a company's industry and competitive environment.

▶ FIGURE 3.1 **The Components of a Company's Macro-Environment**

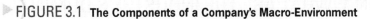

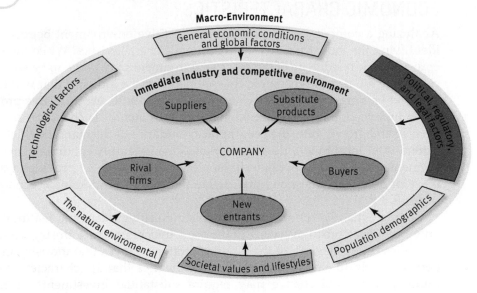

ASSESSING THE COMPANY'S INDUSTRY AND COMPETITIVE ENVIRONMENT

Thinking strategically about a company's industry and competitive environment entails using some well-validated concepts and analytical tools to get clear answers to seven questions:

1. Do the dominant economic characteristics of the industry offer sellers opportunities for growth and attractive profits?
2. What kinds of competitive forces are industry members facing, and how strong is each force?
3. What forces are driving industry change, and what impact will these changes have on competitive intensity and industry profitability?
4. What market positions do industry rivals occupy—who is strongly positioned and who is not?
5. What strategic moves are rivals likely to make next?
6. What are the key factors of competitive success?
7. Does the industry outlook offer good prospects for profitability?

Analysis-based answers to these questions are prerequisites for a strategy offering good fit with the external situation. The remainder of this chapter is devoted to describing the methods of obtaining solid answers to the seven questions above.

Integrative Strategic Experience

QUESTION 1: WHAT ARE THE INDUSTRY'S DOMINANT ECONOMIC CHARACTERISTICS?

Analyzing a company's industry and competitive environment begins with identifying the industry's dominant economic characteristics. While the general economic conditions of the macro-environment may prove to be strategically relevant, it is the economic characteristics of the industry that will have a greater bearing on the industry's prospects for growth and attractive profits. An industry's dominant economic characteristics include such factors as market size and growth rate, the geographic boundaries of the market (which can extend from local to worldwide), market demand-supply conditions, market segmentation, and the pace of technological change. Table 3.1 provides a summary of analytical questions that define the industry's dominant economic features.

Getting a handle on an industry's distinguishing economic features not only provides a broad overview of the attractiveness of the industry, but also promotes understanding of the kinds of strategic moves that industry members are likely to employ. For example, industries that are characterized by rapid technological change may require substantial investments in R&D and the development of strong product innovation capabilities—continuous

▶ TABLE 3.1

What to Consider in Identifying an Industry's Dominant Economic Features

ECONOMIC CHARACTERISTIC	QUESTIONS TO ANSWER
Market size and growth rate	• How big is the industry and how fast is it growing? • What does the industry's position in the life cycle (early development, rapid growth and takeoff, early maturity and slowing growth, saturation and stagnation, decline) reveal about the industry's growth prospects?
Scope of competitive rivalry	• Is the geographic area over which most companies compete local, regional, national, multinational, or global?
Demand-supply conditions	• Is a surplus of capacity pushing prices and profit margins down? • Is the industry overcrowded with too many competitors?
Market segmentation	• Is the industry characterized by various product characteristics or customer wants, needs, or preferences that divide the market into distinct segments?
Pace of technological change	• What role does advancing technology play in this industry? • Do most industry members have or need strong technological capabilities? Why?

product innovation is primarily a survival strategy in such industries as video games, computers, and pharmaceuticals.

QUESTION 2: HOW STRONG ARE THE INDUSTRY'S COMPETITIVE FORCES?

After gaining an understanding of the industry's general economic characteristics, industry and competitive analysis should focus on the competitive dynamics of the industry. The nature and subtleties of competitive forces are never the same from one industry to another and must be wholly understood to accurately form answers to the question *"Where are we now?"* Far and away the most powerful and widely used tool for assessing the strength of the industry's competitive forces is the *five-forces model of competition.*[1] This model, as depicted in Figure 3.2, holds that competitive forces affecting industry

▶**LO2**

Become adept at recognizing the factors that cause competition in an industry to be fierce, more or less normal, or relatively weak.

▶FIGURE 3.2 **The Five-Forces Model of Competition**

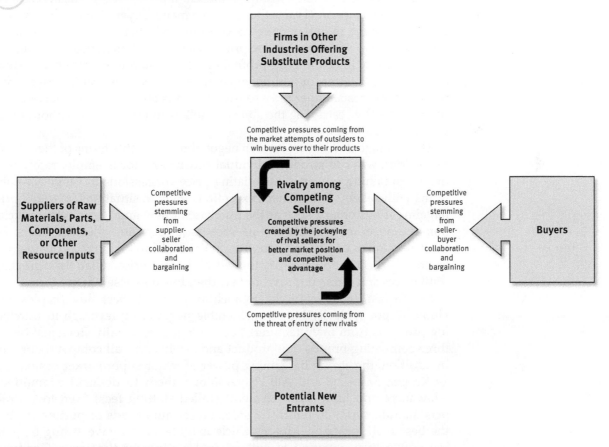

Sources: Based on Michael E. Porter, "How Competitive Forces Shape Strategy," *Harvard Business Review* 57, no. 2 (March–April 1979), pp. 137–45; and Michael E. Porter, "The Five Competitive Forces That Shape Strategy," *Harvard Business Review* 86, no. 1 (January 2008), pp. 80–86.

attractiveness go beyond rivalry among competing sellers and include pressures stemming from four coexisting sources. The five competitive forces affecting industry attractiveness are listed below.

1. Competitive pressures stemming from *buyer* bargaining power.
2. Competitive pressures coming from companies in other industries to win buyers over to *substitute products.*
3. Competitive pressures stemming from *supplier* bargaining power.
4. Competitive pressures associated with the threat of *new entrants* into the market.
5. Competitive pressures associated with *rivalry among competing sellers* to attract customers. This is usually the strongest of the five competitive forces.

The Competitive Force of Buyer Bargaining Power

Whether seller-buyer relationships represent a minor or significant competitive force depends on (1) whether some or many buyers have sufficient bargaining leverage to obtain price concessions and other favorable terms, and (2) the extent to which buyers are price sensitive. Buyers with strong bargaining power can limit industry profitability by demanding price concessions, better payment terms, or additional features and services that increase industry members' costs. Buyer price sensitivity limits the profit potential of industry members by restricting the ability of sellers to raise prices without losing volume or unit sales.

The leverage that buyers have in negotiating favorable terms of the sale can range from weak to strong. Individual consumers, for example, rarely have much bargaining power in negotiating price concessions or other favorable terms with sellers. The primary exceptions involve situations in which price haggling is customary, such as the purchase of new and used motor vehicles, homes, and other big-ticket items such as jewelry and pleasure boats. For most consumer goods and services, individual buyers have no bargaining leverage—their option is to pay the seller's posted price, delay their purchase until prices and terms improve, or take their business elsewhere.

In contrast, large retail chains such as Walmart, Best Buy, Staples, and Home Depot typically have considerable negotiating leverage in purchasing products from manufacturers because retailers usually stock just two or three competing brands of a product and rarely carry all competing brands. In addition, the strong bargaining power of major supermarket chains such as Kroger, Safeway, and Albertsons allows them to demand promotional allowances and lump-sum payments (called slotting fees) from food products manufacturers in return for stocking certain brands or putting them in the best shelf locations. Motor vehicle manufacturers have strong bargaining power in negotiating to buy original equipment tires from Goodyear, Michelin, Bridgestone/Firestone, Continental, and Pirelli not only because they buy in large quantities, but also because tire makers have judged original equipment tires to be important contributors to brand awareness and brand loyalty.

Even if buyers do not purchase in large quantities or offer a seller important market exposure or prestige, they gain a degree of bargaining leverage in the following circumstances:

- *If buyers' costs of switching to competing brands or substitutes are relatively low.* Buyers who can readily switch between several sellers have more negotiating leverage than buyers who have high switching costs. When the products of rival sellers are virtually identical, it is relatively easy for buyers to switch from seller to seller at little or no cost. For example, the screws, rivets, steel, and capacitors used in the production of large home appliances such as washers and dryers are all commodity-like and available from many sellers. The potential for buyers to easily switch from one seller to another encourages sellers to make concessions to win or retain a buyer's business.

- *If the number of buyers is small or if a customer is particularly important to a seller.* The smaller the number of buyers, the less easy it is for sellers to find alternative buyers when a customer is lost to a competitor. The prospect of losing a customer who is not easily replaced often makes a seller more willing to grant concessions of one kind or another. Because of the relatively small number of digital camera brands, the sellers of lenses and other components used in the manufacture of digital cameras are in a weak bargaining position in their negotiations with buyers of their components.

- *If buyer demand is weak.* Weak or declining demand creates a "buyers' market"; conversely, strong or rapidly growing demand creates a "sellers' market" and shifts bargaining power to sellers.

- *If buyers are well informed about sellers' products, prices, and costs.* The more information buyers have, the better bargaining position they are in. The mushrooming availability of product information on the Internet is giving added bargaining power to individuals. It has become common for automobile shoppers to arrive at dealerships armed with invoice prices, dealer holdback information, a summary of incentives, and manufacturers' financing terms.

- *If buyers pose a credible threat of integrating backward into the business of sellers.* Companies such as Anheuser-Busch, Coors, and Heinz have integrated backward into metal can manufacturing to gain bargaining power in obtaining the balance of their can requirements from otherwise powerful metal can manufacturers.

Figure 3.3 summarizes factors causing buyer bargaining power to be strong or weak.

Not all buyers of an industry's product have equal degrees of bargaining power with sellers, and some may be less sensitive than others to price, quality, or service differences. For example, apparel manufacturers confront significant bargaining power when selling to big retailers such as Macy's, T. J. Maxx, or Target, but they can command much better prices selling to small owner-managed apparel boutiques.

▶FIGURE 3.3 **Factors Affecting the Strength of Buyer Bargaining Power**

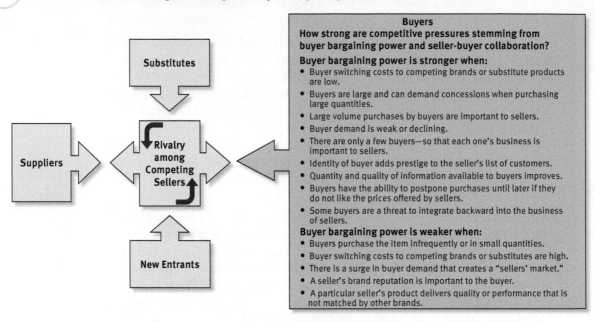

The Competitive Force of Substitute Products

Companies in one industry are vulnerable to competitive pressure from the actions of companies in another industry whenever buyers view the products of the two industries as good substitutes. For instance, the producers of sugar experience competitive pressures from the sales and marketing efforts of the makers of Equal, Splenda, and Sweet'N Low. Similarly, the producers of eyeglasses and contact lenses face competitive pressures from doctors who do corrective laser surgery. First-run movie theater chains are feeling competitive heat as more and more consumers are attracted to simply watch video on demand or movie DVDs at home in media rooms equipped with big-screen, high-definition TVs and surround sound. The producers of metal cans are becoming increasingly engaged in a battle with the makers of retort pouches for the business of companies producing packaged fruits, vegetables, meats, and pet foods. Retort pouches, which are multilayer packages made from polypropylene, aluminum foil, and polyester, are more attractively priced than metal cans because they are less expensive to produce and ship than cans.

Just how strong the competitive pressures are from the sellers of substitute products depends on three factors:

1. *Whether substitutes are readily available and attractively priced.* The presence of readily available and attractively priced substitutes creates competitive pressure by placing a ceiling on the prices industry members can charge. When substitutes are cheaper than an industry's product, industry members come under heavy competitive pressure to reduce their prices and find ways to absorb the price cuts with cost reductions.

2. *Whether buyers view the substitutes as comparable or better in terms of quality, performance, and other relevant attributes.* Customers are prone to compare performance and other attributes as well as price. For example, consumers have found digital cameras to be a superior substitute to film cameras because of the superior ease of use, the ability to download images to a home computer, and the ability to delete bad shots without paying for film developing.

3. *Whether the costs that buyers incur in switching to the substitutes are high or low.* High switching costs deter switching to substitutes while low switching costs make it easier for the sellers of attractive substitutes to lure buyers to their products. Typical switching costs include the inconvenience of switching to a substitute, the costs of additional equipment, the psychological costs of severing old supplier relationships, and employee retraining costs.

Figure 3.4 summarizes the conditions that determine whether the competitive pressures from substitute products are strong, moderate, or weak.

► FIGURE 3.4 **Factors Affecting Competition from Substitute Products**

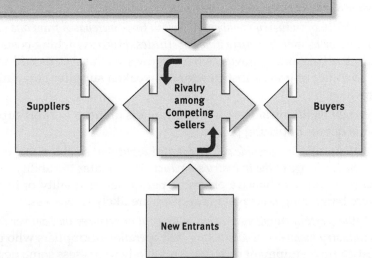

Firms in Other Industries Offering Substitute Products

How strong are competitive pressures coming from substitute products from outside the industry?

Competitive pressures from substitutes are stronger when:
• Good substitutes are readily available or new ones are emerging.
• Substitutes are attractively priced.
• Substitutes have comparable or better performance features.
• End users have low costs in switching to substitutes.
• End users grow more comfortable with using substitutes.

Competitive pressures from substitutes are weaker when:
• Good substitutes are not readily available or don't exist.
• Substitutes are higher priced relative to the performance they deliver.
• End users have high costs in switching to substitutes.

Signs that Competition from Substitutes Is Strong
• Sales of substitutes are growing faster than sales of the industry being analyzed (an indication that the sellers of substitutes are drawing customers away from the industry in question).
• Producers of substitutes are moving to add new capacity.
• Profits of the producers of substitutes are on the rise.

Suppliers

Rivalry among Competing Sellers

Buyers

New Entrants

As a rule, the lower the price of substitutes, the higher their quality and performance, and the lower the user's switching costs, the more intense the competitive pressures posed by substitute products.

The Competitive Force of Supplier Bargaining Power

Whether the suppliers of industry members represent a weak or strong competitive force depends on the degree to which suppliers have sufficient *bargaining power* to influence the terms and conditions of supply in their favor. Suppliers with strong bargaining power can erode industry profitability by charging industry members higher prices, passing costs on to them, and limiting their opportunities to find better deals. For instance, Microsoft and Intel, both of which supply PC makers with essential components, have been known to use their dominant market status not only to charge PC makers premium prices but also to leverage PC makers in other ways. The bargaining power possessed by Microsoft and Intel when negotiating with customers is so great that both companies have faced antitrust charges on numerous occasions. Before a legal agreement ending the practice, Microsoft pressured PC makers to load only Microsoft products on the PCs they shipped. Intel has also defended against antitrust charges resulting from its bargaining strength, but continues to give PC makers that use the biggest percentages of Intel chips in their PC models top priority in filling orders for newly introduced Intel chips. Being on Intel's list of preferred customers helps a PC maker get an early allocation of Intel's latest chips and thus allows a PC maker to get new models to market ahead of rivals.

The factors that determine whether any of the industry suppliers are in a position to exert substantial bargaining power or leverage are fairly clear-cut:

- *If the item being supplied is a commodity that is readily available from many suppliers.* Suppliers have little or no bargaining power or leverage whenever industry members have the ability to source from any of several alternative and eager suppliers.
- *The ability of industry members to switch their purchases from one supplier to another or to switch to attractive substitutes.* High switching costs increase supplier bargaining power, whereas low switching costs and the ready availability of good substitute inputs weaken supplier bargaining power.
- *If certain inputs are in short supply.* Suppliers of items in short supply have some degree of pricing power.
- *If certain suppliers provide a differentiated input that enhances the performance, quality, or image of the industry's product.* The greater the ability of a particular input to enhance a product's performance, quality, or image, the more bargaining leverage its suppliers are likely to possess.
- *Whether certain suppliers provide equipment or services that deliver cost savings to industry members in conducting their operations.* Suppliers who provide cost-saving equipment or services are likely to possess some degree of bargaining leverage.

- *The fraction of the costs of the industry's product accounted for by the cost of a particular input.* The bigger the cost of a specific part or component, the more opportunity for competition in the marketplace to be affected by the actions of suppliers to raise or lower their prices.

- *If industry members are major customers of suppliers.* As a rule, suppliers have less bargaining leverage when their sales to members of this one industry constitute a big percentage of their total sales. In such cases, the well-being of suppliers is closely tied to the well-being of their major customers.

- *Whether it makes good economic sense for industry members to vertically integrate backward.* The make-or-buy decision generally boils down to whether suppliers are able to supply a particular component at a lower cost than industry members could achieve if they were to integrate backward.

Figure 3.5 summarizes the conditions that tend to make supplier bargaining power strong or weak.

The Competitive Force of Potential New Entrants

Several factors determine whether the threat of new companies entering the marketplace presents a significant competitive pressure. One factor relates to the size of the pool of likely entry candidates and the resources at their command. As a rule, the bigger the pool of entry candidates, the stronger the

▶ FIGURE 3.5 **Factors Affecting the Strength of Supplier Bargaining Power**

Suppliers of Resource Inputs

How strong are the competitive pressures stemming from supplier bargaining power and seller-supplier collaboration?

Supplier bargaining power is stronger when:

- Industry members incur high costs in switching their purchases to alternative suppliers.
- Needed inputs are in short supply (which gives suppliers more leverage in setting prices).
- A supplier has a differentiated input that enhances the quality, performance, or image of sellers' products or is a valuable or critical part of sellers' production processes.
- There are only a few suppliers of a particular input.

Supplier bargaining power is weaker when:

- The item being supplied is a "commodity" that is readily available from many suppliers at the going market price.
- Seller switching costs to alternative suppliers are low.
- Good substitute inputs exist or new ones emerge.
- There is a surge in the availability of supplies (thus greatly weakening supplier pricing power).
- Industry members account for a big fraction of suppliers' total sales and continued high volume purchases are important to the well-being of suppliers.
- Industry members are a threat to integrate backward into the business of suppliers and to self-manufacture their own requirements.

Substitutes

Rivalry among Competing Sellers

Buyers

New Entrants

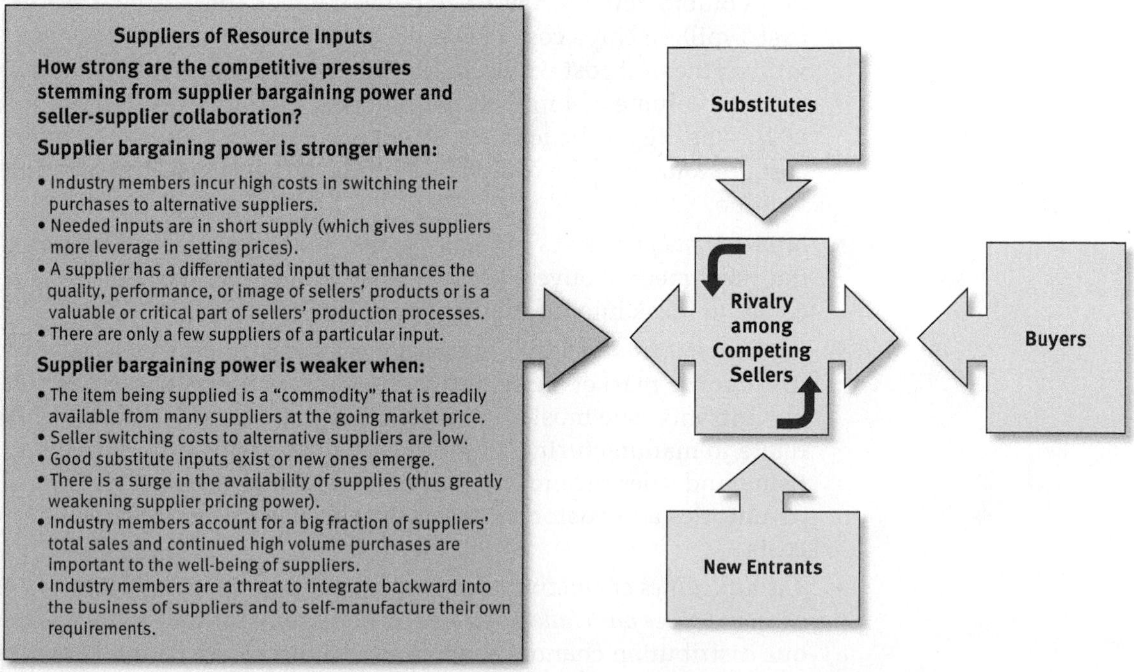

threat of potential entry. This is especially true when some of the likely entry candidates have ample resources to support entry into a new line of business. Frequently, the strongest competitive pressures associated with potential entry come not from outsiders but from current industry participants looking for growth opportunities. *Existing industry members are often strong candidates to enter market segments or geographic areas where they currently do not have a market presence.*

A second factor concerns whether the likely entry candidates face high or low entry barriers. High barriers reduce the competitive threat of potential entry, while low barriers make entry more likely, especially if the industry is growing and offers attractive profit opportunities. The most widely encountered barriers that entry candidates must hurdle include:[2]

- *The presence of sizable economies of scale in production or other areas of operation.* When incumbent companies enjoy cost advantages associated with large-scale operations, outsiders must either enter on a large scale (a costly and perhaps risky move) or accept a cost disadvantage and consequently lower profitability.

- *Cost and resource disadvantages not related to scale of operation.* Aside from enjoying economies of scale, industry incumbents can have cost advantages that stem from the possession of proprietary technology, partnerships with the best and cheapest suppliers, low fixed costs (because they have older facilities that have been mostly depreciated), and experience/learning curve effects. The microprocessor industry is an excellent example of how learning/experience curves put new entrants at a substantial cost disadvantage. Manufacturing unit costs for microprocessors tend to decline about 20 percent each time *cumulative* production volume doubles. With a 20 percent experience curve effect, if the first 1 million chips cost $100 each, once production volume reaches 2 million the unit cost would fall to $80 (80 percent of $100), and by a production volume of 4 million the unit cost would be $64 (80 percent of $80).[3] The bigger the learning or experience curve effect, the bigger the cost advantage of the company with the largest *cumulative* production volume.

- *Strong brand preferences and high degrees of customer loyalty.* The stronger the attachment of buyers to established brands, the harder it is for a newcomer to break into the marketplace.

- *High capital requirements.* The larger the total dollar investment needed to enter the market successfully, the more limited the pool of potential entrants. The most obvious capital requirements for new entrants relate to manufacturing facilities and equipment, introductory advertising and sales promotion campaigns, working capital to finance inventories and customer credit, and sufficient cash to cover start-up costs.

- *The difficulties of building a network of distributors-retailers and securing adequate space on retailers' shelves.* A potential entrant can face numerous distribution channel challenges. Wholesale distributors may be reluctant to take on a product that lacks buyer recognition. Retailers have to be recruited and convinced to give a new brand ample display space and an adequate trial period. Potential entrants sometimes have to "buy" their way into wholesale or retail channels by cutting their prices to provide dealers and distributors with higher markups and profit margins or by giving them big advertising and promotional allowances.

- *Restrictive regulatory policies.* Government agencies can limit or even bar entry by requiring licenses and permits. Regulated industries such as cable TV, telecommunications, electric and gas utilities, and radio and television broadcasting entail government-controlled entry.

- *Tariffs and international trade restrictions.* National governments commonly use tariffs and trade restrictions (antidumping rules, local content requirements, local ownership requirements, quotas, etc.) to raise entry barriers for foreign firms and protect domestic producers from outside competition.

- *The ability and willingness of industry incumbents to launch vigorous initiatives to block a newcomer's successful entry.* Even if a potential entrant has or can acquire the needed competencies and resources to attempt entry, it must still worry about the reaction of existing firms.[4] Sometimes, there's little that incumbents can do to throw obstacles in an entrant's path. But there are times when incumbents use price cuts, increase advertising, introduce product improvements, and launch legal attacks to prevent the entrant from building a clientele. Cable TV companies have vigorously fought the entry of satellite TV into the industry by seeking government intervention to delay satellite providers in offering local stations, offering satellite customers discounts to switch back to cable, and charging satellite customers high monthly rates for cable Internet access.

Figure 3.6 summarizes conditions making the threat of entry strong or weak.

The Competitive Force of Rivalry among Competing Sellers

The strongest of the five competitive forces is nearly always the rivalry among competing sellers of a product or service. In effect, *a market is a competitive battlefield* where there's no end to the campaign for buyer patronage. Rival sellers are prone to employ whatever weapons they have in their business arsenal to improve their market positions, strengthen their market position with buyers, and earn good profits. The strategy-making challenge is to craft a competitive strategy that, at the very least, allows a company to hold its own against rivals and that, ideally, *produces a competitive edge over rivals.* But competitive contests are ongoing and dynamic. When one firm makes a strategic move that produces good results, its rivals typically respond with offensive or defensive countermoves of their own. This pattern of action and reaction produces a continually evolving competitive landscape where the market battle ebbs and flows and produces winners and losers. But the current market leaders have no guarantees of continued leadership. In every industry, the ongoing jockeying of rivals leads to one or more companies

Integrative Strategic Experience

▶FIGURE 3.6 **Factors Affecting the Threat of Entry**

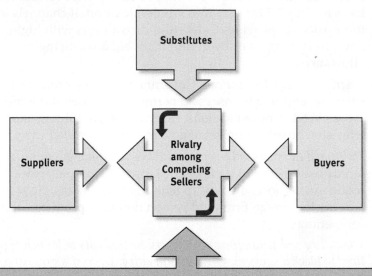

gaining or losing momentum in the marketplace according to whether their latest strategic maneuvers succeed or fail.[5]

Figure 3.7 shows a sampling of competitive weapons that firms can deploy in battling rivals and indicates the factors that influence the intensity of their rivalry. Some of the factors that influence the tempo of rivalry among industry competitors include:

- *Rivalry intensifies when competing sellers regularly launch fresh actions to boost their market standing and business performance.* Normally, competitive jockeying among rival sellers is fairly intense. Indicators of strong competitive rivalry include lively price competition, the rapid introduction of next-generation products, and moves to differentiate products by offering better performance features, higher quality, improved customer service, or a wider product selection. Other common tactics used to temporarily boost

▶ FIGURE 3.7 **Factors Affecting the Strength of Competitive Rivalry**

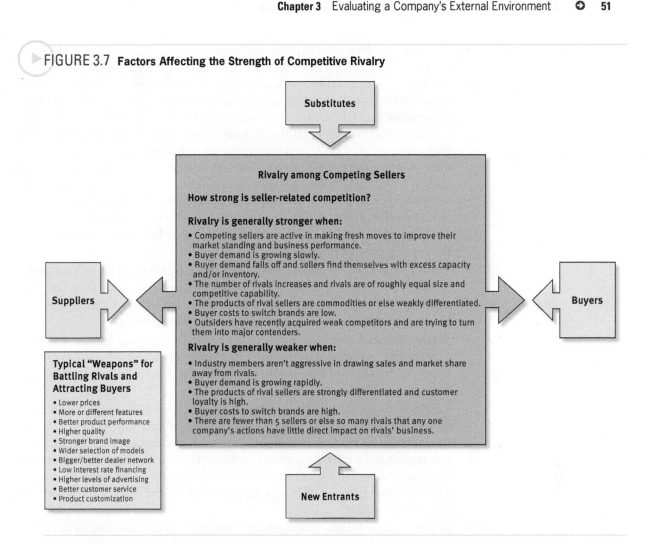

sales include special sales promotions, heavy advertising, rebates, or low-interest-rate financing.

- *Rivalry is stronger in industries where competitors are equal in size and capability.* Competitive rivalry in the quick-service restaurant industry is particularly strong where there are numerous relatively equal-sized hamburger, deli sandwich, chicken, and taco chains. For the most part, McDonald's, Burger King, Taco Bell, KFC, Arby's, and other national fast-food chains have comparable capabilities and are required to compete aggressively to hold their own in the industry.

- *Rivalry is usually stronger in slow-growing markets and weaker in fast-growing markets.* Rapidly expanding buyer demand produces enough new business for all industry members to grow. But in markets where growth is sluggish or where buyer demand drops off unexpectedly, it is not uncommon for competitive rivalry to intensify significantly as rivals battle for market share and volume gains.

- *Rivalry is usually weaker in industries comprised of vast numbers of small rivals; likewise, it is often weak when there are fewer than five competitors.* Head-to-head rivalry tends to be weak once an industry becomes populated with so many rivals that the strategic moves of any one competitor have little discernible impact on the success of rivals. Rivalry also *tends* to be weak if an industry consists of just two to four sellers. In a market with few rivals, each competitor soon learns that aggressive moves to grow its sales and market share can have an immediate adverse impact on rivals' businesses, almost certainly provoking vigorous retaliation. However, some caution must be exercised in concluding that rivalry is weak just because there are only a few competitors. The fierceness of the current battle between Google and Microsoft and the decades-long war between Coca-Cola and Pepsi are prime examples.

- *Rivalry increases when buyer demand falls off and sellers find themselves with excess capacity and/or inventory.* Excess supply conditions create a "buyers' market," putting added competitive pressure on industry rivals to scramble for profitable sales levels (often by price discounting).

- *Rivalry increases as it becomes less costly for buyers to switch brands.* The less expensive it is for buyers to switch their purchases from the seller of one brand to the seller of another brand, the easier it is for sellers to steal customers away from rivals.

- *Rivalry increases as the products of rival sellers become more standardized and diminishes as the products of industry rivals become more differentiated.* When the offerings of rivals are identical or weakly differentiated, buyers have less reason to be brand loyal—a condition that makes it easier for rivals to persuade buyers to switch to their offering. On the other hand, strongly differentiated product offerings among rivals breed high brand loyalty on the part of buyers.

- *Rivalry is more intense when industry conditions tempt competitors to use price cuts or other competitive weapons to boost unit volume.* When a product is perishable, seasonal, or costly to hold in inventory, competitive pressures build quickly any time one or more firms decide to cut prices and dump supplies on the market. Likewise, whenever fixed costs account for a large fraction of total cost, so that unit costs tend to be lowest at or near full capacity, firms come under significant pressure to cut prices or otherwise try to boost sales whenever they are operating below full capacity.

- *Rivalry increases when one or more competitors become dissatisfied with their market position.* Firms that are losing ground or are in financial trouble often pursue aggressive (or perhaps desperate) turnaround strategies that can involve price discounts, greater advertising, or merger with other rivals. Such strategies can turn competitive pressures up a notch.

- *Rivalry increases when strong companies outside the industry acquire weak firms in the industry and launch aggressive, well-funded moves to build market share.* A concerted effort to turn a weak rival into a market leader nearly always entails launching well-financed strategic initiatives to dramatically improve the competitor's product offering, excite buyer interest, and win a much bigger market share—actions that, if successful, put added pressure on rivals to counter with fresh strategic moves of their own.

Rivalry can be characterized as *cutthroat* or *brutal* when competitors engage in protracted price wars or habitually employ other aggressive tactics that are mutually destructive to profitability. Rivalry can be considered *fierce* to *strong* when the battle for market share is so vigorous that the profit margins of most industry members are squeezed to bare-bones levels. Rivalry can be characterized as *moderate* or *normal* when the maneuvering among industry members, while lively and healthy, still allows most industry members to earn acceptable profits. Rivalry is *weak* when most companies in the industry are relatively well satisfied with their sales growth and market share and rarely undertake offensives to steal customers away from one another.

The Collective Strengths of the Five Competitive Forces and Industry Profitability

Scrutinizing each of the five competitive forces one by one provides a powerful diagnosis of what competition is like in a given market. Once the strategist has gained an understanding of the competitive pressures associated with each of the five forces, the next step is to evaluate the collective strength of the five forces and determine if companies in this industry should reasonably expect to earn decent profits.

As a rule, the stronger the collective impact of the five competitive forces, the lower the combined profitability of industry participants. The most extreme case of a "competitively unattractive" industry is when all five forces are producing strong competitive pressures: Rivalry among sellers is vigorous, low entry barriers allow new rivals to gain a market foothold, competition from substitutes is intense, and both suppliers and customers are able to exercise considerable bargaining leverage. Fierce to strong competitive pressures coming from all five directions nearly always drive industry profitability to unacceptably low levels, frequently producing losses for many industry members and forcing some out of business. But an industry can be competitively unattractive without all five competitive forces being strong. Fierce competitive pressures from just one of the five forces, such as brutal price competition among rival sellers, may suffice to destroy the conditions for good profitability.

> The stronger the forces of competition, the harder it becomes for industry members to attractive profits.

In contrast, when the collective impact of the five competitive forces is moderate to weak, an industry is competitively attractive in the sense that industry members can reasonably expect to earn good profits and a nice return on investment. The ideal competitive environment for earning superior profits is one in which both suppliers and customers are in weak bargaining positions, there are no good substitutes, high barriers block further entry, and rivalry among present sellers generates only moderate competitive pressures. Weak competition is the best of all possible worlds for companies with mediocre strategies and second-rate implementation because even they can expect a decent profit.

QUESTION 3: WHAT ARE THE INDUSTRY'S DRIVING FORCES OF CHANGE AND WHAT IMPACT WILL THEY HAVE?

The intensity of competitive forces and the level of industry attractiveness are almost always fluid and subject to change. It is essential for strategy makers to understand the current competitive dynamics of the industry, but it is equally important for strategy makers to consider how the industry is changing and the effect of industry changes that are under way. Any strategies devised by management will play out in a dynamic industry environment, so it's imperative that such plans consider what the industry environment might look like during the near term.

The Concept of Industry Driving Forces

Industry and competitive conditions change because forces are enticing or pressuring certain industry participants (competitors, customers, suppliers) to alter their actions in important ways. The most powerful of the change agents are called **driving forces** because they have the biggest influences in reshaping the industry landscape and altering competitive conditions. Some driving forces originate in the outer ring of the company's macro-environment (see Figure 3.1) but most originate in the company's more immediate industry and competitive environment.

CORE CONCEPT

Driving forces are the major underlying causes of change in industry and competitive conditions.

Driving forces analysis has three steps: (1) identifying what the driving forces are, (2) assessing whether the drivers of change are, individually or collectively, acting to make the industry more or less attractive, and (3) determining what strategy changes are needed to prepare for the impact of the driving forces.

Identifying an Industry's Driving Forces

Many developments can affect an industry powerfully enough to qualify as driving forces, but most drivers of industry and competitive change fall into one of the following categories:

- *Changes in an industry's long-term growth rate.* Shifts in industry growth have the potential to affect the balance between industry supply and buyer demand, entry and exit, and the character and strength of competition. An upsurge in buyer demand triggers a race among established firms and newcomers to capture the new sales opportunities. A slowdown in the growth of demand nearly always brings an increase in rivalry and increased efforts by some firms to maintain their high rates of growth by taking sales and market share away from rivals.

- *Increasing globalization.* Competition begins to shift from primarily a regional or national focus to an international or global focus when industry members begin seeking out customers in foreign markets or when production activities begin to migrate to countries where costs are lowest. The forces of globalization are sometimes such a strong driver that companies find it highly advantageous, if not necessary, to spread their operating reach into more and more country markets. Globalization is very much a driver of industry change in such industries as credit cards, mobile phones, digital cameras, motor vehicles, steel, petroleum, personal computers, and video games.

- *Emerging new Internet capabilities and applications.* Mushrooming Internet use and an ever-growing series of Internet applications and capabilities have been major drivers of change in industry after industry. The ability of companies to reach consumers via the Internet increases the number of rivals a company faces and often escalates rivalry by pitting pure online sellers against local brick-and-mortar sellers. The Internet gives buyers unprecedented ability to research the product offerings of competitors and shop the market for the best value. Widespread use of e-mail has forever eroded the business of providing fax services and the first-class mail delivery revenues of governmental postal services worldwide. Videoconferencing via the Internet erodes the demand for business travel. Online course offerings are profoundly affecting higher education. The Internet of the future will feature faster speeds, dazzling applications, and over a billion connected gadgets performing an array of functions, thus driving further industry and competitive changes. But Internet-related impacts vary from industry to industry. The challenges here are to assess precisely how emerging Internet developments are altering a particular industry's landscape and to factor these impacts into the strategy-making equation.

- *Changes in who buys the product and how they use it.* Shifts in buyer demographics and the ways products are used can alter competition by affecting how customers perceive value, how customers make purchasing decisions, and where customers purchase the product. The burgeoning popularity of downloading and streaming music from the Internet has significantly changed the recording industry. According to IFPI, digital music accounted for more than 25 percent of industry sales in 2009. However, the ability of consumers to purchase individual tracks rather than albums and share files among other users caused industry sales to decline by 30 percent between 2004 and 2009.

- *Product innovation.* An ongoing stream of product innovations tends to alter the pattern of competition in an industry by attracting more first-time buyers, rejuvenating industry growth, and/or creating wider or narrower product differentiation among rival sellers. Product innovation has been a key driving force in such industries as computers, digital cameras, televisions, video games, and prescription drugs.

- *Technological change and manufacturing process innovation.* Advances in technology can dramatically alter an industry's landscape, making it possible to produce new and better products at lower cost and opening new industry frontiers. For instance, Voice over Internet Protocol technology (VoIP) has spawned low-cost, Internet-based phone networks that have begun competing with traditional telephone companies worldwide (whose higher-cost technology depends on hard-wire connections via overhead and underground telephone lines).

- *Marketing innovation.* When firms are successful in introducing *new ways* to market their products, they can spark a burst of buyer interest, widen industry demand, increase product differentiation, and lower unit costs—any or all of which can alter the competitive positions of rival firms and force strategy revisions.

- *Entry or exit of major firms.* The entry of one or more foreign companies into a geographic market once dominated by domestic firms nearly always shakes up competitive conditions. Likewise, when an established domestic firm from another industry attempts entry either by acquisition or by launching its own start-up venture, it usually pushes competition in new directions.

- *Diffusion of technical know-how across more companies and more countries.* As knowledge about how to perform a particular activity or execute a particular manufacturing technology spreads, the competitive advantage held by firms originally possessing this know-how erodes. Knowledge diffusion can occur through scientific journals, trade publications, on-site plant tours, word of mouth among suppliers and customers, employee migration, and Internet sources.

- *Changes in cost and efficiency.* Widening or shrinking differences in the costs among key competitors tend to dramatically alter the state of competition. Declining costs to produce PCs have enabled price cuts and spurred PC sales (especially lower-priced models) by making them more affordable to lower-income households worldwide.

- *Growing buyer preferences for differentiated products instead of a commodity product (or for a more standardized product instead of strongly differentiated products).* When a shift from standardized to differentiated products occurs, rivals must adopt strategies to outdifferentiate one another. However, buyers sometimes decide that a standardized, budget-priced product suits their requirements as well as a premium-priced product with lots of snappy features and personalized services.

- *Regulatory influences and government policy changes.* Government regulatory actions can often force significant changes in industry practices and strategic approaches. Net neutrality rules established by the Federal Communications Commission (FCC) in 2010 had the potential to alter the cost structure, capital budgets, and pricing policies of Internet service providers such as Comcast and AT&T. The FCC net neutrality policy was implemented to prevent Internet service providers from limiting the download speed of bandwidth-consuming content such as video. The requirement to treat all content equally would require greater investments in infrastructure and generate additional costs for such providers. However, the addition of broadband capacity would allow content providers to potentially boost site traffic by making more content requiring a large amount of bandwidth to consumers. In 2011, most content providers were pushing for full implementation of the FCC's net neutrality policies because such policies created new revenue opportunities, while Internet service providers were lobbying Congress to pass legislation restricting the FCC's authority over Internet service to avoid additional capital expenditures, higher operating costs, and price increases to customers.

- *Changing societal concerns, attitudes, and lifestyles.* Emerging social issues and changing attitudes and lifestyles can be powerful instigators of industry change. Consumer concerns about salt, sugar, chemical additives, saturated fat, cholesterol, carbohydrates, and nutritional value have forced food producers to revamp food-processing techniques, redirect R&D efforts into the use of healthier ingredients, and compete in developing nutritious, good-tasting products.

While many forces of change may be at work in a given industry, *no more than three or four* are likely to be true driving forces powerful enough to qualify as the *major determinants* of why and how the industry is changing. Thus, company strategists must resist the temptation to label every change they see as a driving force. Table 3.2 lists the most common driving forces.

Assessing the Impact of the Industry Driving Forces

The second step in driving forces analysis is to determine whether the prevailing driving forces are acting to make the industry environment more or less attractive. Getting a handle on the collective impact of the driving forces usually requires looking at the likely effects of each force separately, because the driving forces may not all be pushing change in the same direction. For example, two driving forces may be acting to spur demand for the industry's product while one driving force may be working to curtail demand. Whether the net effect on industry demand is up or down hinges on which driving forces are the more powerful.

> An important part of driving forces analysis is to determine whether the individual or collective impact of the driving forces will be to increase or decrease market demand, make competition more or less intense, and lead to higher or lower industry profitability.

▶ TABLE 3.2

Common Driving Forces

1. Changes in the long-term industry growth rate.
2. Increasing globalization.
3. Emerging new Internet capabilities and applications.
4. Changes in who buys the product and how they use it.
5. Product innovation.
6. Technological change and manufacturing process innovation.
7. Marketing innovation.
8. Entry or exit of major firms.
9. Diffusion of technical know-how across more companies and more countries.
10. Changes in cost and efficiency.
11. Growing buyer preferences for differentiated products instead of a standardized commodity product (or for a more standardized product instead of strongly differentiated products).
12. Regulatory influences and government policy changes.
13. Changing societal concerns, attitudes, and lifestyles.

Determining Strategy Changes Needed to Prepare for the Impact of Driving Forces

The third step of driving forces analysis—where the real payoff for strategy making comes—is for managers to draw some conclusions about what strategy adjustments will be needed to deal with the impact of the driving forces. Without understanding the forces driving industry change and the impacts these forces will have on the industry environment over the next one to three years, managers are ill prepared to craft a strategy

> The real payoff of driving forces analysis is to help managers understand what strategy changes are needed to prepare for the impacts of the driving forces.

tightly matched to emerging conditions. Similarly, if managers are uncertain about the implications of one or more driving forces, or if their views are off-base, it will be difficult for them to craft a strategy that is responsive to the consequences of driving forces. So driving forces analysis is not something to take lightly; it has practical value and is basic to the task of thinking strategically about where the industry is headed and how to prepare for the changes ahead.

QUESTION 4: HOW ARE INDUSTRY RIVALS POSITIONED?

The nature of competitive strategy inherently positions companies competing in an industry into strategic groups with diverse price/quality ranges, different distribution channels, varying product features, and different geographic coverages. The best technique for revealing the market positions of industry competitors is **strategic group mapping.** This analytical tool is useful for comparing the market positions of industry competitors or for grouping industry combatants into like positions.

> **CORE CONCEPT**
> **Strategic group mapping** is a technique for displaying the different market or competitive positions that rival firms occupy in the industry.

Using Strategic Group Maps to Assess the Positioning of Key Competitors

A **strategic group** consists of those industry members with similar competitive approaches and positions in the market. Companies in the same strategic group can resemble one another in any of several ways—they may have comparable product-line breadth, sell in the same price/quality range, emphasize the same distribution channels, use essentially the same product attributes to appeal to similar types of buyers, depend on identical technological approaches, or offer buyers similar services and technical assistance.[6] An industry with a commodity-like product may contain only one strategic group whereby all sellers pursue essentially identical strategies and have comparable market positions. But even with commodity products, there is

> **CORE CONCEPT**
> A **strategic group** is a cluster of industry rivals that have similar competitive approaches and market positions.

likely some attempt at differentiation occurring in the form of varying delivery times, financing terms, or levels of customer service. Most industries offer a host of competitive approaches that allow companies to find unique industry positioning and avoid fierce competition in a crowded strategic group. Evaluating strategy options entails examining what strategic groups exist, identifying which companies exist within each group, and determining if a competitive "white space" exists where industry competitors are able to create and capture altogether new demand.

The procedure for constructing a *strategic group map* is straightforward:

- Identify the competitive characteristics that delineate strategic approaches used in the industry. Typical variables used in creating strategic group maps are the price/quality range (high, medium, low), geographic coverage (local, regional, national, global), degree of vertical integration (none, partial, full), product-line breadth (wide, narrow), choice of distribution channels (retail, wholesale, Internet, multiple channels), and degree of service offered (no-frills, limited, full).

- Plot firms on a two-variable map based upon their strategic approaches.

- Assign firms occupying the same map location to a common strategic group.

- Draw circles around each strategic group, making the circles proportional to the size of the group's share of total industry sales revenues.

This produces a two-dimensional diagram like the one for the retail chain store industry in Concepts & Connections 3.1.

Several guidelines need to be observed in creating strategic group maps. First, the two variables selected as axes for the map should *not* be highly correlated; if they are, the circles on the map will fall along a diagonal and strategy makers will learn nothing more about the relative positions of competitors than they would by considering just one of the variables. For instance, if companies with broad product lines use multiple distribution channels while companies with narrow lines use a single distribution channel, then looking at product line breadth reveals just as much about industry positioning as looking at the two competitive variables. Second, the variables chosen as axes for the map should reflect key approaches to offering value to customers and expose big differences in how rivals position themselves in the marketplace. Third, the variables used as axes don't have to be either quantitative or continuous; rather, they can be discrete variables or defined in terms of distinct classes and combinations. Fourth, drawing the sizes of the circles on the map proportional to the combined sales of the firms in each strategic group allows the map to reflect the relative sizes of each strategic group. Fifth, if more than two good competitive variables can be used as axes for the map, multiple maps can be drawn to give different exposures to the competitive positioning in the industry. Because there is not necessarily one best map for portraying how competing firms are positioned in the market, it is advisable to experiment with different pairs of competitive variables.

CONCEPTS & CONNECTIONS 3.1

COMPARATIVE MARKET POSITIONS OF SELECTED RETAIL CHAINS: A STRATEGIC GROUP MAP APPLICATION

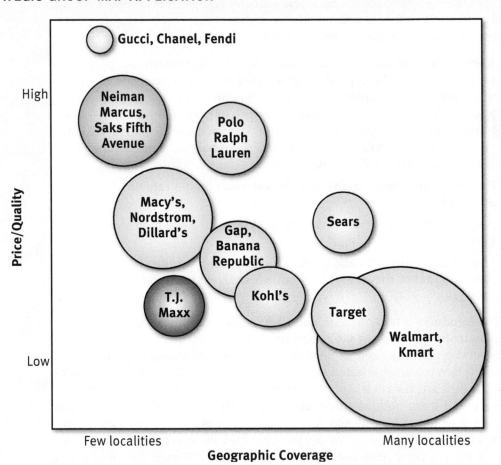

Note: Circles are drawn roughly proportional to the total revenues of the retail chains included in each strategic group.

The Value of Strategic Group Maps

Strategic group maps are revealing in several respects. The *most important* has to do with identifying which rivals are similarly positioned and are thus close rivals and which are distant rivals. Generally, *the closer strategic groups are to each other on the map, the stronger the cross-group competitive rivalry tends to be.* Although firms in the same strategic group are the closest rivals, the next closest rivals are in the immediately adjacent groups.[7] Often, firms in strategic groups that are far apart on the map hardly compete at all. For instance,

Walmart's clientele, merchandise selection, and pricing points are much too different to justify calling them close competitors of Neiman Marcus or Saks Fifth Avenue in retailing. For the same reason, Timex is not a meaningful competitive rival of Rolex, and Kia is not a close competitor of Porsche or Lexus.

> Some strategic groups are more favorably positioned than others because they confront weaker competitive forces and/or because they are more favorably impacted by industry driving forces.

The second thing to be gleaned from strategic group mapping is that *not all positions on the map are equally attractive.* Two reasons account for why some positions can be more attractive than others:

1. *Industry driving forces may favor some strategic groups and hurt others.* Driving forces in an industry may be acting to grow the demand for the products of firms in some strategic groups and shrink the demand for the products of firms in other strategic groups—as is the case in the news industry where Internet news services and cable news networks are gaining ground at the expense of newspapers and network television. The industry driving forces of emerging Internet capabilities and applications, changes in who buys the product and how they use it, and changing societal concerns, attitudes, and lifestyles are making it increasingly difficult for traditional media to increase audiences and attract new advertisers.

2. *Competitive pressures may cause the profit potential of different strategic groups to vary.* The profit prospects of firms in different strategic groups can vary from good to poor because of differing degrees of competitive rivalry within strategic groups, differing degrees of exposure to competition from substitute products outside the industry, and differing degrees of supplier or customer bargaining power from group to group. For instance, the competitive battle between Walmart and Target is more intense (with consequently smaller profit margins) than the rivalry among Versace, Chanel, Fendi, and other high-end fashion retailers.

Thus, part of strategic group analysis always entails drawing conclusions about where on the map is the "best" place to be and why. Which companies or strategic groups are in the best positions to prosper and which might be expected to struggle? And equally important, how might firms in poorly positioned strategic groups reposition themselves to improve their prospects for good financial performance?

QUESTION 5: WHAT STRATEGIC MOVES ARE RIVALS LIKELY TO MAKE NEXT?

As in sports, scouting the business opposition is an essential part of game plan development. **Competitive intelligence** about rivals' strategies, their latest actions and announcements, their resources and organizational capabilities, and the thinking and leadership styles of their executives is valuable for predicting the strategic moves competitors are likely to make next. Having good information to predict the likely moves of key competitors allows a company to prepare defensive countermoves and to exploit any openings that arise from competitors' missteps.

CONCEPTS & CONNECTIONS 3.2

BUSINESS ETHICS AND COMPETITIVE INTELLIGENCE

Those who gather competitive intelligence on rivals can sometimes cross the fine line between honest inquiry and unethical or even illegal behavior. For example, calling rivals to get information about prices, the dates of new-product introductions, or wage and salary levels is legal, but misrepresenting one's company affiliation during such calls is unethical. Pumping rivals' representatives at trade shows is ethical only if one wears a name tag with accurate company affiliation indicated. Avon Products at one point secured information about its biggest rival, Mary Kay Cosmetics (MKC), by having its personnel search through the garbage bins outside MKC's headquarters.[8] When MKC officials learned of the action and sued, Avon claimed it did nothing illegal because a 1988 Supreme Court ruling declared that trash left on public property (in this case, a sidewalk) was anyone's for the taking. Avon even produced a videotape of its removal of the trash at the MKC site. Avon won the lawsuit—but Avon's action, while legal, scarcely qualifies as ethical.

Considerations in trying to predict what strategic moves rivals are likely to make next include the following:

- What executives are saying about where the industry is headed, the firm's situation, and their past actions and leadership styles.
- Identifying trends in the timing of product launches or new marketing promotions.
- Determining which rivals badly need to increase unit sales and market share.
- Considering which rivals have a strong incentive, along with the resources, to make major strategic changes.
- Knowing which rivals are likely to enter new geographic markets.
- Deciding which rivals are strong candidates to expand their product offerings and enter new product segments.

To succeed in predicting a competitor's next moves, company strategists need to have a good understanding of each rival's situation, its pattern of behavior and preferences in responding to prior strategic attacks, what its best strategic options are, and how rival management measures success. Doing the necessary detective work can be tedious and time-consuming, but scouting competitors well enough to anticipate their next moves allows managers to prepare effective countermoves and to take rivals' probable actions into account in crafting their own offensive strategies.[9] Concepts & Connections 3.2 discusses the ethical limits to gathering competitive intelligence.

> Studying competitors' past behavior and preferences provides a valuable assist in anticipating what moves rivals are likely to make next and outmaneuvering them in the marketplace.

QUESTION 6: WHAT ARE THE INDUSTRY KEY SUCCESS FACTORS?

An industry's **key success factors (KSFs)** are those competitive factors that most affect industry members' ability to prosper in the marketplace. Key success factors may include particular strategy elements, product attributes, resources, competitive capabilities, or intangible assets. KSFs by their very nature are so important to future competitive success that *all firms* in the industry must pay close attention to them or risk an eventual exit from the industry.

> **CORE CONCEPT**
>
> **Key success factors** are the strategy elements, product attributes, competitive capabilities, or intangible assets with the greatest impact on future success in the marketplace.

In the ready-to-wear apparel industry, the KSFs are appealing designs and color combinations, low-cost manufacturing, a strong network of retailers or company-owned stores, distribution capabilities that allow stores to keep the best-selling items in stock, and advertisements that effectively convey the brand's image. These attributes and capabilities apply to all brands of apparel ranging from private-label brands sold by discounters to premium-priced ready-to-wear brands sold by upscale department stores. Table 3.3 on the next page lists the most common types of industry key success factors.

An industry's key success factors can usually be deduced through identifying the industry's dominant characteristics, assessing the five competitive forces, considering the impacts of the driving forces, comparing the market positions of industry members, and forecasting the likely next moves of key rivals. In addition, the answers to the following three questions help identify an industry's key success factors:

1. On what basis do buyers of the industry's product choose between the competing brands of sellers? That is, what product attributes are crucial?

2. Given the nature of the competitive forces prevailing in the marketplace, what resources and competitive capabilities does a company need to have to be competitively successful?

3. What shortcomings are almost certain to put a company at a significant competitive disadvantage?

Only rarely are there more than five or six key factors for future competitive success. Managers should therefore resist the temptation to label a factor that has only minor importance a KSF. To compile a list of every factor that matters even a little bit defeats the purpose of concentrating management attention on the factors truly critical to long-term competitive success.

▶**LO3**

Learn how to determine whether an industry's outlook presents a company with sufficiently attractive opportunities for growth and profitability.

QUESTION 7: DOES THE INDUSTRY OFFER GOOD PROSPECTS FOR ATTRACTIVE PROFITS?

The final step in evaluating the industry and competitive environment is boiling down the results of the analyses performed in Questions 1–6 to determine if the industry offers a company strong prospects for attractive profits.

TABLE 3.3

Common Types of Industry Key Success Factors	
Technology-related KSFs	• Expertise in a particular technology or in scientific research (important in pharmaceuticals, Internet applications, mobile communications, and most high-tech industries) • Proven ability to improve production processes (important in industries where advancing technology opens the way for higher manufacturing efficiency and lower production costs)
Manufacturing-related KSFs	• Ability to achieve scale economies and/or capture experience curve effects (important to achieving low production costs) • Quality control know-how (important in industries where customers insist on product reliability) • High utilization of fixed assets (important in capital-intensive/high-fixed-cost industries) • Access to attractive supplies of skilled labor • High labor productivity (important for items with high labor content) • Low-cost product design and engineering (reduces manufacturing costs) • Ability to manufacture or assemble products that are customized to buyer specifications
Distribution-related KSFs	• A strong network of wholesale distributors/dealers • Strong direct sales capabilities via the Internet and/or having company-owned retail outlets • Ability to secure favorable display space on retailer shelves
Marketing-related KSFs	• Breadth of product line and product selection • A well-known and well-respected brand name • Fast, accurate technical assistance • Courteous, personalized customer service • Accurate filling of buyer orders (few back orders or mistakes) • Customer guarantees and warranties (important in mail-order and online retailing, big-ticket purchases, and new-product introductions) • Clever advertising
Skills- and capability-related KSFs	• A talented workforce (superior talent is important in professional services such as accounting and investment banking) • National or global distribution capabilities • Product innovation capabilities (important in industries where rivals are racing to be first to market with new product attributes or performance features) • Design expertise (important in fashion and apparel industries) • Short delivery time capability • Supply chain management capabilities • Strong e-commerce capabilities—a user-friendly website and/or skills in using Internet technology applications to streamline internal operations
Other types of KSFs	• Overall low costs (not just in manufacturing) to be able to meet low-price expectations of customers • Convenient locations (important in many retailing businesses) • Ability to provide fast, convenient, after-the-sale repairs and service • A strong balance sheet and access to financial capital (important in newly emerging industries with high degrees of business risk and in capital-intensive industries) • Patent protection

The important factors on which to base such a conclusion include:

- The industry's growth potential.
- Whether powerful competitive forces are squeezing industry profitability to subpar levels and whether competition appears destined to grow stronger or weaker.
- Whether industry profitability will be favorably or unfavorably affected by the prevailing driving forces.
- The company's competitive position in the industry vis-à-vis rivals. (Well-entrenched leaders or strongly positioned contenders have a much better chance of earning attractive margins than those fighting a steep uphill battle.)
- How competently the company performs industry key success factors.

It is a mistake to think of a particular industry as being equally attractive or unattractive to all industry participants and all potential entrants. Conclusions have to be drawn from the perspective of a particular company. Industries attractive to insiders may be unattractive to outsiders. Industry environments unattractive to weak competitors may be attractive to strong competitors. A favorably positioned company may survey a business environment and see a host of opportunities that weak competitors cannot capture.

> The degree to which an industry is attractive or unattractive is not the same for all industry participants and potential new entrants. The attractiveness of an industry depends on the degree of fit between a company's competitive capabilities and industry key success factors.

When a company decides an industry is fundamentally attractive, a strong case can be made that it should invest aggressively to capture the opportunities it sees. When a strong competitor concludes an industry is relatively unattractive, it may elect to simply protect its present position, investing cautiously if at all, and begin looking for opportunities in other industries. A competitively weak company in an unattractive industry may see its best option as finding a buyer, perhaps a rival, to acquire its business.

KEY POINTS

Thinking strategically about a company's external situation involves probing for answers to the following seven questions:

1. *What are the industry's dominant economic features?* Industries differ significantly on such factors as market size and growth rate, the number and relative sizes of both buyers and sellers, the geographic scope of competitive rivalry, the degree of product differentiation, the speed of product innovation, demand-supply conditions, the extent of vertical integration, and the extent of scale economies and learning curve effects.

2. *What kinds of competitive forces are industry members facing, and how strong is each force?* The strength of competition is a composite of five forces: (1) competitive pressures stemming from buyer bargaining power and seller-buyer collaboration, (2) competitive pressures associated with the sellers of substitutes, (3) competitive pressures stemming from supplier bargaining power and supplier-seller collaboration,

(4) competitive pressures associated with the threat of new entrants into the market, and (5) competitive pressures stemming from the competitive jockeying among industry rivals.

3. *What forces are driving changes in the industry, and what impact will these changes have on competitive intensity and industry profitability?* Industry and competitive conditions change because forces are in motion that create incentives or pressures for change. The first phase is to identify the forces that are driving industry change. The second phase of driving forces analysis is to determine whether the driving forces, taken together, are acting to make the industry environment more or less attractive.

4. *What market positions do industry rivals occupy—who is strongly positioned and who is not?* Strategic group mapping is a valuable tool for understanding the similarities and differences inherent in the market positions of rival companies. Rivals in the same or nearby strategic groups are close competitors, whereas companies in distant strategic groups usually pose little or no immediate threat. Some strategic groups are more favorable than others. The profit potential of different strategic groups may not be the same because industry driving forces and competitive forces likely have varying effects on the industry's distinct strategic groups.

5. *What strategic moves are rivals likely to make next?* Scouting competitors well enough to anticipate their actions can help a company prepare effective countermoves (perhaps even beating a rival to the punch) and allows managers to take rivals' probable actions into account in designing their own company's best course of action.

6. *What are the key factors for competitive success?* An industry's key success factors (KSFs) are the particular product attributes, competitive capabilities, and intangible assets that spell the difference between being a strong competitor and a weak competitor—and sometimes between profit and loss. KSFs by their very nature are so important to competitive success that *all firms* in the industry must pay close attention to them or risk being driven out of the industry.

7. *Does the outlook for the industry present the company with sufficiently attractive prospects for profitability?* Conclusions regarding industry attractiveness are a major driver of company strategy. When a company decides an industry is fundamentally attractive and presents good opportunities, a strong case can be made that it should invest aggressively to capture the opportunities it sees. When a strong competitor concludes an industry is relatively unattractive and lacking in opportunity, it may elect to simply protect its present position, investing cautiously if at all and looking for opportunities in other industries. A competitively weak company in an unattractive industry may see its best option as finding a buyer, perhaps a rival, to acquire its business. On occasion, an industry that is unattractive overall is still very attractive to a favorably situated company with the skills and resources to take business away from weaker rivals.

ASSURANCE OF LEARNING EXERCISES

LO1, LO2

connect
www.mcgrawhillconnect.com

1. Prepare a brief analysis of the coffee industry using the information provided on industry trade association websites. Based upon information provided on the websites of these associations, draw a five-forces diagram for the coffee industry and briefly discuss the nature and strength of each of the five competitive forces.

2. Based on the strategic group map in Concepts & Connections 3.1, who are Nordstrom's closest competitors? Between which two strategic groups is competition the strongest? Why do you think no retail chains are positioned in the upper-right corner of the map? Which company/strategic group faces the weakest competition from the members of other strategic groups?

LO1

www.mcgrawhillconnect.com

3. The Snack Food Association publishes an annual state-of-the-industry report that can be found at www.sfa.org. Based on information in the latest report, does it appear that the economic characteristics of the industry will present industry participants with attractive opportunities for growth and profitability? Explain.

LO1, LO3

>>> EXERCISES FOR SIMULATION PARTICIPANTS

1. Which of the five competitive forces is creating the strongest competitive pressures for your company?

LO1, LO2, LO3

2. What are the "weapons of competition" that rival companies in your industry can use to gain sales and market share? See Figure 3.7 to help you identify the various competitive factors.

3. What are the factors affecting the intensity of rivalry in the industry in which your company is competing? Use Figure 3.7 and the accompanying discussion to help you in pinpointing the specific factors most affecting competitive intensity. Would you characterize the rivalry and jockeying for better market position, increased sales, and market share among the companies in your industry as fierce, very strong, strong, moderate, or relatively weak? Why?

4. Are there any driving forces in the industry in which your company is competing? What impact will these driving forces have? Will they cause competition to be more or less intense? Will they act to boost or squeeze profit margins? List at least two actions your company should consider taking to combat any negative impacts of the driving forces.

5. Draw a strategic group map showing the market positions of the companies in your industry. Which companies do you believe are in the most attractive position on the map? Which companies are the most weakly positioned? Which companies do you believe are likely to try to move to a different position on the strategic group map?

6. What do you see as the key factors for being a successful competitor in your industry? List at least three.

7. Does your overall assessment of the industry suggest that industry rivals have sufficiently attractive opportunities for growth and profitability? Explain.

ENDNOTES

1. Michael E. Porter, *Competitive Strategy: Techniques for Analyzing Industries and Competitors* (New York: Free Press, 1980), chap. 1; Michael E. Porter, "The Five Competitive Forces That Shape Strategy," *Harvard Business Review* 86, no. 1 (January 2008).

2. J. S. Bain, *Barriers to New Competition* (Cambridge, MA: Harvard University Press, 1956); F. M. Scherer, *Industrial Market Structure and Economic Performance* (Chicago: Rand McNally & Co., 1971).

3. Pankaj Ghemawat, "Building Strategy on the Experience Curve," *Harvard Business Review* 64, no. 2 (March–April 1985).

4. Michael E. Porter, "How Competitive Forces Shape Strategy," *Harvard Business Review* 57, no. 2 (March–April 1979)

5. Pamela J. Derfus, Patrick G. Maggitti, Curtis M. Grimm, and Ken G. Smith, "The Red Queen Effect: Competitive Actions and Firm Performance," *Academy of Management Journal* 51, no. 1 (February 2008).

6. Mary Ellen Gordon and George R. Milne, "Selecting the Dimensions That Define Strategic Groups: A Novel Market-Driven Approach," *Journal of Managerial Issues* 11, no. 2 (Summer 1999).

7. Avi Fiegenbaum and Howard Thomas, "Strategic Groups as Reference Groups: Theory, Modeling and Empirical Examination of Industry and Competitive Strategy," *Strategic Management Journal* 16 (1995); and S. Ade Olusoga, Michael P. Mokwa, and Charles H. Noble, "Strategic Groups, Mobility Barriers, and Competitive Advantage," *Journal of Business Research* 33 (1995).

8. Larry Kahaner, *Competitive Intelligence* (New York: Simon and Schuster, 1996).

9. Kevin P. Coyne and John Horn, "Predicting Your Competitor's Reaction," *Harvard Business Review* 87, no. 4 (April 2009).

chapter 4

EVALUATING A COMPANY'S RESOURCES, COST POSITION, AND COMPETITIVENESS

LEARNING OBJECTIVES

LO1 Learn how to assess how well a company's current strategy is working.

LO2 Understand why a company's resources and capabilities are central to its strategic approach and how to evaluate their potential for giving the company a competitive edge over rivals.

LO3 Grasp how and why activities performed internally by a company and those performed externally by its suppliers and forward channel allies determine a company's cost structure and the value it provides to customers.

LO4 Learn how to evaluate a company's competitive strength relative to key rivals.

LO5 Understand how a comprehensive evaluation of a company's external and internal situations can assist managers in making critical decisions about their next strategic moves.

Chapter 3 described how to use the tools of industry and competitive analysis to assess a company's external environment and lay the groundwork for matching a company's strategy to its external situation. This chapter discusses the techniques of evaluating a company's internal situation, including its collection of resources and capabilities, its relative cost position, and its competitive strength versus its rivals. The analytical spotlight will be trained on five questions:

1. How well is the company's strategy working?
2. What are the company's competitively important resources and capabilities?
3. Are the company's cost structure and customer value proposition competitive?
4. Is the company competitively stronger or weaker than key rivals?
5. What strategic issues and problems merit front-burner managerial attention?

The answers to these five questions complete management's understanding of *"Where are we now?"* and position the company for a good strategy-situation fit required by the *"Three Tests of a Winning Strategy"* (see Chapter 1, page 8).

QUESTION 1: HOW WELL IS THE COMPANY'S STRATEGY WORKING?

LO1

Learn how to assess how well a company's current strategy is working.

The two best indicators of how well a company's strategy is working are (1) whether the company is recording gains in financial strength and profitability and (2) whether the company's competitive strength and market standing is improving. Persistent shortfalls in meeting company financial performance targets and weak performance relative to rivals are reliable warning signs that the company suffers from poor strategy making, less-than-competent strategy execution, or both. Other indicators of how well a company's strategy is working include:

- Trends in the company's sales and earnings growth.
- Trends in the company's stock price.
- The company's overall financial strength.
- The company's customer retention rate.
- The rate at which new customers are acquired.
- Changes in the company's image and reputation with customers.
- Evidence of improvement in internal processes such as defect rate, order fulfillment, delivery times, days of inventory, and employee productivity.

The stronger a company's current overall performance, the less likely the need for radical changes in strategy. The weaker a company's financial performance and market standing, the more its current strategy must be questioned. (A compilation of financial ratios most commonly used to evaluate a company's financial performance and balance sheet strength is presented in the Appendix on pages 234–235).

QUESTION 2: WHAT ARE THE COMPANY'S COMPETITIVELY IMPORTANT RESOURCES AND CAPABILITIES?

As discussed in Chapter 1, a company's business model and strategy must be well-matched to its collection of resources and capabilities. An attempt to create and deliver customer value in a manner that depends on resources or capabilities that are deficient and cannot be readily acquired or developed is unwise and positions the company for failure. A company's competitive approach requires a tight fit with a company's internal situation and is strengthened when it exploits resources that are competitively valuable, rare, hard to copy, and not easily trumped by rivals' substitute resources. In addition, long-term competitive advantage requires the ongoing development and expansion of resources and capabilities to pursue emerging market opportunities and defend against future threats to its market standing and profitability.[1]

▶ LO2

Understand why a company's resources and capabilities are central to its strategic approach and how to evaluate their potential for giving the company a competitive edge over rivals.

For example, Dell has put considerable time and money into developing and enhancing its supply chain capabilities to keep its costs low and to allow for the rapid introduction of new models when more powerful PC components become available. Competitively valuable resources and capabilities have also aided cable news channels in strengthening their competitive positions in the media industry. Because Fox News and CNN have the capability to devote more airtime to breaking news stories and get reporters on the scene very quickly compared to the major over-the-air networks ABC, NBC, and CBS, many viewers turn to the cable networks when a major news event occurs.

Identifying Competitively Important Resources and Capabilities

A company's **resources** are competitive assets that are owned or controlled by the company and may either be *tangible resources* such as plants, distribution centers, manufacturing equipment, patents, information systems, and capital reserves or creditworthiness or *intangible assets* such as a well-known brand or a results-oriented organizational culture. Table 4.1 lists the common types of tangible and intangible resources that a company may possess.

> **CORE CONCEPT**
> A **resource** is a competitive asset that is owned or controlled by a company; a **capability** is the capacity of a company to competently perform some internal activity. Capabilities are developed and enabled through the deployment of a company's resources.

A **capability** is the capacity of a firm to competently perform some internal activity. A capability may also be referred to as a **competence**. Capabilities or competences also vary in form, quality, and competitive importance, with some being more competitively valuable than others. *Organizational capabilities are developed and enabled through the deployment of a company's resources or some combination of its resources.*[2] Some capabilities rely heavily on a company's intangible resources, such as human assets and

TABLE 4.1

Common Types of Tangible and Intangible Resources

Tangible Resources

- *Physical resources*—state-of-the-art manufacturing plants and equipment, efficient distribution facilities, attractive real estate locations, or ownership of valuable natural resource deposits.
- *Financial resources*—cash and cash equivalents, marketable securities, and other financial assets such as a company's credit rating and borrowing capacity.
- *Technological assets*—patents, copyrights, superior production technology, and technologies that enable activities.
- *Organizational resources*—information and communication systems (servers, workstations, etc.), proven quality control systems, and strong network of distributors or retail dealers.

Intangible Resources

- *Human assets and intellectual capital*—an experienced and capable workforce, talented employees in key areas, collective learning embedded in the organization, or proven managerial know-how.
- *Brand, image, and reputational assets*—brand names, trademarks, product or company image, buyer loyalty, and reputation for quality, superior service.
- *Relationships*—alliances or joint ventures that provide access to technologies, specialized know-how, or geographic markets, and trust established with various partners.
- *Company culture*—the norms of behavior, business principles, and ingrained beliefs within the company.

intellectual capital. For example, General Mills' brand management capabilities draw upon the knowledge of the company's brand managers, the expertise of its marketing department, and the company's relationships with retailers. Electronic Arts' video game design capabilities result from the creative talents and technological expertise of its game developers and the company's culture that encourages creative thinking.

Determining the Competitive Power of a Company's Resources and Capabilities

What is most telling about a company's aggregation of resources and capabilities is how powerful they are in the marketplace. The competitive power of a resource or capability is measured by how many of the following four tests it can pass:[3]

1. *Is the resource or capability really competitively valuable?* All companies possess a collection of resources and capabilities—some have the potential to contribute to a competitive advantage while others may not. Apple's operating system for its personal computers by some accounts is superior to Windows 7, but Apple has failed miserably in converting its resources devoted to operating system design into competitive success in the global PC market.

A capability that passes the "competitively valuable" test and is *central* to a company's strategy and competitiveness is frequently referred to as a **core competence**. A competitively valuable capability that is performed with a very high level of proficiency is sometimes known as a **distinctive competence**. Most often, *a core competence or distinctive competence is knowledge-based, residing in people and in a company's intellectual capital and not in its assets on the balance sheet.*

> ### CORE CONCEPT
> A **core competence** is a proficiently performed internal activity that is *central* to a company's strategy and competitiveness. A core competence that is performed with a very high level of proficiency is referred to as a **distinctive competence**.

2. *Is the resource or capability rare—is it something rivals lack?* Companies have to guard against pridefully believing that their collection of resources and competitive capabilities is more powerful than that of their rivals. Who can really say whether Coca-Cola's consumer marketing prowess is better than PepsiCo's or whether the Mercedes-Benz brand name is more powerful than that of BMW or Lexus? Although many retailers claim to be quite proficient in product selection and in-store merchandising, a number run into trouble in the marketplace because they encounter rivals whose capabilities in product selection and in-store merchandising are equal to or better than theirs.

3. *Is the resource or capability hard to copy or imitate?* The more difficult and more expensive it is to imitate a company's resource or capability, the greater its potential competitive value. Resources tend to be difficult to copy when they are unique (a fantastic real estate location, patent protection), when they must be built over time (a brand name, a strategy-supportive organizational culture), and when they carry big capital requirements (a cost-effective plant to manufacture cutting-edge microprocessors). Walmart's competitors have failed miserably in their attempts over the past two decades to match its state-of-the-art distribution capabilities.

4. *Can the resource or capability be trumped by substitute resources and competitive capabilities?* Resources that are competitively valuable, rare, and costly to imitate lose their ability to offer competitive advantage if rivals possess equivalent substitute resources. For example, manufacturers relying on automation to gain a cost-based advantage in production activities may find their technology-based advantage nullified by rivals' use of low-wage offshore manufacturing. Resources can contribute to a competitive advantage only when resource substitutes don't exist.

Understanding the nature of competitively important resources allows managers to identify resources or capabilities that should be further developed to play an important role in the company's future strategies. In addition, management may determine that it doesn't possess a resource that independently passes all four tests listed here with high marks, but that it does have a *bundle of resources* that can pass the tests. Although Nike's resources dedicated to research and development, marketing research, and product design are matched relatively well by rival Adidas, its cross-functional design process allows it to set the pace for innovation in athletic apparel and footwear and consistently outperform Adidas and other rivals in the marketplace. Nike's footwear designers get ideas for new performance features from the professional athletes who endorse its products and then work alongside footwear materials researchers, consumer trend analysts, color designers, and marketers to design new models that are presented to a review committee. Nike's review committee is made up of hundreds of individuals who evaluate prototype details such as shoe proportions and color designs, the size of the swoosh, stitching patterns, sole color and tread pattern, and insole design. About 400 models are approved by the committee each year, which are sourced from contract manufacturers and marketed in more than 180 countries. The bundling of Nike's professional endorsements, R&D activities, marketing research efforts, styling expertise, and managerial know-how has become an important source of the company's competitive advantage and has allowed it to remain number one in the athletic footwear and apparel industry for more than 20 years.

> **CORE CONCEPT**
>
> Companies that lack a stand-alone resource that is competitively powerful may nonetheless develop a competitive advantage through **resource bundles** that enable the superior performance of important cross-functional capabilities.

Companies lacking certain resources needed for competitive success in an industry may be able to adopt strategies directed at eroding or at least neutralizing the competitive potency of a particular rival's resources and capabilities by identifying and developing **substitute resources** to accomplish the same purpose. For example, Amazon.com lacks a big network of retail stores to compete with those operated by rival Barnes & Noble, but Amazon's much larger, readily accessible, and searchable book inventory—coupled with its short delivery times and free shipping on orders over $25—are more attractive to many busy consumers than visiting a big-box bookstore. In other words, Amazon has carefully and consciously developed a set of competitively valuable resources that are proving to be effective substitutes for competing head-to-head against Barnes & Noble without having to invest in hundreds of brick-and-mortar retail stores.[4]

> Rather than try to match the resources possessed by a rival company, a company may develop entirely different resources that substitute for the strengths of the rival.

A Company's Resources and Capabilities Must Be Managed Dynamically

Resources and capabilities must be continually strengthened and nurtured to sustain their competitive power and, at times, may need to be broadened and deepened to allow the company to position itself to pursue emerging market opportunities.[5] Organizational resources and capabilities that grow stale can impair competitiveness unless they are refreshed, modified, or even phased out and replaced in response to ongoing market changes and shifts in company strategy. In addition, disruptive environmental change may destroy the value of key strategic assets, turning resources and capabilities "from diamonds to rust."[6] Management's organization-building challenge has two elements: (1) attending to ongoing recalibration of existing capabilities and resources, and (2) casting a watchful eye for opportunities to develop totally new capabilities for delivering better customer value and/or outcompeting rivals. Such expertise, in itself, qualifies as a unique and valuable organizational capability. A company possessing a **dynamic capability** is adept in modifying, upgrading, or deepening existing resources and capabilities to solidify its standing in the marketplace and prepare it to seize market opportunities and defend against external threats to its vitality.[7]

Management at Toyota has aggressively upgraded the company's capabilities in fuel-efficient hybrid engine technology and constantly fine-tuned the famed Toyota Production System to enhance the company's already proficient capabilities in manufacturing top-quality vehicles at relatively low costs. Likewise, management at Honda has recently accelerated the company's efforts to broaden its expertise and capabilities in hybrid engines to stay close to Toyota. Microsoft retooled the manner in which its programmers attacked the task of writing code for its Windows 7 operating systems for PCs and servers.

> **CORE CONCEPT**
>
> A **dynamic capability** is developed when a company has become proficient in modifying, upgrading, or deepening its resources and capabilities to sustain its competitiveness and prepare it to seize future market opportunities and nullify external threats to its well-being.

> A company requires a dynamically evolving portfolio of resources and capabilities in order to sustain its competitiveness and position itself to pursue future market opportunities.

Are Company Resources and Capabilities Sufficient to Allow It to Seize Market Opportunities and Nullify External Threats?

An essential element in evaluating a company's overall situation entails examining the company's resources and competitive capabilities in terms of the degree to which they enable it to pursue its best market opportunities and defend against the external threats to its future well-being. The simplest and most easily applied tool for conducting this examination is widely known as *SWOT analysis,* so named because it zeros in on a company's internal **S**trengths and **W**eaknesses, market **O**pportunities, and external **T**hreats. A first-rate SWOT analysis provides the basis for crafting a strategy that capitalizes on the company's strengths, aims squarely at capturing the company's best opportunities, and defends against the threats to its well-being.

> **CORE CONCEPT**
>
> **SWOT analysis** is a simple but powerful tool for sizing up a company's internal strengths and competitive deficiencies, its market opportunities, and the external threats to its future well-being.

Identifying a Company's Internal Strengths A company's strengths determine whether its competitive power in the marketplace will be impressively strong or disappointingly weak. A company that is well endowed with strengths stemming from potent resources and core competencies normally has considerable competitive power—especially when its management team skillfully utilizes the company's resources in ways that build sustainable competitive advantage. Companies with modest or

> Basing a company's strategy on its strengths resulting from most competitively valuable resources and capabilities gives the company its best chance for market success.

weak competitive assets nearly always are relegated to a trailing position in the industry. Table 4.2 lists the kinds of factors to consider in compiling a company's resource strengths and weaknesses.

▶ TABLE 4.2

Factors to Consider When Identifying a Company's Strengths, Weaknesses, Opportunities, and Threats

Potential Internal Strengths and Competitive Capabilities

- Core competencies in _____.
- A strong financial condition; ample financial resources to grow the business.
- Strong brand name image/company reputation.
- Economies of scale and/or learning and experience curve advantages over rivals.
- Proprietary technology/superior technological skills/important patents.
- Cost advantages over rivals.
- Product innovation capabilities.
- Proven capabilities in improving production processes.
- Good supply chain management capabilities.
- Good customer service capabilities.
- Better product quality relative to rivals.
- Wide geographic coverage and/or strong global distribution capability.
- Alliances/joint ventures with other firms that provide access to valuable technology, competencies, and/or attractive geographic markets.

Potential Market Opportunities

- Serving additional customer groups or market segments.
- Expanding into new geographic markets.
- Expanding the company's product line to meet a broader range of customer needs.
- Utilizing existing company skills or technological know-how to enter new product lines or new businesses.
- Falling trade barriers in attractive foreign markets.
- Acquiring rival firms or companies with attractive technological expertise or capabilities.

Potential Internal Weaknesses and Competitive Deficiencies

- No clear strategic direction.
- No well-developed or proven core competencies.
- A weak balance sheet; burdened with too much debt.
- Higher overall unit costs relative to key competitors.
- A product/service with features and attributes that are inferior to those of rivals.
- Too narrow a product line relative to rivals.
- Weak brand image or reputation.
- Weaker dealer network than key rivals.
- Behind on product quality, R&D, and/or technological know-how.
- Lack of management depth.
- Short on financial resources to grow the business and pursue promising initiatives.

Potential External Threats to a Company's Future Prospects

- Increasing intensity of competition among industry rivals—may squeeze profit margins.
- Slowdowns in market growth.
- Likely entry of potent new competitors.
- Growing bargaining power of customers or suppliers.
- A shift in buyer needs and tastes away from the industry's product.
- Adverse demographic changes that threaten to curtail demand for the industry's product.
- Vulnerability to unfavorable industry driving forces.
- Restrictive trade policies on the part of foreign governments.
- Costly new regulatory requirements.

Identifying Company Resource Weaknesses and Competitive Deficiencies   A *weakness* or *competitive deficiency* is something a company lacks or does poorly or a condition that puts it at a disadvantage in the marketplace. As a rule, strategies that place heavy demands on areas where the company is weakest or has unproven ability are suspect and should be avoided. A company's weaknesses can relate to:

- Deficiencies in competitively important tangible or intangible resources.
- Missing or competitively inferior capabilities in key areas.

Nearly all companies have competitive deficiencies of one kind or another. Whether a company's weaknesses make it competitively vulnerable depends on how much they matter in the marketplace and whether they are offset by the company's strengths. Sizing up a company's complement of strengths and deficiencies is akin to constructing a *strategic balance sheet,* where strengths represent *competitive assets* and weaknesses represent *competitive liabilities.*

Identifying a Company's Market Opportunities   Market opportunity is a big factor in shaping a company's strategy. Indeed, managers can't properly tailor strategy to the company's situation without first identifying its market opportunities and appraising the growth and profit potential each one holds. (See Table 4.2, under "Potential Market Opportunities.") Depending on the prevailing circumstances, a company's opportunities can be plentiful or scarce and can range from wildly attractive to unsuitable.

In evaluating the attractiveness of a company's market opportunities, managers have to guard against viewing every *industry* opportunity as a suitable opportunity. Not every company is equipped with the resources to successfully pursue each opportunity that exists in its industry. Some companies are more capable of going after particular opportunities than others. *The market opportunities most relevant to a company are those that match up well with the company's financial and organizational resources and capabilities, offer the best growth and profitability, and present the most potential for competitive advantage.*

Identifying Threats to a Company's Future Profitability   Often, certain factors in a company's external environment pose *threats* to its profitability and competitive well-being. Threats can stem from the emergence of cheaper or better technologies, rivals' introduction of new or improved products, the entry of lower-cost foreign competitors into a company's market stronghold, new regulations that are more burdensome to a company than to its competitors, vulnerability to a rise in interest rates, the potential of a hostile takeover, unfavorable demographic shifts, or adverse changes in foreign exchange rates. (See Table 4.2, under "Potential External Threats to a Company's Future Prospects.")

External threats may pose no more than a moderate degree of adversity or they may be so imposing as to make a company's situation and outlook quite tenuous. On rare occasions, market shocks can throw a company into an immediate crisis and battle to survive. Many of the world's major airlines have been plunged into unprecedented financial crisis because of a combination of factors: rising prices for jet fuel, a global economic slowdown that has affected business and leisure travel, mounting competition from low-fare carriers, shifting traveler preferences for low fares as opposed to lots of in-flight amenities, and "out-of-control" labor costs. It is management's job to identify the threats to the company's future prospects and to evaluate what strategic actions can be taken to neutralize or lessen their impact.

The Value of a SWOT Analysis   A SWOT analysis involves more than making four lists. The most important parts of SWOT analysis are:

> Simply listing a company's strengths, weaknesses, opportunities, and threats is not enough; the payoff from SWOT analysis comes from the conclusions about a company's situation and the implications for strategy improvement that flow from the four lists.

1. Drawing conclusions from the SWOT listings about the company's overall situation.

2. Translating these conclusions into strategic actions to better match the company's strategy to its strengths and market opportunities, correcting problematic weaknesses, and defending against worrisome external threats.

QUESTION 3: ARE THE COMPANY'S COST STRUCTURE AND CUSTOMER VALUE PROPOSITION COMPETITIVE?

▶ LO3

Grasp how and why activities performed internally by a company and those performed externally by its suppliers and forward channel allies determine a company's cost structure and the value it provides to customers.

Company managers are often stunned when a competitor cuts its prices to "unbelievably low" levels or when a new market entrant comes on strong with a great new product offered at a surprisingly low price. Such competitors may not, however, be buying market positions with prices that are below costs. They may simply have substantially lower costs and therefore are able to offer prices that result in more appealing customer value propositions. One of the most telling signs of whether a company's business position is strong or precarious is whether its cost structure and customer value proposition are competitive with industry rivals.

Cost comparisons are especially critical in industries where price competition is typically the ruling market force. But even in industries where products are differentiated, rival companies have to keep their costs in line with rivals offering value propositions based upon a similar mix of differentiating features. Two analytical tools are particularly useful in determining whether a company's value proposition and costs are competitive: value chain analysis and benchmarking.

Company Value Chains

Every company's business consists of a collection of activities undertaken in the course of designing, producing, marketing, delivering, and supporting its product or service. All of the various activities that a company performs internally combine to form a **value chain**, so-called because the underlying intent of a company's activities is to do things that ultimately *create value for buyers*. The value chain includes a profit margin component since delivering customer value profitably (with a sufficient return on invested capital) is the essence of a sound business model.

> **CORE CONCEPT**
>
> A company's **value chain** identifies the primary activities that create customer value and related support activities.

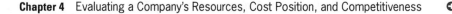

▶ FIGURE 4.1 **A Representative Company Value Chain**

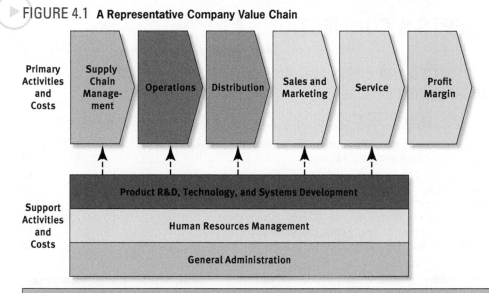

PRIMARY ACTIVITIES

- **Supply Chain Management**—Activities, costs, and assets associated with purchasing fuel, energy, raw materials, parts and components, merchandise, and consumable items from vendors; receiving, storing, and disseminating inputs from suppliers; inspection; and inventory management.

- **Operations**—Activities, costs, and assets associated with converting inputs into final product form (production, assembly, packaging, equipment maintenance, facilities, operations, quality assurance, environmental protection).

- **Distribution**—Activities, costs, and assets dealing with physically distributing the product to buyers (finished goods warehousing, order processing, order picking and packing, shipping, delivery vehicle operations, establishing and maintaining a network of dealers and distributors).

- **Sales and Marketing**—Activities, costs, and assets related to sales force efforts, advertising and promotion, market research and planning, and dealer/distributor support.

- **Service**—Activities, costs, and assets associated with providing assistance to buyers, such as installation, spare parts delivery, maintenance and repair, technical assistance, buyer inquiries, and complaints.

SUPPORT ACTIVITIES

- **Product R&D, Technology, and Systems Development**—Activities, costs, and assets relating to product R&D, process R&D, process design improvement, equipment design, computer software development, telecommunications systems, computer-assisted design and engineering, database capabilities, and development of computerized support systems.

- **Human Resources Management**—Activities, costs, and assets associated with the recruitment, hiring, training, development, and compensation of all types of personnel; labor relations activities; and development of knowledge-based skills and core competencies.

- **General Administration**—Activities, costs, and assets relating to general management, accounting and finance, legal and regulatory affairs, safety and security, management information systems, forming strategic alliances and collaborating with strategic partners, and other "overhead" functions.

Source: Based on the discussion in Michael E. Porter, *Competitive Advantage* (New York: Free Press, 1985), pp. 37–43.

As shown in Figure 4.1, a company's value chain consists of two broad categories of activities that drive costs and create customer value: the *primary activities* that are foremost in creating value for customers and the requisite *support activities* that facilitate and enhance the performance of the primary

CONCEPTS & CONNECTIONS 4.1

VALUE CHAIN ACTIVITIES AND COSTS FOR JUST COFFEE, A PRODUCER OF FAIR TRADE ORGANIC COFFEE

Value Chain Activities and Costs in Producing, Roasting, and Selling a Pound of Fair Trade Organic Coffee	
1. Average cost of procuring the coffee from coffee grower cooperatives	$2.30
2. Import fees, storage costs, and freight charges	.73
3. Labor cost of roasting and bagging	.89
4. Cost of labels and bag	.45
5. Average overhead costs	$3.03
6. Total company costs	7.40
7. Average retail markup over company costs (company operating profit)	$2.59
8. Average price to consumer at retail	$9.99

Source: Developed by the authors from information on Just Coffee's website, www.justcoffee.coop/the_coffee_dollar_breakdown; accessed June 16, 2010.

activities.[8] For example, the primary activities and cost drivers for a big-box retailer such as Target include merchandise selection and buying, store layout and product display, advertising, and customer service; its support activities that affect customer value and costs include site selection, hiring and training, store maintenance, plus the usual assortment of administrative activities. A hotel chain's primary activities and costs are mainly comprised of reservations and hotel operations (check-in and check-out, maintenance and housekeeping, dining and room service, and conventions and meetings); principal support activities that drive costs and impact customer value include accounting, hiring and training hotel staff, and general administration. Supply chain management is a crucial activity for Nissan or Amazon.com but is not a value chain component at Google or CBS. Sales and marketing are dominant activities at Procter & Gamble and Sony but have minor roles at oil-drilling companies and natural gas pipeline companies. Whether an activity is classified as primary or supporting varies with each company's business model and strategy, so it is important to view the listing of the primary and support activities in Figure 4.1 as illustrative rather than definitive. Concepts & Connections 4.1 shows representative costs for various activities performed by Just Coffee, a cooperative producer and roaster of fair trade organic coffee.

Benchmarking: A Tool for Assessing Whether a Company's Value Chain Activities Are Competitive

Benchmarking entails comparing how different companies perform various value chain activities—how materials are purchased, how inventories are managed, how products are assembled, how customer orders are filled and shipped, and how maintenance is performed—and then making cross-company comparisons of the costs and effectiveness of these activities.[9] The objectives of benchmarking are to identify the best practices in performing an activity and to emulate those best practices when they are possessed by others.

Xerox became one of the first companies to use benchmarking in 1979 when Japanese manufacturers began selling midsize copiers in the United States for $9,600 each—less than Xerox's production costs.[10] Xerox management sent a team of line managers and its head of manufacturing to Japan to study competitors' business processes

> **CORE CONCEPT**
> **Benchmarking** is a potent tool for learning which companies are best at performing particular activities and then using their techniques (or "best practices") to improve the cost and effectiveness of a company's own internal activities.

and costs. With the aid of Xerox's joint-venture partner in Japan (Fuji-Xerox), who knew the competitors well, the team found that Xerox's costs were excessive due to gross inefficiencies in the company's manufacturing processes and business practices. The findings triggered a major internal effort at Xerox to become cost-competitive and prompted Xerox to begin benchmarking 67 of its key work processes. Xerox quickly decided not to restrict its benchmarking efforts to its office equipment rivals but to extend them to any company regarded as "world class" in performing *any activity* relevant to Xerox's business. Other companies quickly picked up on Xerox's approach. Toyota managers got their idea for just-in-time inventory deliveries by studying how U.S. supermarkets replenished their shelves. Southwest Airlines reduced the turnaround time of its aircraft at each scheduled stop by studying pit crews on the auto racing circuit. Over 80 percent of Fortune 500 companies reportedly use benchmarking for comparing themselves against rivals on cost and other competitively important measures.

The tough part of benchmarking is not whether to do it, but rather how to gain access to information about other companies' practices and costs. Sometimes benchmarking can be accomplished by collecting information from published reports, trade groups, and industry research firms and by talking to knowledgeable industry analysts, customers, and suppliers. Sometimes field trips to the facilities of competing or noncompeting companies can be arranged to observe how things are done, compare practices and processes, and perhaps exchange data on productivity and other cost components. However, such companies, even if they agree to host facilities tours and answer questions, are unlikely to share competitively sensitive cost information. Furthermore, comparing two companies' costs may not involve comparing apples to apples if the two companies employ different cost accounting principles to calculate the costs of particular activities.

However, a fairly reliable source of benchmarking information has emerged. The explosive interest of companies in benchmarking costs and identifying best practices has prompted consulting organizations (e.g., Accenture, A. T. Kearney, Benchnet—The Benchmarking Exchange, Towers Watson, and Best Practices, LLC) and several councils and associations (e.g., the APQC, the Qualserve Benchmarking Clearinghouse, and the Strategic Planning Institute's Council on Benchmarking) to gather benchmarking data, distribute information about best practices, and provide comparative cost data without identifying the names of particular companies. Having an independent group gather the information and report it in a manner that disguises the names of individual companies avoids the disclosure of competitively sensitive data and lessens the potential for unethical behavior on the part of company personnel in gathering their own data about competitors.

The Value Chain System for an Entire Industry

A company's value chain is embedded in a larger system of activities that includes the value chains of its suppliers and the value chains of whatever distribution channel allies it utilizes in getting its product or service to end users. The value chains of forward channel partners are relevant because (1) the costs and margins of a company's distributors and retail dealers are part of the price the consumer ultimately pays, and (2) the activities that distribution allies perform affect customer value. For these reasons, companies normally work closely with their suppliers and forward channel allies to perform value chain activities in mutually beneficial ways. For instance, motor vehicle manufacturers work closely with their forward channel allies (local automobile dealers) to ensure that owners are satisfied with dealers' repair and maintenance services.[11] Also, many automotive parts suppliers have built plants near the auto assembly plants they supply to facilitate just-in-time deliveries, reduce warehousing and shipping costs, and promote close collaboration on parts design and production scheduling. Irrigation equipment companies, suppliers of grape-harvesting and winemaking equipment, and firms making barrels, wine bottles, caps, corks, and labels all have facilities in the California wine country to be close to the nearly 700 winemakers they supply.[12] The lesson here is that a company's value chain activities are often closely linked to the value chains of their suppliers and the forward allies.

> → A company's customer value proposition and cost competitiveness depend not only on internally performed activities (its own company value chain), but also on the value chain activities of its suppliers and forward channel allies.

As a consequence, *accurately assessing the competitiveness of a company's cost structure and value proposition requires that company managers understand an industry's entire value chain system for delivering a product or service to customers, not just the company's own value chain.* A typical industry value chain that incorporates the value-creating activities, costs, and margins of suppliers and forward channel allies (if any) is shown in Figure 4.2. However, industry value chains vary significantly by industry. For example, the primary value chain activities in the bottled water industry (spring operation or water purification, processing of basic ingredients used in flavored or vitamin-enhanced water, bottling, wholesale distribution, advertising, and retail merchandising) differ from those for the computer software industry (programming, disk loading, marketing, distribution). Producers of bathroom and kitchen faucets depend heavily on the activities of wholesale distributors and building supply retailers in winning sales to home builders and do-it-yourselfers but producers of papermaking machines internalize their distribution activities by selling directly to the operators of paper plants.

▶ FIGURE 4.2 **Representative Value Chain for an Entire Industry**

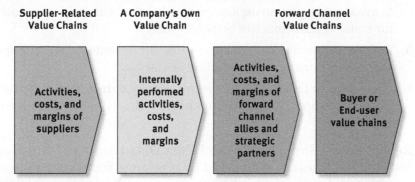

Source: Based in part on the single-industry value chain displayed in Michael E. Porter, *Competitive Advantage* (New York: Free Press, 1985), p. 35.

Strategic Options for Remedying a Cost or Value Disadvantage

The results of value chain analysis and benchmarking may disclose cost or value disadvantages relative to key rivals. These competitive disadvantages are likely to lower a company's relative profit margin or weaken its customer value proposition. In such instances, actions to improve a company's cost structure are called for to boost profitability or to allow for the addition of new features that drive customer value. There are three main areas in a company's overall value chain where important differences between firms in costs and value can occur: a company's own internal activities, the suppliers' part of the industry value chain, and the forward channel portion of the industry chain.

Remedying an Internal Cost or Value Disadvantage Managers can pursue any of several strategic approaches to restore cost parity or rectify a deficiency in customer value when the disadvantage stems from the performance of internal value chain activities:

1. *Implement the use of best practices* throughout the company, particularly for high-cost activities.

2. *Try to eliminate some cost-producing activities* by revamping the value chain. Many retailers have found that donating returned items to charitable organizations and taking the appropriate tax deduction results in a smaller loss than incurring the costs of the value chain activities involved in reverse logistics.

3. *Relocate high-cost activities* (such as manufacturing) to geographic areas such as China, Latin America, or Eastern Europe where they can be performed more cheaply.

4. *See if certain internally performed activities can be outsourced* from vendors or performed by contractors more cheaply than they can be done in-house.

5. *Invest in productivity-enhancing, cost-saving technological improvements* (robotics, flexible manufacturing techniques, state-of-the-art electronic networking).

6. *Find ways to detour around the activities or items where costs are high*—computer chip makers regularly design around the patents held by others to avoid paying royalties; automakers have substituted lower-cost plastic for metal at many exterior body locations.

7. *Redesign the product* and/or some of its components to facilitate speedier and more economical manufacture or assembly.

8. *Try to make up the internal cost disadvantage* by reducing costs in the supplier or forward channel portions of the industry value chain—usually a last resort.

Remedying a Supplier-Related Cost Disadvantage   Supplier-related cost disadvantages can be attacked by pressuring suppliers for lower prices, switching to lower-priced substitute inputs, and collaborating closely with suppliers to identify mutual cost-saving opportunities.[13] For example, just-in-time deliveries from suppliers can lower a company's inventory and internal logistics costs, eliminate capital expenditures for additional warehouse space, and improve cash flow and financial ratios by reducing accounts payable. In a few instances, companies may find that it is cheaper to integrate backward into the business of high-cost suppliers and make the item in-house instead of buying it from outsiders.

Remedying a Cost Disadvantage Associated with Activities Performed by Forward Channel Allies   There are three main ways to combat a cost disadvantage in the forward portion of the industry value chain: (1) Pressure dealer-distributors and other forward channel allies to reduce their costs and markups; (2) work closely with forward channel allies to identify win-win opportunities to reduce costs—for example, a chocolate manufacturer learned that by shipping its bulk chocolate in liquid form in tank cars instead of 10-pound molded bars, it could not only save its candy bar manufacturing customers the costs associated with unpacking and melting but also eliminate its own costs of molding bars and packing them; and (3) change to a more economical distribution strategy or perhaps integrate forward into company-owned retail outlets. Dell has eliminated all activities, costs, and margins of forward channel allies by adopting a direct sales business model that allows buyers to purchase customized PCs directly from the manufacturer. The direct sales model allows Dell to easily match competitors' prices, while earning larger profit margins.

QUESTION 4: WHAT IS THE COMPANY'S COMPETITIVE STRENGTH RELATIVE TO KEY RIVALS?

▶ **LO4**

Learn how to evaluate a company's competitive strength relative to key rivals.

An additional component of evaluating a company's situation is developing a comprehensive assessment of the company's overall competitive strength. Making this determination requires answers to two questions:

1. How does the company rank relative to competitors on each of the important factors that determine market success?

2. All things considered, does the company have a net competitive advantage or disadvantage versus major competitors?

Step 1 in doing a competitive strength assessment is to list the industry's key success factors and other telling measures of competitive strength or weakness (6 to 10 measures usually suffice). Step 2 is to assign a weight to each measure of competitive strength based on its perceived importance in shaping competitive success. (The sum of the weights for each measure must add up to 1.0.) Step 3 is to calculate weighted strength ratings by scoring each competitor on each strength measure (using a 1 to 10 rating scale where 1 is very weak and 10 is very strong) and multiplying the assigned rating by the assigned weight. Step 4 is to sum the weighted strength ratings on each factor to get an overall measure of competitive strength for each company being rated. Step 5 is to use the overall strength ratings to draw conclusions about the size and extent of the company's net competitive advantage or disadvantage and to take specific note of areas of strength and weakness. Table 4.3 provides an example of a competitive strength assessment, using the hypothetical ABC Company against four rivals. ABC's total score of 5.95 signals a net competitive advantage over Rival 3 (with a score of 2.10) and Rival 4 (with a score of 3.70), but indicates a net competitive disadvantage against Rival 1 (with a score of 7. 70) and Rival 2 (with an overall score of 6.85).

Interpreting the Competitive Strength Assessments

Competitive strength assessments provide useful conclusions about a company's competitive situation. The ratings show how a company compares against rivals, factor by factor or capability by capability, thus revealing where it is strongest and weakest. Moreover, the overall competitive strength scores indicate whether the company is at a net competitive advantage or disadvantage against each rival.

> A company's competitive strength scores pinpoint its strengths and weaknesses against rivals and point to offensive and defensive strategies capable of producing first-rate results.

In addition, the strength ratings provide guidelines for designing wise offensive and defensive strategies. For example, consider the ratings and weighted scores in Table 4.3. If ABC Co. wants to go on the offensive to win additional sales and market share, such an offensive probably needs to be aimed directly at winning customers away from Rivals 3 and 4 (which have lower overall strength scores) rather than Rivals 1 and 2 (which have higher overall strength scores). ABC's advantages over Rival 4 tend to be in areas that are moderately important to competitive success in the industry, but ABC outclasses Rival 3 on the two most heavily weighted strength factors—relative cost position and customer service capabilities. Therefore, Rival 3 should be viewed as the primary target of ABC's offensive strategies, with Rival 4 being a secondary target.

A competitively astute company should utilize the strength scores in deciding what strategic moves to make. When a company has important competitive strengths in areas where one or more rivals are weak, it makes sense to

TABLE 4.3

Illustration of a Competitive Strength Assessment

Key Success Factor/Strength Measure	Importance Weight	ABC CO.		RIVAL 1		RIVAL 2		RIVAL 3		RIVAL 4	
		Strength Rating	Score	Strength Rating	Score	Strength Rating	Score	Strength Rating	Score	Strength Rating	Score
Quality/product performance	0.10	8	0.80	5	0.50	10	1.00	1	0.10	6	0.60
Reputation/image	0.10	8	0.80	7	0.70	10	1.00	1	0.10	6	0.60
Manufacturing capability	0.10	2	0.20	10	1.00	4	0.40	5	0.50	1	0.10
Technological skills	0.05	10	0.50	1	0.05	7	0.35	3	0.15	8	0.40
Dealer network/distribution capability	0.05	9	0.45	4	0.20	10	0.50	5	0.25	1	0.05
New-product innovation capability	0.05	9	0.45	4	0.20	10	0.50	5	0.25	1	0.05
Financial resources	0.10	5	0.50	10	1.00	7	0.70	3	0.30	1	0.10
Relative cost position	0.30	5	1.50	10	3.00	3	0.95	1	0.30	4	1.20
Customer service capabilities	0.15	5	0.75	7	1.05	10	1.50	1	0.15	4	0.60
Sum of importance weights	1.00										
Weighted overall strength rating			5.95		7.70		6.85		2.10		3.70

(Rating scale: 1 = very weak; 10 = very strong)

consider offensive moves to exploit rivals' competitive weaknesses. When a company has competitive weaknesses in important areas where one or more rivals are strong, it makes sense to consider defensive moves to curtail its vulnerability.

QUESTION 5: WHAT STRATEGIC ISSUES AND PROBLEMS MUST BE ADDRESSED BY MANAGEMENT?

The final and most important analytical step is to zero in on exactly what strategic issues company managers need to address. This step involves drawing on the results of both industry and competitive analysis and the evaluations of the company's internal situation. The task here is to get a clear fix on exactly what industry and competitive challenges confront the company, which of the company's internal weaknesses need fixing, and what specific problems merit front-burner attention by company managers. *Pinpointing the precise things that management needs to worry about sets the agenda for deciding what actions to take next to improve the company's performance and business outlook.*

▶ **LO5**

Understand how a comprehensive evaluation of a company's external and internal situations can assist managers in making critical decisions about their next strategic moves.

If the items on management's "worry list" are relatively minor, which suggests the company's strategy is mostly on track and reasonably well matched to the company's overall situation, company managers seldom need to go much beyond fine-tuning the present strategy. If, however, the issues and problems confronting the company are serious and indicate the present strategy is not well suited for the road ahead, the task of crafting a better strategy has got to go to the top of management's action agenda.

> Compiling a "worry list" of problems and issues creates an agenda for managerial strategy making.

KEY POINTS

In analyzing a company's own particular competitive circumstances and its competitive position vis-à-vis key rivals consider five key questions:

1. *How well is the present strategy working?* This involves evaluating the strategy from a qualitative standpoint (completeness, internal consistency, rationale, and suitability to the situation) and also from a quantitative standpoint (the strategic and financial results the strategy is producing). The stronger a company's current overall performance, the less likely the need for radical strategy changes. The weaker a company's performance and/or the faster the changes in its external situation (which can be gleaned from industry and competitive analysis), the more its current strategy must be questioned.

2. *What are the company's competitively important resources and capabilities?* A company's resources, competitive capabilities, and core competencies are strategically relevant because they are the most logical and appealing building blocks for strategy. The most potent resources are *competitively valuable, rare, hard to copy or imitate, and are not easily trumped by substitute resources.* Organizational resources

and capabilities must be continually strengthened and nurtured to sustain their competitive power. In addition, resources and capabilities may need to be broadened and deepened to position the company to seize market opportunities and defend against emerging threats to its well-being. A *SWOT analysis* is a simple but powerful tool for sizing up a company's resource strengths and competitive deficiencies, its market opportunities, and the external threats to its future well-being. Resource weaknesses are important because they may represent vulnerabilities that need correction. External opportunities and threats come into play because a good strategy necessarily aims at capturing a company's most attractive opportunities and at defending against threats to its well-being.

3. *Are the company's prices and costs competitive?* One telling sign of whether a company's situation is strong or precarious is whether its prices and costs are competitive with those of industry rivals. Value chain analysis and benchmarking are essential tools in determining whether the company is performing particular functions and activities cost-effectively, learning whether its costs are in line with competitors, and deciding which internal activities and business processes need to be scrutinized for improvement. Value chain analysis teaches that how competently a company manages its value chain activities relative to rivals is a key to building a competitive advantage based on either better competencies and competitive capabilities or lower costs than rivals.

4. *Is the company competitively stronger or weaker than key rivals?* The key appraisals here involve how the company matches up against key rivals on industry key success factors and other chief determinants of competitive success and whether and why the company has a competitive advantage or disadvantage. Quantitative competitive strength assessments, using the method presented in Table 4.3, indicate where a company is competitively strong and weak and provide insight into the company's ability to defend or enhance its market position. As a rule a company's competitive strategy should be built around its competitive strengths and should aim at shoring up areas where it is competitively vulnerable. When a company has important competitive strengths in areas where one or more rivals are weak, it makes sense to consider offensive moves to exploit rivals' competitive weaknesses. When a company has important competitive weaknesses in areas where one or more rivals are strong, it makes sense to consider defensive moves to curtail its vulnerability.

5. *What strategic issues and problems merit front-burner managerial attention?* This analytical step zeros in on the strategic issues and problems that stand in the way of the company's success. It involves using the results of both industry and competitive analysis and company situation analysis to identify a "worry list" of issues to be resolved for the company to be financially and competitively successful in the years ahead. Actually deciding upon a strategy and what specific actions to take comes after the list of strategic issues and problems that merit front-burner management attention has been developed.

Good company situation analysis, like good industry and competitive analysis, is a valuable precondition for good strategy making.

ASSURANCE OF LEARNING EXERCISES

1. Using the financial ratios provided in the Appendix and the financial statement information for Avon Products, Inc., below, calculate the following ratios for Avon for both 2009 and 2010:

   a. Gross profit margin.

   b. Operating profit margin.

   c. Net profit margin.

   d. Times interest earned coverage.

   e. Return on shareholders' equity.

   f. Return on assets.

   g. Debt-to-equity ratio.

   h. Days of inventory.

   i. Inventory turnover ratio.

   j. Average collection period.

   Based on these ratios, did Avon's financial performance improve, weaken, or remain about the same from 2009 to 2010?

LO1

connect
www.mcgrawhillconnect.com

Consolidated Statements of Income for Avon Products, Inc., 2009–2010 (in millions, except per share data)

YEARS ENDED DECEMBER 31	2010	2009
Net sales	$10,731.3	$10,084.8
Other revenue	131.5	120.4
Total revenue	10,862.8	10,205.2
Costs, expenses and other:		
Cost of sales	4,041.3	3,825.5
Selling, general, and administrative expenses	5,748.4	5,374.1
Operating profit	1,073.1	1,005.6
Interest expense	87.1	104.8
Interest income	(14.0)	(20.2)
Other expense, net	54.6	7.3
Total other expenses	127.7	91.9
Income from continuing operations, before taxes	945.4	913.7
Income taxes	350.2	294.5
Income from continuing operations, net of tax	595.2	619.2
Discontinued operations, net of tax	14.1	9.0
Net income	$ 609.3	$ 628.2
Earnings per share:		
Basic from continuing operations	$ 1.37	$ 1.43
Diluted from continuing operations	$ 1.36	$ 1.43
Weighted-average shares outstanding:		
Basic	428.75	426.90
Diluted	431.35	428.54

Consolidated Balance Sheets for Avon Products, Inc., 2009–2010
(in millions, except per share data)

DECEMBER 31	2010	2009
Assets		
Current assets		
Cash, including cash equivalents of $572.0 and $670.5	$1,179.9	$ 963.4
Accounts receivable (less allowances of $232.0 and $165.1)	826.3	765.7
Inventories	1,152.9	1,049.8
Prepaid expenses and other	1,025.2	1,042.3
Current assets of discontinued operations	--	50.3
Total current assets	4,184.3	4,206.2
Property, plant and equipment, at cost Land	69.2	115.9
Buildings and improvements	1,140.2	954.2
Equipment	1,541.5	1,435.8
	2,750.9	2,505.9
Less accumulated depreciation	(1,123.5)	(1,036.9)
	1,627.4	1,469.0
Other assets	1,018.6	846.1
Total assets	$7,873.7	$6,823.4
Liabilities and Shareholders' Equity Current liabilities		
Debt maturing within one year	$ 727.6	$ 137.8
Accounts payable	809.8	739.0
Accrued compensation	293.2	282.6
Other accrued liabilities	771.6	706.3
Sales and taxes other than income	207.6	254.1
Income taxes	146.5	134.5
Total current liabilities	2,956.3	2,291.7
Long-term debt	2,408.6	2,307.2
Employee benefit plans	561.3	577.8
Long-term income taxes	128.9	147.6
Other liabilities	146.0	186.5
Total liabilities	$6,201.1	$5,510.8
Commitments and contingencies		
Shareholders' equity		
Common stock, par value $.25–authorized 1,500 shares; issued 743.3 and 740.9 shares	$ 186.6	$ 186.1
Additional paid-in capital	2,024.2	1,941.0
Retained earnings	4,610.8	4,383.9
Accumulated other comprehensive loss	(605.8)	(692.6)
Treasury stock, at cost –313.8 and 313.4 shares	(4,559.3)	(4,545.8)
Noncontrolling interest	16.1	40.0
Total shareholders' equity	$1,672.6	$1,312.6
Total liabilities and shareholders' equity	$7,873.7	$6,823.4

Source: Avon Products, Inc., 2010, 10-K.

LO2   2.   Starbucks operates more than 17,000 stores in more than 50 countries. How many of the four tests of the competitive power of a resource does the store network pass? Explain your answer.

3. Review the information in Concepts & Connections 4.1 concerning producing and selling fair trade coffee. Then answer the following questions:

    a. Companies that do not sell fair trade coffee can buy coffee direct from small farmers for as little as $0.75 per pound. By paying substandard wages, they can also reduce their labor costs of roasting and bagging coffee to $0.70 per pound and reduce their overhead by 20 percent. If they sell their coffee at the same average price as Just Coffee, what would their profit margin be and how would this compare to Just Coffee's?

    b. How can Just Coffee respond to this type of competitive threat? Does it have any valuable competitive assets that can help it respond or will it need to acquire new ones. Would your answer change the company's value chain in any way?

4. Using the methodology illustrated in Table 4.3 and your knowledge as an automobile owner, prepare a competitive strength assessment for General Motors and its rivals Ford, Chrysler, Toyota, and Honda. Each of the five automobile manufacturers should be evaluated on the key success factors/strength measures of: cost competitiveness, product line breadth, product quality and reliability, financial resources and profitability, and customer service. What does your competitive strength assessment disclose about the overall competitiveness of each automobile manufacturer? What factors account most for Toyota's competitive success? Does Toyota have competitive weaknesses that were disclosed by your analysis? Explain.

LO3

www.mcgrawhillconnect.com

LO4

EXERCISES FOR SIMULATION PARTICIPANTS

1. Using the formulas in the Appendix and the data in your company's latest financial statements, calculate the following measures of financial performance for your company:

    a. Operating profit margin

    b. Return on total assets

    c. Current ratio

    d. Working capital

    e. Long-term debt-to-capital ratio

    f. Price-earnings ratio

LO1

2. Based on your company's latest financial statements and all of the other available data regarding your company's performance that appear in the Industry Report, list the three measures of financial performance on which your company did "best" and the three measures on which your company's financial performance was "worst."

LO1

3. What hard evidence can you cite that indicates your company's strategy is working fairly well (or perhaps not working so well, if your company's performance is lagging that of rival companies)?

LO1

4. What internal strengths and weaknesses does your company have? What external market opportunities for growth and increased profitability exist for your company? What external threats to your company's future well-being and

LO2

profitability do you and your co-managers see? What does the preceding SWOT analysis indicate about your company's present situation and future prospects—where on the scale from "exceptionally strong" to "alarmingly weak" does the attractiveness of your company's situation rank?

LO2

5. Does your company have any core competencies? If so, what are they?

LO3

6. What are the key elements of your company's value chain? Refer to Figure 4.1 in developing your answer.

LO4

7. Using the methodology illustrated in Table 4.3, do a weighted competitive strength assessment for your company and two other companies that you and your co-managers consider to be very close competitors.

ENDNOTES

1. Birger Wernerfelt, "A Resource-Based View of the Firm," *Strategic Management Journal* 5, no. 5 (September–October 1984); Jay Barney, "Firm Resources and Sustained Competitive Advantage," *Journal of Management* 17, no. 1 (1991); Margaret A. Peteraf, "The Cornerstones of Competitive Advantage: A Resource-Based View," *Strategic Management Journal* 14, no. 3 (March 1993).

2. R. Amit and P. Schoemaker, "Strategic Assets and Organizational Rent," *Strategic Management Journal* 14, no. 1 (1993).

3 David J. Collis and Cynthia A. Montgomery, "Competing on Resources: Strategy in the 1990s," *Harvard Business Review* 73, no. 4 (July–August 1995).

4. George Stalk, Philip Evans, and Lawrence E. Schulman, "Competing on Capabilities: The New Rules of Corporate Strategy," *Harvard Business Review* 70, no. 2 (March–April 1992).

5. David J. Teece, Gary Pisano, and Amy Shuen, "Dynamic Capabilities and Strategic Management," *Strategic Management Journal* 18, no.

7 (1997); and Constance E. Helfat and Margaret A. Peteraf, "The Dynamic Resource-Based View: Capability Lifecycles," *Strategic Management Journal* 24, no. 10 (2003).

6. C. Montgomery, "Of Diamonds and Rust: A New Look at Resources" in *Resource-Based and Evolutionary Theories of the Firm*, ed. C. Montgomery (Boston: Kluwer Academic Publishers, 1995), pp. 251–68.

7. K. Eisenhardt and J. Martin, "Dynamic Capabilities: What are They?" *Strategic Management Journal*, 21, nos. 10–11 (2000); and M. Zollo and S. Winter, "Deliberate Learning and the Evolution of Dynamic Capabilities," *Organization Science* 13 (2002).

8. Michael E. Porter, *Competitive Advantage* (New York: Free Press, 1985).

9. Gregory H. Watson, *Strategic Benchmarking: How to Rate Your Company's Performance Against the World's Best* (New York: John Wiley & Sons, 1993); Robert C. Camp, *Benchmarking: The Search for Industry Best Practices That Lead to Superior Performance* (Milwaukee:

ASQC Quality Press, 1989); Christopher E. Bogan and Michael J. English, *Benchmarking for Best Practices: Winning through Innovative Adaptation* (New York: McGraw-Hill, 1994); and Dawn Iacobucci and Christie Nordhielm, "Creative Benchmarking," *Harvard Business Review* 78, no. 6 (November–December 2000).

10. Jeremy Main, "How to Steal the Best Ideas Around," *Fortune*, October 19, 1992, pp. 102–3.

11. M. Hegert and D. Morris, "Accounting Data for Value Chain Analysis," *Strategic Management Journal* 10 (1989); Robin Cooper and Robert S. Kaplan, "Measure Costs Right: Make the Right Decisions," *Harvard Business Review* 66, no. 5 (September–October 1988); and John K. Shank and Vijay Govindarajan, *Strategic Cost Management* (New York: Free Press, 1993).

12. Michael E. Porter, "Clusters and the New Economics of Competition," *Harvard Business Review* 76, no. 6 (November–December 1998).

13. Reuben E. Stone, "Leading a Supply Chain Turnaround," *Harvard Business Review* 82, no. 10 (October 2004).

chapter 5

THE FIVE GENERIC COMPETITIVE STRATEGIES

LEARNING OBJECTIVES

LO1   Gain an understanding of how each of the five generic competitive strategies goes about building competitive advantage and delivering superior value to customers.

LO2   Learn the major avenues for achieving a competitive advantage based on lower costs.

LO3   Recognize why some generic strategies work better in certain kinds of industry and competitive conditions than others.

LO4   Gain command of the major avenues for developing a competitive advantage based on differentiating a company's product or service offering from the offerings of rivals.

LO5   Recognize the required conditions for delivering superior value to customers through the use of a hybrid of low-cost provider and differentiation strategies.

There are several basic approaches to competing successfully and gaining a competitive advantage, but they all involve giving buyers what they perceive as superior value compared to the offerings of rival sellers. Superior value can mean offering a good product at a lower price, a superior product that is worth paying more for, or a best-value offering that represents an attractive combination of price, features, quality, service, and other appealing attributes.

This chapter describes the five *generic competitive strategy options* for building competitive advantage and delivering superior value to customers. Which of the five to employ is a company's first and foremost choice in crafting an overall strategy and beginning its quest for competitive advantage.

COMPETITIVE STRATEGIES AND MARKET POSITIONING

▶ **LO1**

Gain an understanding of how each of the five generic competitive strategies goes about building competitive advantage and delivering superior value to customers.

A company's **competitive strategy** deals exclusively with the specifics of management's game plan for competing successfully—its specific efforts to please customers, its offensive and defensive moves to counter the maneuvers of rivals, its responses to whatever market conditions prevail at the moment, and its approach to securing a competitive advantage vis-à-vis rivals. There are countless variations in the competitive strategies that companies employ, mainly because each company's strategic approach entails custom-designed actions to fit its own circumstances and industry environment. The custom-tailored nature of each company's strategy is also the result of management's efforts to uniquely position the company in its market. Companies are much more likely to achieve competitive advantage and earn above-average profits if they find a unique way of delivering superior value to customers. For example, the iPod's attractive styling, easy-to-use controls, attention-grabbing ads, and extensive collection of music available at Apple's iTunes Store have given Apple a competitive advantage in the digital media player industry. Microsoft has attempted to imitate Apple's competitive strategy with introduction of its Zune music player and store, but Microsoft has fared no better in its attack on the iPod than any of the other makers of digital media players. By choosing a unique approach to providing value to customers, Apple has achieved an enduring brand loyalty that makes it difficult for others to triumph by merely copying its strategic approach. "Me too" strategies can rarely be expected to deliver competitive advantage and stellar performance unless the imitator possesses resources or competencies that allow it to provide greater value to customers than that offered by firms with similar strategic approaches.

> **CORE CONCEPT**
>
> A **competitive strategy** concerns the specifics of management's game plan for competing successfully and securing a competitive advantage over rivals in the marketplace.

Competitive strategies that provide distinctive industry positioning and competitive advantage in the marketplace involve choosing between (1) a market target that is either broad or narrow, and (2) whether the company should pursue a competitive advantage linked to low costs or product

▶ FIGURE 5.1 **The Five Generic Competitive Strategies**

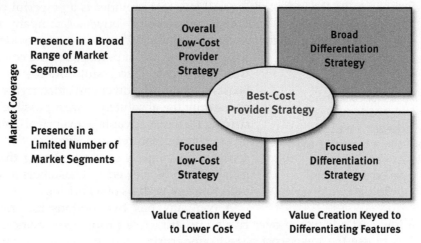

Source: This is an author-expanded version of a three-strategy classification discussed in Michael E. Porter, *Competitive Strategy* (New York: Free Press, 1980), pp. 35–40.

differentiation. These two factors give rise to the five competitive strategy options shown in Figure 5.1 and listed below.[1]

1. *A low-cost provider strategy*—striving to achieve lower overall costs than rivals and appealing to a broad spectrum of customers, usually by underpricing rivals.

2. *A broad differentiation strategy*—seeking to differentiate the company's product or service from rivals' in ways that will appeal to a broad spectrum of buyers.

3. *A focused low-cost strategy*—concentrating on a narrow buyer segment (or market niche) and outcompeting rivals by having lower costs than rivals and thus being able to serve niche members at a lower price.

4. *A focused differentiation strategy*—concentrating on a narrow buyer segment (or market niche) and outcompeting rivals by offering niche members customized attributes that meet their tastes and requirements better than rivals' products.

5. *A best-cost provider strategy*—giving customers more value for the money by satisfying buyers' expectations on key quality/features/ performance/service attributes while beating their price expectations. This option is a *hybrid* strategy that blends elements of low-cost provider and differentiation strategies; the aim is to have the lowest (best) costs and prices among sellers offering products with comparable differentiating attributes.

The remainder of this chapter explores the ins and outs of the five generic competitive strategies and how they differ.

LOW-COST PROVIDER STRATEGIES

Striving to be the industry's overall low-cost provider is a powerful competitive approach in markets with many price-sensitive buyers. A company achieves low-cost leadership when it becomes the industry's lowest-cost provider rather than just being one of perhaps several competitors with low costs. Successful low-cost providers boast meaningfully lower costs than rivals, but not necessarily the absolutely lowest possible cost. In striving for a cost advantage over rivals, managers must include features and services that buyers consider essential. A product offering that is too frills-free can be viewed by consumers as offering little value, regardless of its pricing.

> **CORE CONCEPT**
>
> A **low-cost leader**'s basis for competitive advantage is lower overall costs than competitors. Success in achieving a low-cost edge over rivals comes from eliminating and/or curbing "nonessential" activities and/or outmanaging rivals in performing essential activities.

A company has two options for translating a low-cost advantage over rivals into attractive profit performance. Option 1 is to use the lower-cost edge to underprice competitors and attract price-sensitive buyers in great enough numbers to increase total profits. Option 2 is to maintain the present price, be content with the present market share, and use the lower-cost edge to earn a higher profit margin on each unit sold, thereby raising the firm's total profits and overall return on investment.

The Two Major Avenues for Achieving Low-Cost Leadership

LO2

Learn the major avenues for achieving a competitive advantage based on lower costs.

To achieve a low-cost edge over rivals, a firm's cumulative costs across its overall value chain must be lower than competitors' cumulative costs. There are two major avenues for accomplishing this:[2]

1. Performing essential value chain activities more cost-effectively than rivals.

2. Revamping the firm's overall value chain to eliminate or bypass some cost-producing activities.

Cost-Efficient Management of Value Chain Activities   For a company to do a more cost-efficient job of managing its value chain than rivals, managers must launch a concerted, ongoing effort to ferret out cost-saving opportunities in every part of the value chain. No activity can escape cost-saving scrutiny, and all company personnel must be expected to use their talents and ingenuity to come up with innovative and effective ways to keep costs down. All avenues for performing value chain activities at a lower cost than rivals must be explored. These can include:

- *Striving to capture all available economies of scale.* Economies of scale stem from an ability to lower unit costs by increasing the scale of operation. For example, occasions may arise when a large plant is more economical to operate than a small or medium-sized plant or when a large distribution center is more cost efficient than a small one.

- *Taking full advantage of experience and learning curve effects.* The cost of performing an activity can decline over time as the learning and experience of company personnel build.

- *Trying to operate facilities at full capacity.* Whether a company is able to operate at or near full capacity has a big impact on unit costs when its value chain contains activities associated with substantial fixed costs. Higher rates of capacity utilization allow depreciation and other fixed costs to be spread over a larger unit volume, thereby lowering fixed costs per unit.

- *Pursuing efforts to boost sales volumes and thus spread outlays for R&D, advertising, and general administration over more units.* The more units a company sells, the more it lowers cost per unit for expenses such as new-product development, sales promotion campaigns, and administrative support activities.

- *Substituting lower cost inputs whenever there's little or no sacrifice in product quality or product performance.* If the costs of certain raw materials and parts are "too high," a company can switch to using lower-cost alternatives when they exist.

- *Employing advanced production technology and process design to improve overall efficiency.* Often production costs can be cut by utilizing design for manufacture (DFM) procedures and computer-assisted design (CAD) techniques that enable more integrated and efficient production methods, investing in highly automated robotic production technology, and shifting to production processes that enable manufacturing multiple versions of a product as cost efficiently as mass producing a single version. A number of companies are ardent users of total quality management systems, business process reengineering, Six Sigma methodology, and other business process management techniques that aim at boosting efficiency and reducing costs.

- *Using communication systems and information technology to achieve operating efficiencies.* For example sharing data and production schedules with suppliers, coupled with the use of enterprise resource planning (ERP) and manufacturing execution system (MES) software, can reduce parts inventories, trim production times, and lower labor requirements.

- *Pursuing ways to reduce workforce size and lower overall compensation costs.* A company can economize on labor costs by installing labor-saving technology, shifting production from geographic areas where pay scales are high to geographic areas where pay scales are low, using incentive compensation systems that promote high labor productivity, and avoiding the use of union labor where possible (because costly work rules can stifle productivity and because of "unreasonable" union demands for above-market pay scales and costly fringe benefits).

- *Using the company's bargaining power vis-à-vis suppliers to gain concessions.* A company may have sufficient bargaining clout with suppliers to win price discounts on large-volume purchases or realize other cost-savings.

- *Being alert to the cost advantages of outsourcing and vertical integration.* Outsourcing the performance of certain value chain activities can be more economical than performing them in-house if outside specialists, by virtue of their expertise and volume, can perform the activities at lower cost.

Revamping the Value Chain Dramatic cost advantages can often emerge from reengineering the company's value chain in ways that eliminate costly work steps and bypass certain cost-producing value chain activities. Such value chain revamping can include:

- *Selling directly to consumers and cutting out the activities and costs of distributors and dealers.* To circumvent the need for distributors–dealers, a company can (1) create its own direct sales force (which adds the costs of maintaining and supporting a sales force but may be cheaper than utilizing independent distributors and dealers to access buyers), and/or (2) conduct sales operations at the company's website (costs for website operations and shipping may be a substantially cheaper way to make sales to customers than going through distributor–dealer channels). Costs in the wholesale/retail portions of the value chain frequently represent 35 to 50 percent of the price final consumers pay, so establishing a direct sales force or selling online may offer big cost savings.

- *Streamlining operations by eliminating low value-added or unnecessary work steps and activities.* At Walmart, some items supplied by manufacturers are delivered directly to retail stores rather than being routed through Walmart's distribution centers and delivered by Walmart trucks. In other instances, Walmart unloads incoming shipments from manufacturers' trucks arriving at its distribution centers directly onto outgoing Walmart trucks headed to particular stores without ever moving the goods into the distribution center.

- *Reducing materials handling and shipping costs by having suppliers locate their plants or warehouses close to a company's own facilities.* Having suppliers locate their plants or warehouses very close to a company's own plant not only lowers inbound shipping costs, but also facilitates just-in-time deliveries of parts and components.

Concepts & Connections 5.1 describes Walmart's broad approach to managing its value chain in the retail grocery portion of its business to achieve a dramatic cost advantage over rival supermarket chains and become the world's biggest grocery retailer.

When a Low-Cost Provider Strategy Works Best

▶ **LO3**

Recognize why some generic strategies work better in certain kinds of industry and competitive conditions than others.

A competitive strategy predicated on low-cost leadership is particularly powerful when:

1. *Price competition among rival sellers is especially vigorous.* Low-cost providers are in the best position to compete offensively on the basis of price and to survive price wars.

2. *The products of rival sellers are essentially identical and are readily available from several sellers.* Commodity-like products and/or ample supplies set the stage for lively price competition; in such markets, it is the less efficient, higher-cost companies that are most vulnerable.

3. *There are few ways to achieve product differentiation that have value to buyers.* When the product or service differences between brands do not matter much to buyers, buyers nearly always shop the market for the best price.

CONCEPTS & CONNECTIONS 5.1

HOW WALMART MANAGED ITS VALUE CHAIN TO ACHIEVE A LOW-COST ADVANTAGE OVER RIVAL SUPERMARKET CHAINS

Walmart has achieved a very substantial cost and pricing advantage over rival supermarket chains by both revamping portions of the grocery retailing value chain and outmanaging its rivals in efficiently performing various value chain activities. Its cost advantage stems from a series of initiatives and practices:

- Instituting extensive information sharing with vendors via online systems that relay sales at its checkout counters directly to suppliers of the items, thereby providing suppliers with real-time information on customer demand and preferences (creating an estimated 6 percent cost advantage).

- Pursuing global procurement of some items and centralizing most purchasing activities so as to leverage the company's buying power (creating an estimated 2.5 percent cost advantage).

- Investing in state-of-the-art automation at its distribution centers, efficiently operating a truck fleet that makes daily deliveries to Walmart's stores, and putting assorted other cost-saving practices into place at its headquarters, distribution centers, and stores (resulting in an estimated 4 percent cost advantage).

- Striving to optimize the product mix and achieve greater sales turnover (resulting in about a 2 percent cost advantage).

- Installing security systems and store operating procedures that lower shrinkage rates (producing a cost advantage of about 0.5 percent).

- Negotiating preferred real estate rental and leasing rates with real estate developers and owners of its store sites (yielding a cost advantage of 2 percent).

- Managing and compensating its workforce in a manner that produces lower labor costs (yielding an estimated 5 percent cost advantage).

Altogether, these value chain initiatives give Walmart an approximately 22 percent cost advantage over Kroger, Safeway, and other leading supermarket chains. With such a sizable cost advantage, Walmart has been able to underprice its rivals and become the world's leading supermarket retailer.

Source: www.walmart.com; and Marco Iansiti and Roy Levien, "Strategy as Ecology," *Harvard Business Review* 82, no. 3 (March 2004), p. 70.

4. *Buyers incur low costs in switching their purchases from one seller to another.* Low switching costs give buyers the flexibility to shift purchases to lower-priced sellers having equally good products. A low-cost leader is well positioned to use low price to induce its customers not to switch to rival brands.

5. *The majority of industry sales are made to a few, large-volume buyers.* Low-cost providers are in the best position among sellers in bargaining with high-volume buyers because they are able to beat rivals' pricing to land a high-volume sale while maintaining an acceptable profit margin.

6. *Industry newcomers use introductory low prices to attract buyers and build a customer base.* The low-cost leader can use price cuts of its own to make it harder for a new rival to win customers.

As a rule, the more price-sensitive buyers are, the more appealing a low-cost strategy becomes. A low-cost company's ability to set the industry's price floor and still earn a profit erects protective barriers around its market position.

Pitfalls to Avoid in Pursuing a Low-Cost Provider Strategy

Perhaps the biggest pitfall of a low-cost provider strategy is getting carried away with *overly aggressive price cutting* and ending up with lower, rather than higher, profitability. A low-cost/low-price advantage results in superior profitability only if (1) prices are cut by less than the size of the cost advantage or (2) the added volume is large enough to bring in a bigger total profit despite lower margins per unit sold. Thus, a company with a 5 percent cost advantage cannot cut prices 20 percent, end up with a volume gain of only 10 percent, and still expect to earn higher profits!

A second big pitfall is *relying on an approach to reduce costs that can be easily copied by rivals.* The value of a cost advantage depends on its sustainability. Sustainability, in turn, hinges on whether the company achieves its cost advantage in ways difficult for rivals to replicate or match. If rivals find it relatively easy or inexpensive to imitate the leader's low-cost methods, then the leader's advantage will be too short-lived to yield a valuable edge in the marketplace.

A third pitfall is becoming *too fixated on cost reduction.* Low costs cannot be pursued so zealously that a firm's offering ends up being too features-poor to gain the interest of buyers. Furthermore, a company driving hard to push its costs down has to guard against misreading or ignoring increased buyer preferences for added features or declining buyer price sensitivity. Even if these mistakes are avoided, a low-cost competitive approach still carries risk. Cost-saving technological breakthroughs or process improvements by rival firms can nullify a low-cost leader's hard-won position.

BROAD DIFFERENTIATION STRATEGIES

Differentiation strategies are attractive whenever buyers' needs and preferences are too diverse to be fully satisfied by a standardized product or service.

> **CORE CONCEPT**
>
> The essence of a **broad differentiation strategy** is to offer unique product or service attributes that a wide range of buyers find appealing and worth paying for.

A company attempting to succeed through differentiation must study buyers' needs and behavior carefully to learn what buyers think has value and what they are willing to pay for. Then the company must include these desirable features to clearly set itself apart from rivals lacking such product or service attributes.

Successful differentiation allows a firm to:

- Command a premium price, and/or
- Increase unit sales (because additional buyers are won over by the differentiating features), and/or
- Gain buyer loyalty to its brand (because some buyers are strongly attracted to the differentiating features and bond with the company and its products).

Differentiation enhances profitability whenever the extra price the product commands outweighs the added costs of achieving the differentiation.

Company differentiation strategies fail when buyers don't value the brand's uniqueness and/or when a company's approach to differentiation is easily copied or matched by its rivals.

Approaches to Differentiation

Companies can pursue differentiation from many angles: a unique taste (Red Bull, Listerine), multiple features (Microsoft Office, Apple iPhone), wide selection and one-stop shopping (Home Depot, Amazon.com), superior service (Ritz-Carlton, Nordstrom), spare parts availability (Caterpillar guarantees 48-hour spare parts delivery to any customer anywhere in the world or else the part is furnished free), engineering design and performance (Mercedes-Benz, BMW), luxury and prestige (Rolex, Gucci, Chanel), product reliability (Whirlpool and Bosch in large home appliances), quality manufacturing (Michelin in tires, Toyota and Honda in automobiles), technological leadership (3M Corporation in bonding and coating products), a full range of services (Charles Schwab in stock brokerage), and a complete line of products (Campbell soups, Frito-Lay snack foods).

► **LO4**

Gain command of the major avenues for developing a competitive advantage based on differentiating a company's product or service offering from the offerings of rivals.

The most appealing approaches to differentiation are those that are hard or expensive for rivals to duplicate. Resourceful competitors can, in time, clone almost any product or feature or attribute. If Coca-Cola introduces a vitamin-enhanced bottled water, so can Pepsi; if Firestone offers customers attractive financing terms, so can Goodyear. As a rule, differentiation yields a longer-lasting and more profitable competitive edge when it is based on product innovation, technical superiority, product quality and reliability, comprehensive customer service, and unique competitive capabilities. Such differentiating attributes tend to be tough for rivals to copy or offset profitably and buyers widely perceive them as having value.

> Easy-to-copy differentiating features cannot produce sustainable competitive advantage; differentiation based on hard-to-copy competencies and capabilities tends to be more sustainable.

Delivering Superior Value via a Differentiation Strategy

While it is easy enough to grasp that a successful differentiation strategy must offer value in ways unmatched by rivals, a big issue in crafting a differentiation strategy is deciding what is valuable to customers. Typically, value can be delivered to customers in three basic ways.

1. *Include product attributes and user features that lower the buyer's costs.* Commercial buyers value products that can reduce their cost of doing business. For example, making a company's product more economical for a buyer to use can be done by reducing the buyer's raw materials waste (providing cut-to-size components), reducing a buyer's inventory requirements (providing just-in-time deliveries), increasing product reliability to lower a buyer's repair and maintenance costs, and providing free technical support. Similarly, consumers find value in differentiating features that will reduce their expenses. Rising costs for gasoline prices have spurred the efforts of motor vehicle manufacturers worldwide to introduce models with better fuel economy.

2. *Incorporate tangible features that improve product performance.* Commercial buyers and consumers alike value higher levels of performance in many types of products. Product reliability, output, durability, convenience, and ease of use are aspects of product performance that differentiate products offered to buyers. Mobile phone manufacturers are currently in a race to improve the performance of their products through the introduction of next-generation phones with a more appealing, trend-setting array of user features and options.

3. *Incorporate intangible features that enhance buyer satisfaction in noneconomic ways.* Toyota's Prius appeals to environmentally conscious motorists who wish to help reduce global carbon dioxide emissions. Bentley, Ralph Lauren, Louis Vuitton, Tiffany, Cartier, and Rolex have differentiation-based competitive advantages linked to buyer desires for status, image, prestige, upscale fashion, superior craftsmanship, and the finer things in life. L.L. Bean makes its mail-order customers feel secure in their purchases by providing an unconditional guarantee with no time limit.

 Differentiation can be based on *tangible* or *intangible* features and attributes.

Managing the Value Chain in Ways That Enhance Differentiation

Differentiation is not necessarily something hatched in marketing and advertising departments, nor is it limited to quality and service. Differentiation opportunities can exist in activities all along the value chain. Value chain activities that affect the value of a product or service include the following:

- *Supplier and purchasing activities* that ultimately spill over to affect the performance or quality of the company's end product. Starbucks gets high ratings on its coffees partly because it has very strict specifications on the coffee beans purchased from suppliers.

- *Product R&D activities* that aim at improved product designs and performance, expanded end uses and applications, more frequent first-to-market victories, added user safety, greater recycling capability, or enhanced environmental protection.

- *Production R&D and technology-related activities* that permit the manufacture of customized products at an efficient cost; make production methods safer for the environment; or improve product quality, reliability, and appearance. Many manufacturers have developed flexible manufacturing systems that allow different models and product versions to be made on the same assembly line. Being able to provide buyers with made-to-order products can be a potent differentiating capability.

- *Manufacturing activities* that reduce product defects, extend product life, allow better warranty coverages, or enhance product appearance. The quality edge enjoyed by Japanese automakers stems partly from their distinctive competence in performing assembly line activities.

- *Distribution and shipping activities* that allow for fewer warehouse and on-the-shelf stockouts, quicker delivery to customers, more accurate order filling, and/or lower shipping costs.

- *Marketing, sales, and customer service activities* that result in superior technical assistance to buyers, faster maintenance and repair services, better credit terms, quicker order processing, or greater customer convenience.

Perceived Value and the Importance of Signaling Value

The price premium commanded by a differentiation strategy reflects *the value actually delivered* to the buyer and *the value perceived* by the buyer. The value of certain differentiating features is rather easy for buyers to detect, but in some instances buyers may have trouble assessing what their experience with the product will be. Successful differentiators go to great lengths to make buyers knowledgeable about a product's value and incorporate signals of value such as attractive packaging; extensive ad campaigns; the quality of brochures and sales presentations; the seller's list of customers; the length of time the firm has been in business; and the professionalism, appearance, and personality of the seller's employees. Such signals of value may be as important as actual value (1) when the nature of differentiation is subjective or hard to quantify, (2) when buyers are making a first-time purchase, (3) when repurchase is infrequent, and (4) when buyers are unsophisticated.

When a Differentiation Strategy Works Best

Differentiation strategies tend to work best in market circumstances where:

▶**LO3**

Recognize why some generic strategies work better in certain kinds of industry and competitive conditions than others.

1. *Buyer needs and uses of the product are diverse.* Diverse buyer preferences allow industry rivals to set themselves apart with product attributes that appeal to particular buyers. For instance, the diversity of consumer preferences for menu selection, ambience, pricing, and customer service gives restaurants exceptionally wide latitude in creating differentiated concepts. Other industries offering opportunities for differentiation based upon diverse buyer needs and uses include magazine publishing, automobile manufacturing, footwear, kitchen appliances, and computers.

2. *There are many ways to differentiate the product or service that have value to buyers.* Industries that allow competitors to add features to product attributes are well suited to differentiation strategies. For example, hotel chains can differentiate on such features as location, size of room, range of guest services, in-hotel dining, and the quality and luxuriousness of bedding and furnishings. Similarly, cosmetics producers are able to differentiate based upon prestige and image, formulations that fight the signs of aging, UV light protection, exclusivity of retail locations, the inclusion of antioxidants and natural ingredients, or prohibitions against animal testing.

3. *Few rival firms are following a similar differentiation approach.* The best differentiation approaches involve trying to appeal to buyers on the basis of attributes that rivals are not emphasizing. A differentiator encounters less head-to-head rivalry when it goes its own separate way to create uniqueness and does not try to outdifferentiate rivals on the very same attributes. When many rivals are all claiming "ours tastes better than theirs" or "ours gets your clothes cleaner than theirs," competitors tend to end up chasing the same buyers with very similar product offerings.

4. *Technological change is fast-paced and competition revolves around rapidly evolving product features.* Rapid product innovation and frequent introductions of next-version products heighten buyer interest and provide space for companies to pursue distinct differentiating paths. In video game hardware and video games, golf equipment, PCs, mobile phones, and automobile navigation systems, competitors are locked into an ongoing battle to set themselves apart by introducing the best next-generation products; companies that fail to come up with new and improved products and distinctive performance features quickly lose out in the marketplace.

Pitfalls to Avoid in Pursuing a Differentiation Strategy

Differentiation strategies can fail for any of several reasons. *A differentiation strategy keyed to product or service attributes that are easily and quickly copied is always suspect.* Rapid imitation means that no rival achieves meaningful differentiation, because whatever new feature one firm introduces that strikes the fancy of buyers is almost immediately added by rivals. This is why a firm must search out sources of uniqueness that are time-consuming or burdensome for rivals to match if it hopes to use differentiation to win a sustainable competitive edge over rivals.

Differentiation strategies can also falter when buyers see little value in the unique attributes of a company's product. Thus even if a company sets the attributes of its brand apart from its rivals' brands, its strategy can fail because of trying to differentiate on the basis of something that does not deliver adequate value to buyers. Any time many potential buyers look at a company's differentiated product offering and conclude "so what," the company's differentiation strategy is in deep trouble; buyers will likely decide the product is not worth the extra price and sales will be disappointingly low.

Overspending on efforts to differentiate is a strategy flaw that can erode profitability. Company efforts to achieve differentiation nearly always raise costs. The trick to profitable differentiation is either to keep the costs of achieving differentiation below the price premium the differentiating attributes can command in the marketplace or to offset thinner profit margins by selling enough additional units to increase total profits. If a company goes overboard in pursuing costly differentiation, it could be saddled with unacceptably thin profit margins or even losses. The need to contain differentiation costs is why many companies add little touches of differentiation that add to buyer satisfaction but are inexpensive to institute.

Other common pitfalls and mistakes in crafting a differentiation strategy include:

- *Overdifferentiating so that product quality or service levels exceed buyers' needs.* Buyers are unlikely to pay extra for features and attributes that will go unused. For example, consumers are unlikely to purchase programmable large appliances such as washers, dryers, and ovens if they are satisfied with manually controlled appliances.

- *Trying to charge too high a price premium.* Even if buyers view certain extras or deluxe features as "nice to have," they may still conclude that the added benefit or luxury is not worth the price differential over that of lesser differentiated products.

- *Being timid and not striving to open up meaningful gaps in quality or service or performance features vis-à-vis the products of rivals.* Tiny differences between rivals' product offerings may not be visible or important to buyers.

A low-cost provider strategy can always defeat a differentiation strategy when buyers are satisfied with a basic product and don't think "extra" attributes are worth a higher price.

FOCUSED (OR MARKET NICHE) STRATEGIES

What sets focused strategies apart from low-cost leadership or broad differentiation strategies is a concentration on a narrow piece of the total market. The targeted segment, or niche, can be defined by geographic uniqueness or by special product attributes that appeal only to niche members. The advantages of focusing a company's entire competitive effort on a single market niche are considerable, especially for smaller and medium-sized companies that may lack the breadth and depth of resources to tackle going after a national customer base with a "something for everyone" lineup of models, styles, and product selection. Community Coffee, the largest family-owned specialty coffee retailer in the United States, has a geographic focus on the state of Louisiana and communities across the Gulf of Mexico. Community holds only a 1.1 percent share of the national coffee market, but has recorded sales in excess of $100 million and has won a 50 percent share of the coffee business in the 11-state region where it is distributed. Examples of firms that concentrate on a well-defined market niche keyed to a particular product or buyer segment include Discovery Channel and Comedy Central (in cable TV), Google (in Internet search engines), Porsche (in sports cars), and CGA, Inc. (a specialist in providing insurance to cover the cost of lucrative hole-in-one prizes at golf tournaments). Microbreweries, local bakeries, bed-and-breakfast inns, and local owner-managed retail boutiques are all good examples of enterprises that have scaled their operations to serve narrow or local customer segments.

A Focused Low-Cost Strategy

A focused strategy based on low cost aims at securing a competitive advantage by serving buyers in the target market niche at a lower cost and a lower price than rival competitors. This strategy has considerable attraction when a firm can lower costs significantly by limiting its customer base to a well-defined buyer segment. The avenues to achieving a cost advantage over rivals also serving the target market niche are the same as for low-cost leadership—outmanage rivals in keeping the costs to a bare minimum and searching for innovative ways to bypass or reduce nonessential activities. The only real difference between a low-cost provider strategy and a focused low-cost strategy is the size of the buyer group to which a company is appealing.

Focused low-cost strategies are fairly common. Producers of private-label goods are able to achieve low costs in product development, marketing, distribution, and advertising by concentrating on making generic items similar to name-brand merchandise and selling directly to retail chains wanting a low-priced store brand. The Perrigo Company has become a leading

CONCEPTS & CONNECTIONS 5.2

VIZIO'S FOCUSED LOW-COST STRATEGY

California-based Vizio, Inc., designs flat-panel LCD and plasma TVs, which are sold only by big box discount retailers such as Walmart, Sam's Club, Costco Wholesale, and Best Buy. If you've shopped for a flat-panel TV recently, you've probably noticed that Vizio is among the lowest-priced brands and that its picture quality is surprisingly good considering the price. The company keeps its cost low by designing TVs and then sourcing production to a limited number of contract manufacturers in Taiwan. In fact, 80 percent of its production is handled by AmTran Technology. Such a dependence on a supplier can place a buyer in a precarious situation by making it vulnerable to price increases or product shortages, but Vizio has countered this possible threat by making AmTran a major stockholder. AmTran Technology owns a 23 percent stake in Vizio and earns about 80 percent of its revenues from its sales of televisions to Vizio. This close relationship with its major supplier and its focus on a single product category sold through limited distribution channels allow Vizio to offer its customers deep price discounts.

Vizio's first major account was landed in 2003 when it approached Costco buyers with a 46-inch plasma TV with a wholesale price that was half the price of the next-lowest-price competitor. Within two months, Costco was carrying Vizio flat-screen TVs in 320 of its warehouse stores in the United States. In October 2007, Vizio approached buyers for Sam's Club with a 20-inch LCD TV that could be sold at retail for less than $350. The price and quality of the 20-inch TV led Sam's Club buyers to place an order for 20,000 TVs for a March 2008 delivery. Vizio has since expanded its product line to include HDTVs as large as 65 inches and planned a 2011 launch of a 3DTV line that would sell for less than $500. In 2010, Vizio was the largest seller of flat-panel HDTVs in the United States with a market share of 28 percent.

Source: Vizio's rapid success was highlighted in "Picture Shift: U.S. Upstart Takes On TV Giants in Price War," *The Wall Street Journal*, April 15, 2008, p. A1; and "Vizio Takes Top Spot for 2010 LCD TV Sales," Vizio press release, February 25, 2011.

manufacturer of over-the-counter health care products with 2010 sales of more than $2.2 billion by focusing on producing private-label brands for retailers such as Walmart, CVS, Walgreens, Rite Aid, and Safeway. Even though Perrigo doesn't make branded products, a focused low-cost strategy is appropriate for the makers of branded products as well. Concepts & Connections 5.2 describes how Vizio's low costs and focus on big box retailers have allowed it to become the largest seller of flat-panel HDTVs in the United States.

A Focused Differentiation Strategy

Focused differentiation strategies are keyed to offering carefully designed products or services to appeal to the unique preferences and needs of a narrow, well-defined group of buyers (as opposed to a broad differentiation strategy aimed at many buyer groups and market segments). Companies such as Four Seasons Hotels and Resorts, Chanel, Gucci, and Louis Vuitton employ successful differentiation-based focused strategies targeted at affluent buyers wanting products and services with world-class attributes. Indeed, most markets contain a buyer segment willing to pay a price premium for the very finest items available, thus opening the strategic window for some competitors to pursue differentiation-based focused strategies aimed at the very top of the market pyramid. Ferrari markets its 1,500 cars sold in North America each year to a list of just 20,000 highly affluent car enthusiasts.

CONCEPTS & CONNECTIONS 5.3

NESTLÉ NESPRESSO'S FOCUSED DIFFERENTIATION STRATEGY IN THE COFFEE INDUSTRY

Nestlé's strategy in the gourmet coffee industry has allowed its Nespresso brand of espresso coffee to become the fastest-growing billion-dollar brand in its broad lineup of chocolates and confectionery, bottled waters, coffee, ready-to-eat cereals, frozen food, dairy products, ice cream, and baby foods. The Nespresso concept was developed in 1986 to allow consumers to create a perfect cup of espresso coffee, equal to that of a skilled barista, with the use of a proprietary line of coffeemakers designed to accommodate Nespresso's single-serving coffee capsules. Nespresso capsules were available in 16 different roasts and aromatic profiles and could be purchased online at Nestlé's Nespresso Club website, in any of Nestlé's 200 lavish Nespresso boutiques located in the world's most exclusive shopping districts, and in select upscale retailers across the globe. Nespresso coffee machines were designed for ease-of-use while having advanced technological features that maximized the aroma of the coffee and automated the entire process even down to creating a thick and creamy froth from cold milk for cappuccinos. Nespresso coffeemakers also set standards for aesthetics with classic, sleek models, avant-garde models, and retro-modern models.

The ease-of-use of the stylish Nespresso coffeemakers and the high-quality coffee selected by Nestlé for its single-serving coffee pods allowed coffee drinkers with little experience in preparing gourmet coffees to master great-tasting lattes, cappuccinos, and espresso drinks. Nespresso was sold in more than 50 countries in 2011 and had averaged annual growth in revenues of 30 percent since 2000 to reach sales of more than $3 billion Swiss francs in 2010.

Nestlé's focus differentiation strategy for Nespresso includes the following primary elements:

- **Unsurpassed product quality and proven coffee expertise.** Through its unique business model, Nespresso has the ability to guarantee highest quality at every stage of the coffee value chain. Nespresso's team of passionate green coffee experts, agronomists, and supply partners regularly crisscross the globe in search of the highest-quality beans from specialty farms in the finest countries of origin. They work with a variety of other Nespresso coffee experts including coffee sensory, aroma, and flavor experts who create the Nespresso Grand Crus at state-of-the-art coffee production facilities in Orbe and Avenches, Switzerland.

- **Unstoppable drive for innovation and distinctive design.** Obsessed about innovation, compulsive about the fine details, and passionate about the fusion between technology and design, the Nespresso in-house research and development team has pioneered many award-winning machine innovations and cutting-edge designs, in collaboration with external design and machine experts. These breakthroughs have resulted in more than 1,700 patents.

- **Inspirational, iconic global reputation of the brand.** Nespresso is continually infusing itself with original ideas, flavors, and innovations from around the world to define its own unique lifestyle. Its journey toward becoming an iconic brand has made it a well-recognized and respected reference for highest quality around the world. Through Nespresso's network of more than 200 exclusive boutiques in key cities around the world, coffee lovers can come together to experience the brand with all senses, such as tasting Nespresso's luxurious coffees or learning more about the coffee countries of origin. These stylish sanctuaries are the perfect destinations for people who love the very best coffee.

- **Global brand community thanks to direct customer relationships.** Much of the success Nespresso has enjoyed in recent years can be attributed to the privileged relationships the brand has developed with its consumers and the reciprocal enthusiasm consumers have consistently shown for the brand. More than 50 percent of all new Nespresso Club Members first experience the brand through existing members. Between 2001 and 2009, the number of Nespresso Club Members worldwide jumped from 600,000 to more than 6 million.

- **Exclusive routes to market.** The Nespresso business model enables the company to maintain direct relationships with its customers through three channels. A global Internet boutique is available at www.nespresso.com; a global retail boutique network gives consumers the opportunity to experience the brand with all senses; and Customer Relationship Centers help consumers connect with friendly coffee specialists by phone.

- **Expertise in sustainable quality development.** Nespresso and its key suppliers work closely with more than 30,000 farmers who are part of the AAA Sustainable Quality Program to ensure they are implementing farming practices that lead to the highest-quality beans and economic viability, while respecting the environment. Coffee farmers who are part of the program are rewarded not only with higher compensation but also with a long-term partnership with Nespresso. Approximately 50 percent of the coffee Nespresso buys is AAA Sustainable Quality.

Source: Nestlé press releases, June 9, 2009, September 21, 2009, and August 11, 2010.

Another successful focused differentiator is "fashion food retailer" Trader Joe's, a 300-store, 25-state chain that is a combination gourmet deli and food warehouse. Customers shop Trader Joe's as much for entertainment as for conventional grocery items; the store stocks out-of-the-ordinary culinary treats such as raspberry salsa, salmon burgers, and jasmine fried rice, as well as the standard goods normally found in supermarkets. What sets Trader Joe's apart is not just its unique combination of food novelties and competitively priced grocery items but also its capability to turn an otherwise mundane grocery excursion into a whimsical treasure hunt that is just plain fun. Concepts & Connections 5.3 describes Nestlé's focused differentiation strategy for Nespresso.

When a Focused Low-Cost or Focused Differentiation Strategy Is Viable

LO3

Recognize why some generic strategies work better in certain kinds of industry and competitive conditions than others.

A focused strategy aimed at securing a competitive edge based either on low cost or differentiation becomes increasingly attractive as more of the following conditions are met:

- The target market niche is big enough to be profitable and offers good growth potential.
- Industry leaders have chosen not to compete in the niche—focusers can avoid battling head-to-head against the industry's biggest and strongest competitors.
- It is costly or difficult for multisegment competitors to meet the specialized needs of niche buyers and at the same time satisfy the expectations of mainstream customers.
- The industry has many different niches and segments, thereby allowing a focuser to pick a niche suited to its resource strengths and capabilities.
- Few, if any, rivals are attempting to specialize in the same target segment.

The Risks of a Focused Low-Cost or Focused Differentiation Strategy

Focusing carries several risks. The *first major risk* is the chance that competitors will find effective ways to match the focused firm's capabilities in serving the target niche. In the lodging business, large chains such as Marriott and Hilton have launched multibrand strategies that allow them to compete effectively in several lodging segments simultaneously. Marriott has flagship hotels with a full complement of services and amenities that allow it to attract travelers and vacationers going to major resorts; it has J.W. Marriott and Ritz-Carlton hotels that provide deluxe comfort and service to business and leisure travelers; it has Courtyard by Marriott and SpringHill Suites brands for business travelers looking for moderately priced lodging; it has Marriott Residence Inns and TownePlace Suites designed as a "home away from home" for travelers staying five or more nights; and it has more than 650 Fairfield Inn locations that cater to travelers looking for quality lodging at an "affordable" price.

Similarly, Hilton has a lineup of brands (Waldorf Astoria, Conrad Hotels, Doubletree Hotels, Embassy Suites Hotels, Hampton Inns, Hilton Hotels, Hilton Garden Inns, and Homewood Suites) that enable it to compete in multiple segments and compete head-to-head against lodging chains that operate only in a single segment. Multibrand strategies are attractive to large companies such as Marriott and Hilton precisely because they enable a company to enter a market niche and siphon business away from companies that employ a focus strategy.

A *second risk* of employing a focus strategy is the potential for the preferences and needs of niche members to shift over time toward the product attributes desired by the majority of buyers. An erosion of the differences across buyer segments lowers entry barriers into a focuser's market niche and provides an open invitation for rivals in adjacent segments to begin competing for the focuser's customers. A *third risk* is that the segment may become so attractive it is soon inundated with competitors, intensifying rivalry and splintering segment profits.

BEST-COST PROVIDER STRATEGIES

▶**LO5**

Recognize the required conditions for delivering superior value to customers through the use of a hybrid of low-cost provider and differentiation strategies.

As Figure 5.1 indicates, **best-cost provider strategies** are a *hybrid* of low-cost provider and differentiation strategies that aim at satisfying buyer expectations on key quality/features/performance/service attributes and beating customer expectations on price. Companies pursuing best-cost strategies aim squarely at the sometimes great mass of value-conscious buyers looking for a good-to-very-good product or service at an economical price. The essence of a best-cost provider strategy is giving customers *more value for the money* by satisfying buyer desires for appealing features/ performance/quality/service and charging a lower price for these attributes compared to rivals with similar caliber product offerings.[3]

> **CORE CONCEPT**
>
> **Best-cost provider strategies** are a *hybrid* of low-cost provider and differentiation strategies that aim at satisfying buyer expectations on key quality/features/performance/service attributes and beating customer expectations on price.

To profitably employ a best-cost provider strategy, a company *must have the capability to incorporate attractive or upscale attributes at a lower cost than rivals.* This capability is contingent on (1) a superior value chain configuration that eliminates or minimizes activities that do not add value, (2) unmatched efficiency in managing essential value chain activities, and (3) core competencies that allow differentiating attributes to be incorporated at a low cost. When a company can incorporate appealing features, good-to-excellent product performance or quality, or more satisfying customer service into its product offering *at a lower cost than rivals,* then it enjoys "best-cost" status—it is the low-cost provider of a product or service with *upscale attributes.* A best-cost provider can use its low-cost advantage to underprice rivals whose products or services have similar upscale attributes and still earn attractive profits.

Concepts & Connections 5.4 describes how Toyota has applied the principles of a best-cost provider strategy in producing and marketing its Lexus brand.

CONCEPTS & CONNECTIONS 5.4

TOYOTA'S BEST-COST PRODUCER STRATEGY FOR ITS LEXUS LINE

Toyota Motor Company is widely regarded as a low-cost producer among the world's motor vehicle manufacturers. Despite its emphasis on product quality, Toyota has achieved low-cost leadership because it has developed considerable skills in efficient supply chain management and low-cost assembly capabilities, and because its models are positioned in the low-to-medium end of the price spectrum, where high production volumes are conducive to low unit costs. But when Toyota decided to introduce its new Lexus models to compete in the luxury-car market, it employed a classic best-cost provider strategy. Toyota took the following four steps in crafting and implementing its Lexus strategy:

- Designing an array of high-performance characteristics and upscale features into the Lexus models so as to make them comparable in performance and luxury to other high-end models and attractive to Mercedes-Benz, BMW, Audi, Jaguar, Cadillac, and Lincoln buyers.

- Transferring its capabilities in making high-quality Toyota models at low cost to making premium-quality Lexus models at costs below other luxury-car makers. Toyota's supply chain capabilities and low-cost assembly know-how allowed it to incorporate high-tech performance features

and upscale quality into Lexus models at substantially less cost than comparable Mercedes and BMW models.

- Using its relatively lower manufacturing costs to underprice comparable Mercedes and BMW models. Toyota believed that with its cost advantage it could price attractively equipped Lexus cars low enough to draw price-conscious buyers away from Mercedes and BMW. Toyota's pricing policy also allowed it to induce Toyota, Honda, Ford, or GM owners desiring more luxury to switch to a Lexus. Lexus's pricing advantage over Mercedes and BMW was sometimes quite significant. For example, in 2011 the Lexus RX 350, a midsize SUV, carried a sticker price in the $39,000–$52,000 range (depending on how it was equipped), whereas variously equipped Mercedes ML 350 SUVs had price tags in the $46,000–$92,000 range, and a BMW X5 SUV could range anywhere from $47,000 to $86,000, depending on the optional equipment chosen.

- Establishing a new network of Lexus dealers, separate from Toyota dealers, dedicated to providing a level of personalized, attentive customer service unmatched in the industry.

Lexus's best-cost strategy allowed it to become the number-one-selling luxury car brand worldwide in 2000—a distinction it has held through 2010.

When a Best-Cost Provider Strategy Works Best

LO3

Recognize why some generic strategies work better in certain kinds of industry and competitive conditions than others.

A best-cost provider strategy works best in markets where product differentiation is the norm and attractively large numbers of value-conscious buyers can be induced to purchase midrange products rather than the basic products of low-cost producers or the expensive products of top-of-the-line differentiators. A best-cost provider usually needs to position itself near the middle of the market with either a medium-quality product at a below-average price or a high-quality product at an average or slightly higher-than-average price. Best-cost provider strategies also work well in recessionary times when great masses of buyers become value-conscious and are attracted to economically priced products and services with especially appealing attributes.

The Danger of an Unsound Best-Cost Provider Strategy

A company's biggest vulnerability in employing a best-cost provider strategy is not having the requisite core competencies and efficiencies in managing value chain activities to support the addition of differentiating features without significantly increasing costs. A company with a modest degree of differentiation and no real cost advantage will most likely find itself squeezed between the firms using low-cost strategies and those using differentiation strategies. Low-cost providers may be able to siphon customers away with the appeal of a lower price (despite having marginally less appealing product attributes). High-end differentiators may be able to steal customers away with the appeal of appreciably better product attributes (even though their products carry a somewhat higher price tag). Thus, a successful best-cost provider must offer buyers *significantly* better product attributes to justify a price above what low-cost leaders are charging. Likewise, it has to achieve significantly lower costs in providing upscale features so that it can outcompete high-end differentiators on the basis of a *significantly* lower price.

SUCCESSFUL COMPETITIVE STRATEGIES ARE RESOURCE BASED

For a company's competitive strategy to succeed in delivering good performance and the intended competitive edge over rivals, it has to be well-matched to a company's internal situation and underpinned by an appropriate set of resources, know-how, and competitive capabilities. To succeed in employing a low-cost provider strategy, a company has to have the resources and capabilities to keep its costs below those of its competitors; this means having the expertise to cost-effectively manage value chain activities better than rivals and/or the innovative capability to bypass certain value chain activities being performed by rivals. To succeed in strongly differentiating its product in ways that are appealing to buyers, a company must have the resources and capabilities (such as better technology, strong skills in product innovation, expertise in customer service) to incorporate unique attributes into its product offering that a broad range of buyers will find appealing and worth paying for. Strategies focusing on a narrow segment of the market require the capability to do an outstanding job of satisfying the needs and expectations of niche buyers. Success in employing a strategy keyed to a best value offering requires the resources and capabilities to incorporate upscale product or service attributes at a lower cost than rivals.

> A company's competitive strategy should be well matched to its internal situation and predicated on leveraging its collection of competitively valuable resources and competencies.

KEY POINTS

1. Early in the process of crafting a strategy, company managers have to decide which of the five basic competitive strategies to employ—overall low-cost, broad differentiation, focused low-cost, focused differentiation, or best-cost provider.

2. In employing a low-cost provider strategy, a company must do a better job than rivals of cost-effectively managing internal activities and/or it must find innovative ways to eliminate or bypass cost-producing activities. Low-cost provider strategies work particularly well when price competition is strong and the products of rival sellers are very weakly differentiated. Other conditions favoring a low-cost provider strategy are when supplies are readily available from eager

sellers, when there are not many ways to differentiate that have value to buyers, when the majority of industry sales are made to a few large buyers, when buyer switching costs are low, and when industry newcomers are likely to use a low introductory price to build market share.

3. Broad differentiation strategies seek to produce a competitive edge by incorporating attributes and features that set a company's product/service offering apart from rivals in ways that buyers consider valuable and worth paying for. Successful differentiation allows a firm to (1) command a premium price for its product, (2) increase unit sales (because additional buyers are won over by the differentiating features), and/or (3) gain buyer loyalty to its brand (because some buyers are strongly attracted to the differentiating features and bond with the company and its products). Differentiation strategies work best in markets with diverse buyer preferences where there are big windows of opportunity to strongly differentiate a company's product offering from those of rival brands, in situations where few other rivals are pursuing a similar differentiation approach, and in circumstances where technological change is fast-paced and competition centers on rapidly evolving product features. A differentiation strategy is doomed when competitors are able to quickly copy most or all of the appealing product attributes a company comes up with, when a company's differentiation efforts meet with a ho-hum or so-what market reception, or when a company erodes profitability by overspending on efforts to differentiate its product offering.

4. A focus strategy delivers competitive advantage either by achieving lower costs than rivals in serving buyers comprising the target market niche or by offering niche buyers an appealingly differentiated product or service that meets their needs better than rival brands. A focused strategy becomes increasingly attractive when the target market niche is big enough to be profitable and offers good growth potential, when it is costly or difficult for multisegment competitors to put capabilities in place to meet the specialized needs of the target market niche and at the same time satisfy the expectations of their mainstream customers, when there are one or more niches that present a good match with a focuser's resource strengths and capabilities, and when few other rivals are attempting to specialize in the same target segment.

5. Best-cost provider strategies stake out a middle ground between pursuing a low-cost advantage and a differentiation-based advantage and between appealing to the broad market as a whole and a narrow market niche. The aim is to create competitive advantage by giving buyers more value for the money—satisfying buyer expectations on key quality/features/performance/service attributes while beating customer expectations on price. To profitably employ a best-cost provider strategy, a company *must have the capability to incorporate attractive or upscale attributes at a lower cost than rivals*. This capability is contingent on (1) a superior value chain configuration, (2) unmatched efficiency in managing essential value chain activities, and (3) resource strengths and core competencies that allow differentiating attributes to be incorporated at a low cost. A best-cost provider strategy works best in markets where opportunities to differentiate exist and where many buyers are sensitive to price and value.

6. Deciding which generic strategy to employ is perhaps the most important strategic commitment a company makes—it tends to drive the rest of the strategic actions a company decides to undertake and it sets the whole tone for the pursuit of a competitive advantage over rivals.

ASSURANCE OF LEARNING EXERCISES

1. Best Buy is the largest consumer electronics retailer in the United States with 2011 sales of more than $50 billion. The company competes aggressively on price with rivals such as Costco Wholesale, Sam's Club, Walmart, and Target, but is also known by consumers for its first-rate customer service. Best Buy customers have commented that the retailer's sales staff is exceptionally knowledgeable about products and can direct them to the exact location of difficult to find items. Best Buy customers also appreciate that demonstration models of PC monitors, digital media players, and other electronics are fully powered and ready for in-store use. Best Buy's Geek Squad tech support and installation services are additional customer service features valued by many customers.

   LO1, LO2, LO3, LO4, LO5

   How would you characterize Best Buy's competitive strategy? Should it be classified as a low-cost provider strategy? a differentiation strategy? a best-cost strategy? Explain your answer.

2. Concepts & Connections 5.1 discusses Walmart's low-cost advantage in the supermarket industry. Based on information provided in the illustration, explain how Walmart has built its low-cost advantage in the supermarket industry and why a low-cost provider strategy is well-suited to the industry.

   LO2, LO3

   www.mcgrawhillconnect.com

3. Stihl is the world's leading manufacturer and marketer of chain saws with annual sales exceeding $2 billion. With innovations dating to its 1929 invention of the gasoline-powered chain saw, the company holds more than 1,000 patents related to chain saws and outdoor power tools. The company's chain saws, leaf blowers, and hedge trimmers sell at price points well above competing brands and are sold only by its network of some 8,000 independent dealers.

   LO1, LO2, LO3, LO4, LO5

   How would you characterize Stihl's competitive strategy? Should it be classified as a low-cost provider strategy? a differentiation strategy? a best-cost strategy? Also, has the company chosen to focus on a narrow piece of the market or does it appear to pursue a broad market approach? Explain your answer.

4. Explore BMW's website at www.bmwgroup.com and see if you can identify at least three ways in which the company seeks to differentiate itself from rival automakers. Is there reason to believe that BMW's differentiation strategy has been successful in producing a competitive advantage? Why or why not?

   LO3, LO4

   www.mcgrawhillconnect.com

EXERCISES FOR SIMULATION PARTICIPANTS

1. Which one of the five generic competitive strategies best characterizes your company's strategic approach to competing successfully?

   LO1, LO2, LO3, LO4, LO5

2. Which rival companies appear to be employing a low-cost provider strategy?

3. Which rival companies appear to be employing a broad differentiation strategy?

4. Which rival companies appear to be employing a best-cost provider strategy?

5. Which rival companies appear to be employing some type of focus strategy?

6. What is your company's action plan to achieve a sustainable competitive advantage over rival companies? List at least three (preferably more than three) specific kinds of decision entries on specific decision screens that your company has made or intends to make to win this kind of competitive edge over rivals.

ENDNOTES

1. Michael E. Porter, *Competitive Strategy: Techniques for Analyzing Industries and Competitors* (New York: Free Press, 1980), chap. 2; and Michael E. Porter, "What Is Strategy?" *Harvard Business Review* 74, no. 6 (November–December 1996).

2. Michael E. Porter, *Competitive Advantage* (New York: Free Press, 1985).

3. Peter J. Williamson and Ming Zeng, "Value-for-Money Strategies for Recessionary Times," *Harvard Business Review* 87, no. 3 (March 2009).

chapter 6

SUPPLEMENTING THE CHOSEN COMPETITIVE STRATEGY—OTHER IMPORTANT STRATEGY CHOICES

LEARNING OBJECTIVES

LO1   Learn whether and when to pursue offensive strategic moves to improve a company's market position.

LO2   Learn whether and when to employ defensive strategies to protect the company's market position.

LO3   Recognize when being a first mover or a fast follower or a late mover can lead to competitive advantage.

LO4   Learn the advantages and disadvantages of extending a company's scope of operations via vertical integration.

LO5   Understand the conditions that favor farming out certain value chain activities to outside parties.

LO6   Gain an understanding of how strategic alliances and collaborative partnerships can bolster a company's collection of resources and capabilities.

LO7   Become aware of the strategic benefits and risks of mergers and acquisitions.

Once a company has settled on which of the five generic competitive strategies to employ, attention turns to what *other strategic actions* it can take to complement its competitive approach and maximize the power of its overall strategy. Several decisions regarding the company's operating scope and how to best strengthen its market standing must be made:

- Whether and when to go on the offensive and initiate aggressive strategic moves to improve the company's market position.
- Whether and when to employ defensive strategies to protect the company's market position.
- When to undertake strategic moves based upon whether it is advantageous to be a first mover or a fast follower or a late mover.
- Whether to integrate backward or forward into more stages of the industry value chain.
- Which value chain activities, if any, should be outsourced.
- Whether to enter into strategic alliances or partnership arrangements with other enterprises.
- Whether to bolster the company's market position by merging with or acquiring another company in the same industry.

This chapter presents the pros and cons of each of these measures that round out a company's overall strategy.

LAUNCHING STRATEGIC OFFENSIVES TO IMPROVE A COMPANY'S MARKET POSITION

LO1

Learn whether and when to pursue offensive strategic moves to improve a company's market position.

No matter which of the five generic competitive strategies a company employs, there are times when a company *should be aggressive and go on the offensive.* Strategic offensives are called for when a company spots opportunities to gain profitable market share at the expense of rivals or when a company has no choice but to try to whittle away at a strong rival's competitive advantage. Companies such as Walmart, Apple, Southwest Airlines, and Google play hardball, aggressively pursuing competitive advantage and trying to reap the benefits a competitive edge offers—a leading market share, excellent profit margins, and rapid growth.[1]

Choosing the Basis for Competitive Attack

Generally, strategic offensives should be grounded in a company's competitive assets and strong points and should be aimed at exploiting competitor weaknesses.[2] Ignoring the need to tie a strategic offensive to a company's competitive strengths is like going to war with a popgun—the prospects for success are dim. For instance, it is foolish for a company with relatively high costs to employ a price-cutting offensive. Likewise, it is ill advised to pursue a product innovation offensive without having proven expertise in R&D, new-product development, and speeding new or improved products to market.

> The best offensives use a company's most competitively potent resources to attack rivals in those competitive areas where they are weakest.

The principal offensive strategy options include the following:

1. *Attacking the competitive weaknesses of rivals.* For example, a company with especially good customer service capabilities can make special sales pitches to the customers of those rivals who provide subpar customer service. Aggressors with a recognized brand name and strong marketing skills can launch efforts to win customers away from rivals with weak brand recognition.

2. *Offering an equally good or better product at a lower price.* Lower prices can produce market share gains if competitors offering similarly performing products don't respond with price cuts of their own. Price-cutting offensives are best initiated by companies that have *first achieved a cost advantage.*[3]

3. *Pursuing continuous product innovation to draw sales and market share away from less innovative rivals.* Ongoing introductions of new/improved products can put rivals under tremendous competitive pressure, especially when rivals' new-product development capabilities are weak.

4. *Leapfrogging competitors by being the first to market with next-generation technology or products.* Microsoft got its next-generation Xbox 360 to market 12 months ahead of Sony's PlayStation 3 and Nintendo's Wii, helping it build a sizable market share and develop a reputation for cutting-edge innovation in the video game industry.

5. *Adopting and improving on the good ideas of other companies (rivals or otherwise).* The idea of warehouse-type home improvement centers did not originate with Home Depot co-founders Arthur Blank and Bernie Marcus; they got the "big box" concept from their former employer, Handy Dan Home Improvement. But they were quick to improve on Handy Dan's business model and strategy and take Home Depot to a higher plateau in terms of product-line breadth and customer service.

6. *Deliberately attacking those market segments where a key rival makes big profits.* Toyota has launched a hardball attack on General Motors, Ford, and Chrysler in the U.S. market for light trucks and SUVs, the very market arena where the Detroit automakers typically earn their big profits (roughly $10,000 to $15,000 per vehicle). Toyota's pickup trucks and SUVs have weakened the Big 3 U.S. automakers by taking away sales and market share that they desperately need.

7. *Maneuvering around competitors to capture unoccupied or less contested market territory.* Examples include launching initiatives to build strong positions in geographic areas or product categories where close rivals have little or no market presence.

8. *Using hit-and-run or guerrilla warfare tactics to grab sales and market share from complacent or distracted rivals.* Options for "guerrilla offensives" include occasional lowballing on price (to win a big order or steal a key account from a rival) or surprising key rivals with sporadic but intense bursts of promotional activity (offering a 20 percent discount for one week to draw customers away from rival brands).[4] Guerrilla offensives

are particularly well suited to small challengers who have neither the resources nor the market visibility to mount a full-fledged attack on industry leaders.

9. *Launching a preemptive strike to capture a rare opportunity or secure an industry's limited resources.*[5] What makes a move preemptive is its one-of-a-kind nature—whoever strikes first stands to acquire competitive assets that rivals can't readily match. Examples of preemptive moves include (1) securing the best distributors in a particular geographic region or country; (2) moving to obtain the most favorable site at a new interchange or intersection, in a new shopping mall, and so on; and (3) tying up the most reliable, high-quality suppliers via exclusive partnerships, long-term contracts, or even acquisition. To be successful, a preemptive move doesn't have to totally block rivals from following or copying; it merely needs to give a firm a prime position that is not easily circumvented.

Choosing Which Rivals to Attack

Offensive-minded firms need to analyze which of their rivals to challenge as well as how to mount that challenge. The following are the best targets for offensive attacks:

- *Market leaders that are vulnerable.* Offensive attacks make good sense when a company that leads in terms of size and market share is not a true leader in terms of serving the market well. Signs of leader vulnerability include unhappy buyers, an inferior product line, a weak competitive strategy with regard to low-cost leadership or differentiation, a preoccupation with diversification into other industries, and mediocre or declining profitability.

- *Runner-up firms with weaknesses in areas where the challenger is strong.* Runner-up firms are an especially attractive target when a challenger's resource strengths and competitive capabilities are well suited to exploiting their weaknesses.

- *Struggling enterprises that are on the verge of going under.* Challenging a hard-pressed rival in ways that further sap its financial strength and competitive position can hasten its exit from the market.

- *Small local and regional firms with limited capabilities.* Because small firms typically have limited expertise and resources, a challenger with broader capabilities is well positioned to raid their biggest and best customers.

Blue Ocean Strategy—A Special Kind of Offensive

A **blue ocean strategy** seeks to gain a dramatic and durable competitive advantage *by abandoning efforts to beat out competitors in existing markets and, instead, inventing a new industry or distinctive market segment that renders existing competitors largely irrelevant and allows a company to create and capture altogether new demand.*[6] This strategy views the business universe as consisting of two distinct types of market space. One is where industry boundaries are defined and accepted, the competitive rules of the game are well understood by all industry members, and companies try to outperform rivals by capturing a bigger share of existing demand; in such markets, lively competition constrains a company's prospects for rapid growth and superior profitability since rivals move quickly to either imitate or counter the successes of competitors. The second type of market space is a "blue ocean" where the industry does not really exist yet, is untainted by competition, and offers wide open opportunity for profitable and rapid growth if a company can come up with a product offering

> **CORE CONCEPT**
>
> **Blue ocean strategies** offer growth in revenues and profits by discovering or inventing new industry segments that create altogether new demand.

and strategy that allows it to create new demand rather than fight over existing demand. A terrific example of such wide open or blue ocean market space is the online auction industry that eBay created and now dominates.

Other examples of companies that have achieved competitive advantages by creating blue ocean market spaces include Starbucks in the coffee shop industry, Dollar General in extreme discount retailing, FedEx in overnight package delivery, and Cirque du Soleil in live entertainment. Cirque du Soleil "reinvented the circus" by creating a distinctively different market space for its performances (Las Vegas nightclubs and theater-type settings) and pulling in a whole new group of customers—adults and corporate clients—who were willing to pay several times more than the price of a conventional circus ticket to have an "entertainment experience" featuring sophisticated clowns and star-quality acrobatic acts in a comfortable atmosphere. Companies that create blue ocean market spaces can usually sustain their initially won competitive advantage without encountering major competitive challenges for 10 to 15 years because of high barriers to imitation and the strong brand name awareness that a blue ocean strategy can produce.

USING DEFENSIVE STRATEGIES TO PROTECT A COMPANY'S MARKET POSITION AND COMPETITIVE ADVANTAGE

▶**LO2**

Learn whether and when to employ defensive strategies to protect the company's market position.

In a competitive market, all firms are subject to offensive challenges from rivals. The purposes of defensive strategies are to lower the risk of being attacked, weaken the impact of any attack that occurs, and influence challengers to aim their efforts at other rivals. While defensive strategies usually don't enhance a firm's competitive advantage, they can definitely help fortify its competitive position. Defensive strategies can take either of two forms: actions to block challengers and actions signaling the likelihood of strong retaliation.

> Good defensive strategies can help protect competitive advantage but rarely are the basis for creating it.

Blocking the Avenues Open to Challengers

The most frequently employed approach to defending a company's present position involves actions to restrict a competitive attack by a challenger. A number of obstacles can be put in the path of would-be challengers.[7] A defender can introduce new features, add new models, or broaden its product line to close off vacant niches to opportunity-seeking challengers. It can thwart the efforts of rivals to attack with a lower price by maintaining economy-priced options of its own. It can try to discourage buyers from trying competitors' brands by making early announcements about upcoming new products or planned price changes. Finally, a defender can grant volume discounts or better financing terms to dealers and distributors to discourage them from experimenting with other suppliers.

Signaling Challengers that Retaliation Is Likely

The goal of signaling challengers that strong retaliation is likely in the event of an attack is either to dissuade challengers from attacking or to divert them to less threatening options. Either goal can be achieved by letting challengers know the battle will cost more than it is worth. Would-be challengers can be signaled by:

- Publicly announcing management's commitment to maintain the firm's present market share.
- Publicly committing the company to a policy of matching competitors' terms or prices.
- Maintaining a war chest of cash and marketable securities.
- Making an occasional strong counter response to the moves of weak competitors to enhance the firm's image as a tough defender.

TIMING A COMPANY'S OFFENSIVE AND DEFENSIVE STRATEGIC MOVES

LO3

Recognize when being a first mover or a fast follower or a late mover can lead to competitive advantage.

When to make a strategic move is often as crucial as *what* move to make. Timing is especially important when *first-mover advantages* or *disadvantages* exist. Being first to initiate a strategic move can have a high payoff when (1) pioneering helps build a firm's image and reputation with buyers; (2) early commitments to new technologies, new-style components, new or emerging distribution channels, and so on, can produce an absolute cost advantage over rivals; (3) first-time customers remain strongly loyal to pioneering firms in making repeat purchases; and (4) moving first constitutes a preemptive strike, making imitation extra hard or unlikely. The bigger the first-mover advantages, the more attractive making the first move becomes.[8]

> **CORE CONCEPT**
>
> Because of **first-mover advantages and disadvantages,** competitive advantage can spring from *when* a move is made as well as from *what* move is made.

Sometimes, though, markets are slow to accept the innovative product offering of a first mover, in which case a fast follower with substantial resources and marketing muscle can overtake a first mover (as Fox News has done in competing against CNN to become the leading cable news network). Sometimes furious technological change or product innovation makes a first mover vulnerable to quickly appearing next-generation technology or products. For instance, former market leaders in mobile phones Nokia and Research in Motion (Blackberry) have been victimized by Apple's far more innovative iPhone models and new smartphones based on Google's Android operating system. Hence, there are no guarantees that a first mover will win sustainable competitive advantage.[9]

To sustain any advantage that may initially accrue to a pioneer, a first mover needs to be a fast learner and continue to move aggressively to capitalize on any initial pioneering advantage. If a first mover's skills, know-how, and actions are easily copied or even surpassed, then followers and even late movers can catch or overtake the first mover in a relatively short period. What makes being a first mover strategically important is not being the first company to do something but rather being the first competitor to put together the precise combination of features, customer value, and sound revenue/cost/ profit economics that gives it an edge over rivals in the battle for market leadership.[10] If the marketplace quickly takes to a first mover's innovative product offering, a first mover must have large-scale production, marketing, and distribution capabilities if it is to stave off fast followers that possess similar resources capabilities. If technology is advancing at a torrid pace, a first mover cannot hope to sustain its lead without having strong capabilities in R&D, design, and new-product development, along with the financial strength to fund these activities. Concepts & Connections 6.1 describes how Amazon.com achieved a first-mover advantage in online retailing.

The Potential for Late-Mover Advantages or First-Mover Disadvantages

There are instances when there are actually *advantages* to being an adept follower rather than a first mover. Late-mover advantages (or *first-mover disadvantages*) arise in four instances:

- When pioneering leadership is more costly than followership and only negligible experience or learning curve benefits accrue to the leader—a condition that allows a follower to end up with lower costs than the first mover.

- When the products of an innovator are somewhat primitive and do not live up to buyer expectations, thus allowing a clever follower to win disenchanted buyers away from the leader with better-performing products.

- When potential buyers are skeptical about the benefits of a new technology or product being pioneered by a first mover.

- When rapid market evolution (due to fast-paced changes in either technology or buyer needs and expectations) gives fast followers and maybe even cautious late movers the opening to leapfrog a first mover's products with more attractive next-version products.

Deciding Whether to Be an Early Mover or Late Mover

In weighing the pros and cons of being a first mover versus a fast follower versus a slow mover, it matters whether the race to market leadership in a particular industry is a marathon or a sprint. In marathons, a slow mover is not unduly penalized—first-mover advantages can be fleeting, and there's

CONCEPTS & CONNECTIONS 6.1

AMAZON.COM'S FIRST-MOVER ADVANTAGE IN ONLINE RETAILING

Amazon.com's path to world's largest online retailer began in 1994 when Jeff Bezos, a Manhattan hedge fund analyst at the time, noticed the number of Internet users was increasing by 2,300 percent annually. Bezos saw the tremendous growth as an opportunity to sell products online that would be demanded by a large number of Internet users and could be easily shipped. Bezos launched the online bookseller, Amazon.com, in 1995. The start-up's revenues soared to $148 million in 1997, $610 million in 1998, and $1.6 billion in 1999. Bezo's business plan, hatched while on a cross-country trip with his wife in 1994, made him *Time*'s Person of the Year in 1999.

Amazon.com's early entry into online retailing had delivered a first-mover advantage, but between 2000 and 2011, Bezos undertook a series of additional strategic initiatives to solidify the company's number-one ranking in the industry. Bezos undertook a massive $300 million building program in the late 1990s that added five new warehouses and fulfillment centers. The additional warehouse space was added years before it was needed, but Bezos wanted to ensure that, as demand continued to grow, the company could continue to offer its customers the best selection, the lowest prices, and the cheapest and most convenient delivery. The company also expanded its product line to include Kindle readers, sporting goods, tools, toys, automotive parts, appliances, electronics, and digital music downloads. Amazon.com's 2010 revenues of $34.2 billion made it the world's largest Internet retailer, and Jeff Bezos' shares in Amazon.com made him the 12th wealthiest person in the United States with an estimated net worth of $12.6 billion.

Not all of Bezos' efforts to maintain a first-mover advantage in online retailing were a success. Bezos commented in a 2008 *Fortune* article profiling the company, "We were investors in every bankrupt, 1999-vintage e-commerce start-up. Pets.com, living.com, kozmo.com. We invested in a lot of high-profile flameouts." He went on to specify that although the ventures were a "waste of money," they "didn't take us off our own mission." Bezos also suggested that gaining advantage as a first mover is "taking a million tiny steps—and learning quickly from your missteps."

Sources: Mark Brohan, "The Top 500 Guide," *Internet Retailer,* June 2009, accessed at www.internetretailer.com on June 17, 2009; and Josh Quittner, "How Jeff Bezos Rules the Retail Space," *Fortune,* May 5, 2008, pp. 126–34.

ample time for fast followers and sometimes even late movers to catch up.[11] Thus the speed at which the pioneering innovation is likely to catch on matters considerably as companies struggle with whether to pursue a particular emerging market opportunity aggressively or cautiously. For instance, it took 5.5 years for worldwide mobile phone use to grow from 10 million to 100 million worldwide and close to 10 years for the number of at-home broadband subscribers to grow to 100 million worldwide. The lesson here is that there is a market-penetration curve for every emerging opportunity; typically, the curve has an inflection point at which all the pieces of the business model fall into place, buyer demand explodes, and the market takes off. The inflection point can come early on a fast-rising curve (like use of e-mail) or farther on up a slow-rising curve (such as use of broadband). Any company that seeks competitive advantage by being a first mover thus needs to ask some hard questions:

- Does market takeoff depend on the development of complementary products or services that currently are not available?
- Is new infrastructure required before buyer demand can surge?

- Will buyers need to learn new skills or adopt new behaviors? Will buyers encounter high switching costs?

- Are there influential competitors in a position to delay or derail the efforts of a first mover?

When the answers to any of these questions are yes, then a company must be careful not to pour too many resources into getting ahead of the market opportunity—the race is likely going to be more of a 10-year marathon than a 2-year sprint.

VERTICAL INTEGRATION: OPERATING ACROSS MORE INDUSTRY VALUE CHAIN SEGMENTS

Vertical integration extends a firm's competitive and operating scope within the same industry. It involves expanding the firm's range of value chain activities backward into sources of supply and/or forward toward end users. Thus, if a manufacturer invests in facilities to produce certain component parts that it formerly purchased from outside suppliers or if it opens its own chain of retail stores to market its products to consumers, it remains in essentially the same industry as before. The only change is that it has operations in two stages of the industry value chain. For example, paint manufacturer Sherwin-Williams remains in the paint business even though it has integrated forward into retailing by operating nearly 4,000 retail stores that market its paint products directly to consumers.

▶ **LO4**

Learn the advantages and disadvantages of extending a company's scope of operations via vertical integration.

> **CORE CONCEPT**
>
> A **vertically integrated** firm is one that performs value chain activities along more than one stage of an industry's overall value chain.

A firm can pursue vertical integration by starting its own operations in other stages of the vertical activity chain, by acquiring a company already performing the activities it wants to bring in-house, or by means of a strategic alliance or joint venture. Vertical integration strategies can aim at *full integration* (participating in all stages of the vertical chain) or *partial integration* (building positions in selected stages of the vertical chain). Companies may choose to pursue *tapered integration,* a strategy that involves both outsourcing and performing the activity internally. Oil companies' practice of supplying their refineries with both crude oil produced from their own wells and crude oil supplied by third-party operators and well owners is an example of tapered backward integration. Boston Beer Company, the maker of Samuel Adams, engages in tapered forward integration since it operates brew pubs, but sells the majority of its products through third-party distributors.

> **CORE CONCEPT**
>
> **Backward integration** involves performing industry value chain activities previously performed by suppliers or other enterprises engaged in earlier stages of the industry value chain; **forward integration** involves performing industry value chain activities closer to the end user.

The Advantages of a Vertical Integration Strategy

The two best reasons for investing company resources in vertical integration are to strengthen the firm's competitive position and/or to boost its profitability.[12] Vertical integration has no real payoff unless it produces sufficient cost savings to justify the extra investment, adds materially to a company's technological and competitive strengths, and/or helps differentiate the company's product offering.

Integrating Backward to Achieve Greater Competitiveness   It is harder than one might think to generate cost savings or boost profitability by integrating backward into activities such as parts and components manufacture. For backward integration to be a viable and profitable strategy, a company must be able to (1) achieve the same scale economies as outside suppliers and (2) match or beat suppliers' production efficiency with no decline in quality. Neither outcome is easily achieved. To begin with, a company's in-house requirements are often too small to reach the optimum size for low-cost operation—for instance, if it takes a minimum production volume of 1 million units to achieve scale economies and a company's in-house requirements are just 250,000 units, then it falls way short of being able to match the costs of outside suppliers (who may readily find buyers for 1 million or more units).

But that said, there are still occasions when a company can improve its cost position and competitiveness by performing a broader range of value chain activities in-house rather than having these activities performed by outside suppliers. The best potential for being able to reduce costs via a backward integration strategy exists in situations where suppliers have very large profit margins, where the item being supplied is a major cost component, and where the requisite technological skills are easily mastered or acquired. Backward vertical integration can produce a differentiation-based competitive advantage when performing activities internally contributes to a better-quality product/service offering, improves the caliber of customer service, or in other ways enhances the performance of a final product. Other potential advantages of backward integration include sparing a company the uncertainty of being dependent on suppliers for crucial components or support services and lessening a company's vulnerability to powerful suppliers inclined to raise prices at every opportunity. Apple recently decided to integrate backward into producing its own chips for iPhones, chiefly because chips are a major cost component, have big profit margins, and in-house production would help protect Apple's proprietary iPhone technology.

Integrating Forward to Enhance Competitiveness   Vertical integration into forward stages of the industry value chain allows manufacturers to gain better access to end users, improve market visibility, and include the end user's purchasing experience as a differentiating feature. In many industries, independent sales agents, wholesalers, and retailers handle competing brands of the same product and have no allegiance to any one company's brand—they tend to push whatever offers the biggest profits. An independent insurance agency, for example, represents a number of different insurance companies and tries to find the best match between a customer's insurance requirements and the policies of alternative insurance companies. Under this arrangement, it is possible an agent will develop a preference for one company's policies or underwriting practices and neglect other represented insurance companies. An insurance company may conclude, therefore, that it is better off integrating forward and setting up its own local sales offices. The insurance company also has the ability to make consumers' interactions with local agents and office personnel a differentiating feature. Likewise, apparel manufacturers as varied as Polo Ralph Lauren, Ann Taylor, and Nike have integrated forward into retailing by operating full-price stores, factory outlet stores, and Internet retailing websites.

Forward Vertical Integration and Internet Retailing Bypassing regular wholesale/retail channels in favor of direct sales and Internet retailing can have appeal if it lowers distribution costs, produces a relative cost advantage over certain rivals, offers higher margins, or results in lower selling prices to end users. In addition, sellers are compelled to include the Internet as a retail channel when a sufficiently large number of buyers in an industry prefer to make purchases online. However, a company that is vigorously pursuing online sales to consumers at the same time that it is also heavily promoting sales to consumers through its network of wholesalers and retailers *is competing directly against its distribution allies.* Such actions constitute *channel conflict* and create a tricky route to negotiate. A company that is actively trying to grow online sales to consumers is signaling *a weak strategic commitment to its dealers* and *a willingness to cannibalize dealers' sales and growth potential.* The likely result is angry dealers and loss of dealer goodwill. Quite possibly, a company may stand to lose more sales by offending its dealers than it gains from its own online sales effort. Consequently, in industries where the strong support and goodwill of dealer networks is essential, companies may conclude that it is important to avoid channel conflict and that *their website should be designed to partner with dealers rather than compete with them.*

The Disadvantages of a Vertical Integration Strategy

Vertical integration has some substantial drawbacks beyond the potential for channel conflict.[13] The most serious drawbacks to vertical integration include:

- Vertical integration *increases a firm's capital investment* in the industry.

- Integrating into more industry value chain segments *increases business risk* if industry growth and profitability sour.

- Vertically integrated companies are often *slow to embrace technological advances* or more efficient production methods when they are saddled with older technology or facilities.

- Integrating backward potentially results in less flexibility in accommodating shifting buyer preferences when a new product design doesn't include parts and components that the company makes in-house.

CONCEPTS & CONNECTIONS 6.2

AMERICAN APPAREL'S VERTICAL INTEGRATION STRATEGY

American Apparel—known for its hip line of basic garments and its provocative advertisements—is no stranger to the concept of "doing it all." The Los Angeles-based casual wear company has made both forward and backward vertical integration a central part of its strategy, making it a rarity in the fashion industry. Not only does it do all its own fabric cutting and sewing, but it also owns several knitting and dyeing facilities in Southern California, as well as a distribution warehouse, a wholesale operation, and more than 270 retail stores in 20 countries. American Apparel even does its own clothing design, marketing, and advertising, often using its employees as photographers and clothing models.

Founder and CEO Dov Charney claims the company's vertical integration strategy lets American Apparel respond more quickly to rapid market changes, allowing the company to bring an item from design to its stores worldwide in the span of a week. End-to-end coordination also improves inventory control, helping prevent common problems in the fashion business such as stock-outs and steep markdowns. The company capitalizes on its California-based vertically integrated operations by using taglines such as "Sweatshop Free. Made in the USA" to bolster its "authentic" image.

However, this strategy is not without risks and costs. In an industry where 97 percent of goods are imported,

American Apparel pays its workers wages and benefits above the relatively high mandated American minimum. Furthermore, operating in so many key vertical chain activities makes it impossible to be expert in all of them, and creates optimal scale and capacity mismatches—problems with which the firm has partly dealt by tapering its backward integration into knitting and dyeing. Lastly, while the company can respond quickly to new fashion trends, its vertical integration strategy may make it more difficult for the company to scale back in an economic downturn or respond to radical change in the industry environment. Ultimately, only time will tell whether American Apparel will dilute or capitalize on its vertical integration strategy in its pursuit of profitable growth.

Developed with John R. Moran.

Sources: American Apparel website, www.americanapparel.net, accessed June 16, 2010; American Apparel investor presentation, June 2009, http://files.shareholder.com/downloads/APP/938846703x0x300331/3dd0b7ca-e458-45b8-8516-e25ca272016d/NYC%20JUNE%202009.pdf; YouTube, "American Apparel—Dov Charney Interview," CBS News, http://youtube.com/watch?v=hYqR8UII8A4; and Christopher Palmeri, "Living on the Edge at American Apparel," *BusinessWeek,* June 27, 2005.

- Vertical integration poses all kinds of *capacity matching problems.* In motor vehicle manufacturing, for example, the most efficient scale of operation for making axles is different from the most economic volume for radiators, and different yet again for both engines and transmissions. Consequently, integrating across several production stages in ways that achieve the lowest feasible costs can be a monumental challenge.

- Integration forward or backward often requires the *development of new skills and business capabilities.* Parts and components manufacturing, assembly operations, wholesale distribution and retailing, and direct sales via the Internet are different businesses with different key success factors.

 A vertical integration strategy has appeal *only* if it significantly strengthens a firm's competitive position and/or boosts its profitability.

American Apparel, the largest U.S. clothing manufacturer, has made vertical integration a central part of its strategy, as described in Concepts & Connections 6.2.

OUTSOURCING STRATEGIES: NARROWING THE SCOPE OF OPERATIONS

Outsourcing forgoes attempts to perform certain value chain activities internally and instead farms them out to outside specialists and strategic allies. Outsourcing makes strategic sense whenever:

▶ **LO5**

Understand the conditions that favor farming out certain value chain activities to outside parties.

- *An activity can be performed better or more cheaply by outside specialists.* A company should generally *not* perform any value chain activity internally that can be performed more efficiently or effectively by outsiders. The chief exception is when a particular activity is strategically crucial and internal control over that activity is deemed essential.

> **CORE CONCEPT**
>
> **Outsourcing** involves contracting out certain value chain activities to outside specialists and strategic allies.

- *The activity is not crucial to the firm's ability to achieve sustainable competitive advantage and won't hollow out its capabilities, core competencies, or technical know-how.* Outsourcing of support activities such as maintenance services, data processing and data storage, fringe benefit management, and website operations has become common. Colgate-Palmolive, for instance, has been able to reduce its information technology operational costs by more than 10 percent per year through an outsourcing agreement with IBM.

- *It improves organizational flexibility and speeds time to market.* Outsourcing gives a company the flexibility to switch suppliers in the event that its present supplier falls behind competing suppliers. Also, to the extent that its suppliers can speedily get next-generation parts and components into production, a company can get its own next-generation product offerings into the marketplace quicker.

- *It reduces the company's risk exposure to changing technology and/or buyer preferences.* When a company outsources certain parts, components, and services, its suppliers must bear the burden of incorporating state-of-the-art technologies and/or undertaking redesigns and upgrades to accommodate a company's plans to introduce next-generation products.

- *It allows a company to concentrate on its core business, leverage its key resources and core competencies, and do even better what it already does best.* A company is better able to build and develop its own competitively valuable competencies and capabilities when it concentrates its full resources and energies on performing those activities. Nike, for example, devotes its energy to designing, marketing, and distributing athletic footwear, sports apparel, and sports equipment, while outsourcing the manufacture of all its products to some 600 contract factories in 46 countries. Apple also outsources production of its iPod, iPhone, and iPad models to Chinese contract manufacturer Foxconn. Hewlett-Packard and others have sold some of their manufacturing plants to outsiders and contracted to repurchase the output from the new owners.

> A company should guard against outsourcing activities that hollow out the resources and capabilities that it needs to be a master of its own destiny.

The Big Risk of an Outsourcing Strategy The biggest danger of outsourcing is that a company will farm out the wrong types of activities and thereby hollow out its own capabilities.[14] In such cases, a company loses touch with the very activities and expertise that over the long run determine its success. But most companies are alert to this danger and take actions to protect against being held hostage by outside suppliers. Cisco Systems guards against loss of control and protects its manufacturing expertise by designing the production methods that its contract manufacturers must use. Cisco keeps the source code for its designs proprietary, thereby controlling the initiation of all improvements and safeguarding its innovations from imitation. Further, Cisco uses the Internet to monitor the factory operations of contract manufacturers around the clock and can know immediately when problems arise and decide whether to get involved.

STRATEGIC ALLIANCES AND PARTNERSHIPS

▶ LO6

Gain an understanding of how strategic alliances and collaborative partnerships can bolster a company's collection of resources and capabilities.

Companies in all types of industries have elected to form strategic alliances and partnerships to complement their accumulation of resources and capabilities and strengthen their competitiveness in domestic and international markets. A **strategic alliance** is a formal agreement between two or more separate companies in which there is strategically relevant collaboration of some sort, joint contribution of resources, shared risk, shared control, and mutual dependence. Collaborative relationships between partners may entail a contractual agreement but they commonly stop short of formal ownership ties between the partners (although there are a few strategic alliances where one or more allies have minority ownership in certain of the other alliance members). Collaborative arrangements involving shared ownership are called joint ventures. A **joint venture** is a partnership involving the establishment of an independent corporate entity that is jointly owned and controlled by two or more companies. Since joint ventures involve setting up a mutually owned business, they tend to be more durable but also riskier than other arrangements.

> **CORE CONCEPT**
>
> A **strategic alliance** is a formal agreement between two or more companies to work cooperatively toward some common objective.

The most common reasons companies enter into strategic alliances are to expedite the development of promising new technologies or products, to overcome deficits in their own technical and manufacturing expertise, to bring together the personnel and expertise needed to create desirable new skill sets and capabilities, to improve supply chain efficiency, to gain economies of scale in production and/or marketing, and to acquire or improve market access through joint marketing agreements.[15] Because of the varied benefits of strategic alliances, many large corporations have become involved in 30 to 50 alliances, and a number have formed hundreds of alliances. Most automakers have forged long-term strategic partnerships with suppliers of automotive parts and components, both to achieve lower costs and to improve the quality and reliability of their vehicles. Microsoft collaborates very closely with independent software developers to ensure their programs will run on the next-generation versions of Windows. Over the past 10 years, South Korean giant

Samsung Electronics has entered into more than 30 strategic alliances with such companies as Sony, Yahoo, Hewlett-Packard, Nokia, Motorola, Intel, Microsoft, Dell, Mitsubishi, Disney, IBM, Maytag, Cisco, Rockwell Automation, and Giorgio Armani. Samsung's alliances have involved joint investments, technology transfer arrangements, joint R&D projects, and agreements to supply parts and components, with most having the objective of facilitating the company's strategic efforts to establish itself as a leader in the worldwide electronics industry.

> **CORE CONCEPT**
>
> A **joint venture** is a type of strategic alliance that involves the establishment of an independent corporate entity that is jointly owned and controlled by the two partners.

Failed Strategic Alliances and Cooperative Partnerships

Most alliances with an objective of technology sharing or providing market access turn out to be temporary, fulfilling their purpose after a few years because the benefits of mutual learning have occurred. Although long-term alliances sometimes prove mutually beneficial, most partners don't hesitate to terminate the alliance and go it alone when the payoffs run out. Alliances are more likely to be long lasting when (1) they involve collaboration with suppliers or distribution allies, or (2) both parties conclude that continued collaboration is in their mutual interest, perhaps because new opportunities for learning are emerging.

A surprisingly large number of alliances never live up to expectations. A 1999 study by Accenture, a global business consulting organization, revealed that 61 percent of alliances were either outright failures or "limping along." In 2004, McKinsey & Co. estimated the overall success rate of alliances was about 50 percent, based on whether the alliance achieved the stated objectives. Another study, published in 2007, found that while the number of strategic alliances was increasing about 25 percent annually, some 60 to 70 percent of alliances failed each year. The high "divorce rate" among strategic allies has several causes, the most common of which are:[16]

- Diverging objectives and priorities.
- An inability to work well together.
- Changing conditions that make the purpose of the alliance obsolete.
- The emergence of more attractive technological paths.
- Marketplace rivalry between one or more allies.

Experience indicates that *alliances stand a reasonable chance of helping a company reduce competitive disadvantage but very rarely have they proved a strategic option for gaining a durable competitive edge over rivals.*

The Strategic Dangers of Relying on Alliances for Essential Resources and Capabilities

The Achilles' heel of alliances and cooperative strategies is becoming dependent on other companies for *essential* expertise and capabilities. To be a market leader (and perhaps even a serious market contender), a company must ultimately develop its own resources and capabilities in areas where internal strategic control is pivotal to protecting its competitiveness and building competitive advantage. Moreover, some alliances hold only limited potential because the partner guards its most valuable skills and expertise; in such instances, acquiring or merging with a company possessing the desired know-how and resources is a better solution.

MERGER AND ACQUISITION STRATEGIES

LO7

Become aware of the strategic benefits and risks of mergers and acquisitions.

Mergers and acquisitions are well suited for situations in which strategic alliances or joint ventures do not go far enough in providing a company with access to needed resources and capabilities. Resources that are deemed to be essential to a company's competitive capabilities and its strength in the marketplace are more dependably and permanently deployed when owned and autonomously controlled. A **merger** is the combining of two or more companies into a single corporate entity, with the newly created company often taking on a new name. An **acquisition** is a combination in which one company, the acquirer, purchases and absorbs the operations of another, the acquired. The difference between a merger and an acquisition relates more to the details of ownership, management control, and financial arrangements than to strategy and competitive advantage. The resources and competitive capabilities of the newly created enterprise end up much the same whether the combination is the result of acquisition or merger.

> Combining the operations of two companies, via merger or acquisition, is an attractive strategic option for achieving operating economies, strengthening the resulting company's competencies and competitiveness, and opening avenues of new market opportunity.

Merger and acquisition strategies typically set sights on achieving any of five objectives:[17]

1. *To create a more cost-efficient operation out of the combined companies.* When a company acquires another company in the same industry, there's usually enough overlap in operations that certain inefficient plants can be closed or distribution and sales activities can be partly combined and downsized. The combined companies may also be able to reduce supply chain costs because of buying in greater volume from common suppliers. Likewise, it is usually feasible to squeeze out cost savings in administrative activities, again by combining and downsizing such activities as finance and accounting, information technology, human resources, and so on.

2. *To expand a company's geographic coverage.* One of the best and quickest ways to expand a company's geographic coverage is to acquire rivals with operations in the desired locations. Food products companies such as Nestlé, Kraft, Unilever, and Procter & Gamble have made acquisitions an integral part of their strategies to expand internationally.

3. *To extend the company's business into new product categories.* Many times a company has gaps in its product line that need to be filled. Acquisition can be a quicker and more potent way to broaden a company's product line than going through the exercise of introducing a company's own new product to fill the gap. PepsiCo acquired Quaker Oats chiefly to bring Gatorade into the Pepsi family of beverages. While Coca-Cola has expanded its beverage lineup by introducing its own new products

(such as Powerade and Dasani), it has also expanded its offerings by acquiring Minute Maid, Glacéau VitaminWater, and Hi-C.

4. *To gain quick access to new technologies or other resources and competitive capabilities.* Making acquisitions to bolster a company's technological know-how or to expand its skills and capabilities allows a company to bypass a time-consuming and perhaps expensive *internal effort* to build desirable new resource strengths. From 2000 through April 2011, Cisco Systems purchased 97 companies to give it more technological reach and product breadth, thereby enhancing its standing as the world's biggest provider of hardware, software, and services for building and operating Internet networks.

5. *To lead the convergence of industries whose boundaries are being blurred by changing technologies and new market opportunities.* Such acquisitions are the result of a company's management betting that two or more distinct industries are converging into one and deciding to establish a strong position in the consolidating markets by bringing together the resources and products of several different companies. News Corporation has prepared for the convergence of media services with the purchase of satellite TV companies to complement its media holdings in TV broadcasting (the Fox network and TV stations in various countries), cable TV (Fox News, Fox Sports, and FX), filmed entertainment (Twentieth Century Fox and Fox Studios), newspapers, magazines, and book publishing.

Why Mergers and Acquisitions Sometimes Fail to Produce Anticipated Results

Companies such as Wells Fargo and Clear Channel Communications have used mergers and acquisitions to catapult themselves into positions of market leadership. But mergers and acquisitions do not always produce the hoped-for outcomes. The managers appointed to oversee the integration of a newly acquired company can make mistakes in deciding what activities to leave alone and what activities to meld into the acquired company's operations. Cost savings may prove smaller than expected. Gains in competitive capabilities may take substantially longer to realize or may never materialize. Efforts to mesh the corporate cultures can stall due to formidable resistance from organization members. Managers and employees at the acquired company may argue forcefully for continuing to do certain things the way they were done before the acquisition. And key employees at the acquired company can quickly become disenchanted and leave.

A number of mergers/acquisitions have been notably unsuccessful. eBay's $2.6 billion acquisition of Skype in 2005 proved to be a mistake—eBay wrote off $900 million of its Skype investment in 2007 and sold 70 percent of its ownership in Skype in September 2009 to a group of investors. The merger of Daimler-Benz (Mercedes) and Chrysler was a failure, as was Ford's $2.5 billion acquisition of Jaguar and its $2.5 billion acquisition of Land Rover (both were sold to India's Tata Motors in 2008 for $2.3 billion). Several recent mergers/acquisitions have yet to live up to expectations—prominent examples include Oracle's acquisition of Sun Microsystems, the Fiat-Chrysler deal, and Bank of America's acquisition of Countrywide Financial.

KEY POINTS

Once a company has selected which of the five basic competitive strategies to employ in its quest for competitive advantage, then it must decide whether and how to supplement its choice of a basic competitive strategy approach.

1. Companies have a number of offensive strategy options for improving their market positions and trying to secure a competitive advantage: (1) attacking competitors' weaknesses, (2) offering an equal or better product at a lower price, (3) pursuing sustained product innovation, (4) leapfrogging competitors by being first to adopt next-generation technologies or the first to introduce next-generation products, (5) adopting and improving on the good ideas of other companies, (6) deliberately attacking those market segments where key rivals make big profits, (7) going after less contested or unoccupied market territory, (8) using hit-and-run tactics to steal sales away from unsuspecting rivals, and (9) launching preemptive strikes. A blue ocean offensive strategy seeks to gain a dramatic and durable competitive advantage by abandoning efforts to beat out competitors in existing markets and, instead, inventing a new industry or distinctive market segment that renders existing competitors largely irrelevant and allows a company to create and capture altogether new demand.

2. Defensive strategies to protect a company's position usually take the form of making moves that put obstacles in the path of would-be challengers and fortify the company's present position while undertaking actions to dissuade rivals from even trying to attack (by signaling that the resulting battle will be more costly to the challenger than it is worth).

3. The timing of strategic moves also has relevance in the quest for competitive advantage. Company managers are obligated to carefully consider the advantages or disadvantages that attach to being a first mover versus a fast follower versus a wait-and-see late mover.

4. Vertically integrating forward or backward makes strategic sense only if it strengthens a company's position via either cost reduction or creation of a differentiation-based advantage. Otherwise, the drawbacks of vertical integration (increased investment, greater business risk, increased vulnerability to technological changes, and less flexibility in making product changes) are likely to outweigh any advantages.

5. Outsourcing pieces of the value chain formerly performed in-house can enhance a company's competitiveness whenever (1) an activity can be performed better or more cheaply by outside specialists; (2) the activity is not crucial to the firm's ability to achieve sustainable competitive advantage and won't hollow out its core competencies, capabilities, or technical know-how; (3) it improves a company's ability to innovate; and/or (4) it allows a company to concentrate on its core business and do what it does best.

6. Many companies are using strategic alliances and collaborative partnerships to help them in the race to build a global market presence or be a leader in the industries of the future. Strategic alliances are an attractive, flexible, and often cost-effective means by which companies can gain access to missing technology, expertise, and business capabilities.

7. Mergers and acquisitions are another attractive strategic option for strengthening a firm's competitiveness. When the operations of two companies are combined via merger or acquisition, the new company's competitiveness can be enhanced

in any of several ways—lower costs; stronger technological skills; more or better competitive capabilities; a more attractive lineup of products and services; wider geographic coverage; and/or greater financial resources with which to invest in R&D, add capacity, or expand into new areas.

ASSURANCE OF LEARNING EXERCISES

1. Does it appear that Nintendo relies more heavily on offensive or defensive strategies as it competes in the video game industry? Has Nintendo's timing of strategic moves made it an early mover or a fast follower? Could Nintendo's introduction of the Wii be characterized as a blue ocean strategy? You may rely on your knowledge of the video game industry and information provided at Nintendo's investor relations website (www.nintendo.com) to provide justification for your answers to these questions.

   LO1, LO2, LO3

   connect
   www.mcgrawhillconnect.com

2. American Apparel, known for its hip line of basic garments and its provocative advertisements, is no stranger to the concept of "doing it all." Concepts & Connections 6.2 on page 126 describes how American Apparel has made vertical integration a central part of its strategy. What value chain segments has American Apparel chosen to enter and perform internally? How has vertical integration aided the company in building competitive advantage? Has vertical integration strengthened its market position? Explain why or why not.

   LO4

   connect
   www.mcgrawhillconnect.com

3. Perform an Internet search to identify at least two companies in different industries that have entered into outsourcing agreements with firms with specialized services. In addition, describe what value chain activities the companies have chosen to outsource. Do any of these outsourcing agreements seem likely to threaten any of the companies' competitive capabilities?

   LO5

4. Using your university library's subscription to Lexis-Nexis, EBSCO, or a similar database, find two examples of how companies have relied on strategic alliances or joint ventures to substitute for horizontal or vertical integration.

   LO6

5. Using your university library's subscription to Lexis-Nexis, EBSCO, or a similar database, identify at least two companies in different industries that are using mergers and acquisitions to strengthen their market positions. How have these mergers and acquisitions enhanced the acquiring companies' resources and competitive capabilities?

   LO7

EXERCISES FOR SIMULATION PARTICIPANTS

1. Has your company relied more on offensive or defensive strategies to achieve your rank in the industry? What options for being a first mover does your company have? Do any of these first-mover options hold competitive advantage potential?

   LO1, LO2, LO3

2. Is your company vertically integrated? Explain.

   LO4

3. Is your company able to engage in outsourcing? If so, what do you see as the pros and cons of outsourcing?

   LO5

4. Does your company have the option to merge with or acquire other companies? If so, which rival companies would you like to acquire or merge with?

   LO7

ENDNOTES

1. George Stalk, Jr., and Rob Lachenauer, "Hardball: Five Killer Strategies for Trouncing the Competition," *Harvard Business Review* 82, no. 4 (April 2004); Richard D'Aveni, "The Empire Strikes Back: Counterrevolutionary Strategies for Industry Leaders," *Harvard Business Review* 80, no. 11 (November 2002); and David J. Bryce and Jeffrey H. Dyer, "Strategies to Crack Well-Guarded Markets," *Harvard Business Review* 85, no. 5 (May 2007).

2. David B. Yoffie and Mary Kwak, "Mastering Balance: How to Meet and Beat a Stronger Opponent," *California Management Review* 44, no. 2 (Winter 2002).

3. Ian C. MacMillan, Alexander B. van Putten, and Rita Gunther McGrath, "Global Gamesmanship," *Harvard Business Review* 81, no. 5 (May 2003); and Askay R. Rao, Mark E. Bergen, and Scott Davis, "How to Fight a Price War," *Harvard Business Review* 78, no. 2 (March–April 2000).

4. Ming-Jer Chen and Donald C. Hambrick, "Speed, Stealth, and Selective Attack: How Small Firms Differ from Large Firms in Competitive Behavior," *Academy of Management Journal* 38, no. 2 (April 1995); Ian MacMillan, "How Business Strategists Can Use Guerrilla Warfare Tactics," *Journal of Business Strategy* 1, no. 2 (Fall 1980); William E. Rothschild, "Surprise and the Competitive Advantage," *Journal of Business Strategy* 4, no. 3 (Winter 1984); Kathryn R. Harrigan, *Strategic Flexibility* (Lexington, MA: Lexington Books, 1985); and Liam Fahey, "Guerrilla Strategy: The Hit-and-Run Attack," in *The Strategic Management Planning Reader*, ed.

Liam Fahey (Englewood Cliffs, NJ: Prentice Hall, 1989).

5. Ian MacMillan, "Preemptive Strategies," *Journal of Business Strategy* 14, no. 2 (Fall 1983).

6. W. Chan Kim and Renée Mauborgne, "Blue Ocean Strategy," *Harvard Business Review* 82, no. 10 (October 2004).

7. Michael E. Porter, *Competitive Advantage* (New York: Free Press, 1985).

8. Jeffrey G. Covin, Dennis P. Slevin, and Michael B. Heeley, "Pioneers and Followers: Competitive Tactics, Environment, and Growth," *Journal of Business Venturing* 15, no. 2 (March 1999); and Christopher A. Bartlett and Sumantra Ghoshal, "Going Global: Lessons from Late-Movers," *Harvard Business Review* 78, no. 2 (March–April 2000).

9. Fernando Suarez and Gianvito Lanzolla, "The Half-Truth of First-Mover Advantage," *Harvard Business Review* 83 no. 4 (April 2005).

10. Gary Hamel, "Smart Mover, Dumb Mover," *Fortune*, September 3, 2001.

11. Costas Markides and Paul A. Geroski, "Racing to Be 2nd: Conquering the Industries of the Future," *Business Strategy Review* 15, no. 4 (Winter 2004).

12. Kathryn R. Harrigan, "Matching Vertical Integration Strategies to Competitive Conditions," *Strategic Management Journal* 7, no. 6 (November–December 1986); and John Stuckey and David White, "When and When Not to Vertically Integrate," *Sloan Management Review*, Spring 1993.

13. Thomas Osegowitsch and Anoop Madhok, "Vertical Integration Is

Dead, or Is It?" *Business Horizons* 46, no. 2 (March–April 2003).

14. Jérôme Barthélemy, "The Seven Deadly Sins of Outsourcing," *Academy of Management Executive* 17, no. 2 (May 2003); Gary P. Pisano and Willy C. Shih, "Restoring American Competitiveness," *Harvard Business Review* 87, no. 7/8 (July–August 2009); and Ronan McIvor, "What Is the Right Outsourcing Strategy for Your Process?" *European Management Journal* 26, no. 1 (February 2008).

15. Michael E. Porter, *The Competitive Advantage of Nations* (New York: Free Press, 1990); K. M. Eisenhardt and C. B. Schoonhoven, "Resource-Based View of Strategic Alliance Formation: Strategic and Social Effects in Entrepreneurial Firms," *Organization Science* 7, no. 2 (March–April 1996); Nancy J. Kaplan and Jonathan Hurd, "Realizing the Promise of Partnerships," *Journal of Business Strategy* 23, no. 3 (May–June 2002); Salvatore Parise and Lisa Sasson, "Leveraging Knowledge Management across Strategic Alliances," *Ivey Business Journal* 66, no. 4 (March–April 2002); and David Ernst and James Bamford, "Your Alliances Are Too Stable," *Harvard Business Review* 83, no. 6 (June 2005).

16. Yves L. Doz and Gary Hamel, *Alliance Advantage; The Art of Creating Value through Partnering* (Boston: Harvard Business School Press, 1998).

17. Joseph L. Bower, "Not All M&As Are Alike—And That Matters," *Harvard Business Review* 79, no. 3 (March 2001); and O. Chatain and P. Zemsky, "The Horizontal Scope of the Firm: Organizational Trade-offs vs. Buyer-Supplier Relationships," *Management Science* 53, no. 4 (April 2007).

chapter 8

CORPORATE STRATEGY: DIVERSIFICATION AND THE MULTIBUSINESS COMPANY

LEARNING OBJECTIVES

LO1 Understand when and how diversifying into multiple businesses can enhance shareholder value.

LO2 Gain an understanding of how related diversification strategies can produce cross-business strategic fit capable of delivering competitive advantage.

LO3 Become aware of the merits and risks of corporate strategies keyed to unrelated diversification.

LO4 Gain command of the analytical tools for evaluating a company's diversification strategy.

LO5 Understand a diversified company's four main corporate strategy options for solidifying its diversification strategy and improving company performance.

This chapter moves up one level in the strategy-making hierarchy, from strategy making in a single-business enterprise to strategy making in a diversified enterprise. Because a diversified company is a collection of individual businesses, the strategy-making task is more complicated. In a one-business company, managers have to come up with a plan for competing successfully in only a single industry environment—the result is what Chapter 2 labeled as *business strategy* (or *business-level strategy*). But in a diversified company, the strategy-making challenge involves assessing multiple industry environments and developing a *set* of business strategies, one for each industry arena in which the diversified company operates. And top executives at a diversified company must still go one step further and devise a companywide or *corporate strategy* for improving the attractiveness and performance of the company's overall business lineup and for making a rational whole out of its diversified collection of individual businesses.

In most diversified companies, corporate-level executives delegate considerable strategy-making authority to the heads of each business, usually giving them the latitude to craft a business strategy suited to their particular industry and competitive circumstances and holding them accountable for producing good results. But the task of crafting a diversified company's overall corporate strategy falls squarely in the lap of top-level executives and involves four distinct facets:

1. *Picking new industries to enter and deciding on the means of entry.* The decision to pursue business diversification requires that management decide what new industries offer the best growth prospects and whether to enter by starting a new business from the ground up, acquiring a company already in the target industry, or forming a joint venture or strategic alliance with another company.

2. *Pursuing opportunities to leverage cross-business value chain relationships into competitive advantage.* Companies that diversify into businesses with strategic fit across the value chains of their business units have a much better chance of gaining a $1 + 1 = 3$ effect than multibusiness companies lacking strategic fit.

3. *Establishing investment priorities and steering corporate resources into the most attractive business units.* A diversified company's business units are usually not equally attractive, and it is incumbent on corporate management to channel resources into areas where earnings potentials are higher.

4. *Initiating actions to boost the combined performance of the corporation's collection of businesses.* Corporate strategists must craft moves to improve the overall performance of the corporation's business lineup and sustain increases in shareholder value. Strategic options for diversified corporations include *(a)* sticking closely with the existing business lineup and pursuing opportunities presented by these businesses, *(b)* broadening the scope of diversification by entering additional industries, *(c)* retrenching to a narrower scope of diversification by divesting poorly performing businesses, and *(d)* broadly restructuring the business lineup with multiple divestitures and/or acquisitions.

The first portion of this chapter describes the various means a company can use to diversify and explores the pros and cons of related versus unrelated diversification strategies. The second part of the chapter looks at how to evaluate the attractiveness of a diversified company's business lineup, decide whether it has a good diversification strategy, and identify ways to improve its future performance.

WHEN BUSINESS DIVERSIFICATION BECOMES A CONSIDERATION

As long as a single-business company can achieve profitable growth opportunities in its present industry, there is no urgency to pursue diversification. However, a company's opportunities for growth can become limited if the industry becomes competitively unattractive. Consider, for example, what the growing use of debit cards and online bill payment have done to the check printing business and what mobile phone companies and marketers of Voice over Internet Protocol (VoIP) have done to the revenues of long-distance providers such as AT&T, British Telecommunications, and NTT in Japan. Thus, *diversifying into new industries always merits strong consideration whenever a single-business company encounters diminishing market opportunities and stagnating sales in its principal business.*[1]

▶ **LO1**

Understand when and how diversifying into multiple businesses can enhance shareholder value.

BUILDING SHAREHOLDER VALUE: THE ULTIMATE JUSTIFICATION FOR BUSINESS DIVERSIFICATION

Diversification must do more for a company than simply spread its business risk across various industries. In principle, diversification cannot be considered a success unless it results in *added shareholder value*—value that shareholders cannot capture on their own by spreading their investments across the stocks of companies in different industries.

Business diversification stands little chance of building shareholder value without passing the following three tests:[2]

1. *The industry attractiveness test.* The industry to be entered through diversification must offer an opportunity for profits and return on investment that is equal to or better than that of the company's present business(es).

2. *The cost-of-entry test.* The cost to enter the target industry must not be so high as to erode the potential for good profitability. A Catch-22 can prevail here, however. The more attractive an industry's prospects are for growth and good long-term profitability, the more expensive it can be to enter. It's easy for acquisitions of companies in highly attractive industries to fail the cost-of-entry test.

3. *The better-off test.* Diversifying into a new business must offer potential for the company's existing businesses and the new business to perform better together under a single corporate umbrella than they would perform operating as independent, stand-alone businesses. For example, let's say company A diversifies by purchasing company B in another industry. If A and B's consolidated profits in the years to come prove no greater than

what each could have earned on its own, then A's diversification won't provide its shareholders with added value. Company A's shareholders could have achieved the same $1 + 1 = 2$ result by merely purchasing stock in company B. Shareholder value is not created by diversification unless it produces a $1 + 1 = 3$ effect.

> → Creating added value for shareholders via diversification requires building a multibusiness company where the whole is greater than the sum of its parts.

Diversification moves that satisfy all three tests have the greatest potential to grow shareholder value over the long term. Diversification moves that can pass only one or two tests are suspect.

APPROACHES TO DIVERSIFYING THE BUSINESS LINEUP

The means of entering new industries and lines of business can take any of three forms: acquisition, internal development, or joint ventures with other companies.

Diversification by Acquisition of an Existing Business

Acquisition is a popular means of diversifying into another industry. Not only is it quicker than trying to launch a new operation, but it also offers an effective way to hurdle such entry barriers as acquiring technological know-how, establishing supplier relationships, achieving scale economies, building brand awareness, and securing adequate distribution. Buying an ongoing operation allows the acquirer to move directly to the task of building a strong market position in the target industry, rather than getting bogged down in the fine points of launching a start-up.

The big dilemma an acquisition-minded firm faces is whether to pay a premium price for a successful company or to buy a struggling company at a bargain price.[3] If the buying firm has little knowledge of the industry but has ample capital, it is often better off purchasing a capable, strongly positioned firm—unless the price of such an acquisition is prohibitive and flunks the cost-of-entry test. However, when the acquirer sees promising ways to transform a weak firm into a strong one, a struggling company can be the better long-term investment.

Entering a New Line of Business through Internal Development

Achieving diversification through *internal development* involves starting a new business subsidiary from scratch. Generally, forming a start-up subsidiary to enter a new business has appeal only when (1) the parent company already has in-house most or all of the skills and resources needed to compete effectively; (2) there is ample time to launch the business; (3) internal entry has lower costs than entry via acquisition; (4) the targeted industry is populated with many relatively small firms such that the new start-up does not have to compete against large, powerful rivals; (5) adding new production capacity will not adversely impact the supply–demand balance in the industry; and (6) incumbent firms are likely to be slow or ineffective in responding to a new entrant's efforts to crack the market.

Using Joint Ventures to Achieve Diversification

A joint venture to enter a new business can be useful in at least two types of situations.[4] First, a joint venture is a good vehicle for pursuing an opportunity that is too complex, uneconomical, or risky for one company to pursue alone. Second, joint ventures make sense when the opportunities in a new industry require a broader range of competencies and know-how than an expansion-minded company can marshal. Many of the opportunities in biotechnology call for the coordinated development of complementary innovations and tackling an intricate web of technical, political, and regulatory factors simultaneously. In such cases, pooling the resources and competencies of two or more companies is a wiser and less risky way to proceed.

However, as discussed in Chapters 6 and 7, partnering with another company—either in the form of a joint venture or collaborative alliance—has significant drawbacks due to the potential for conflicting objectives, disagreements over how to best operate the venture, culture clashes, and so on. Joint ventures are generally the least durable of the entry options, usually lasting only until the partners decide to go their own ways.

CHOOSING THE DIVERSIFICATION PATH: RELATED VERSUS UNRELATED BUSINESSES

> **CORE CONCEPT**
>
> **Related businesses** possess competitively valuable cross-business value chain and resource matchups; **unrelated businesses** have dissimilar value chains and resources requirements, with no competitively important cross-business value chain relationships.

Once a company decides to diversify, its first big corporate strategy decision is whether to diversify into **related businesses, unrelated businesses,** or some mix of both (see Figure 8.1). *Businesses are said to be related when their value chains possess competitively valuable cross-business relationships.* These value chain matchups present opportunities for the businesses to perform better under the same corporate umbrella than they could by operating as stand-alone entities. *Businesses are said to be unrelated when the activities comprising their respective value chains and resource requirements are so dissimilar that no competitively valuable cross-business relationships are present.*

The next two sections explore the ins and outs of related and unrelated diversification.

▶**LO2**

Gain an understanding of how related diversification strategies can produce cross-business strategic fit capable of delivering competitive advantage.

THE CASE FOR RELATED DIVERSIFICATION

A related diversification strategy involves building the company around businesses whose value chains possess competitively valuable strategic fit, as shown in Figure 8.2. **Strategic fit** exists whenever one or more activities comprising the value chains of different businesses are sufficiently similar to present opportunities for:[5]

> **CORE CONCEPT**
>
> **Strategic fit** exists when the value chains of different businesses present opportunities for cross-business skills transfer, cost sharing, or brand sharing.

- *Transferring competitively valuable resources, expertise, technological know-how, or other*

▶FIGURE 8.1 **Strategic Themes of Multibusiness Corporations**

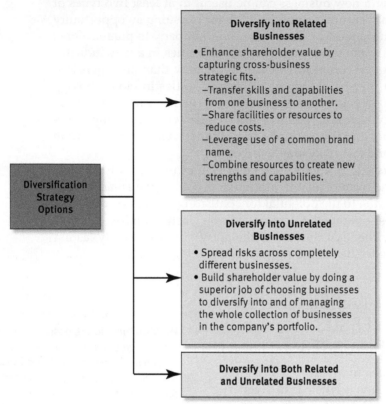

capabilities from one business to another. Google's technological know-how and innovation capabilities refined in its Internet search business have aided considerably in the development of its Android mobile operating system and Chrome operating system for computers. After acquiring Marvel Comics in 2009, Walt Disney Company shared Marvel's iconic characters such as Spider-Man, Iron Man, and the Black Widow with many of the other Disney businesses, including its theme parks, retail stores, motion picture division, and video game business.

- *Cost sharing between separate businesses where value chain activities can be combined.* For instance, it is often feasible to manufacture the products of different businesses in a single plant or have a single sales force for the products of different businesses if they are marketed to the same types of customers.

- *Brand sharing between business units that have common customers or that draw upon common core competencies.* For example, Yamaha's name in motorcycles gave it instant credibility and recognition in entering the personal watercraft business, allowing it to achieve a significant market share without spending large sums on advertising to establish a brand identity for the WaveRunner. Likewise, Apple's reputation for producing easy-to-operate computers was a competitive asset that facilitated the company's diversification into digital music players and smartphones.

FIGURE 8.2 Related Diversification Is Built upon Competitively Valuable Strategic Fit in Value Chain Activities

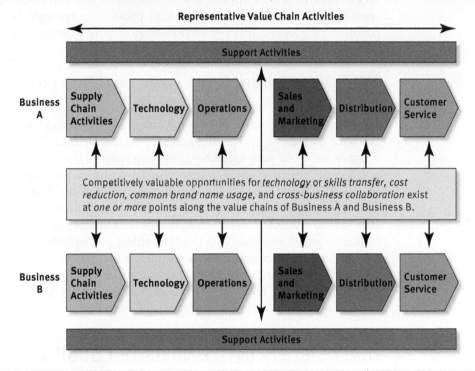

Cross-business strategic fit can exist anywhere along the value chain—in R&D and technology activities, in supply chain activities, in manufacturing, in sales and marketing, or in distribution activities. Likewise, different businesses can often use the same administrative and customer service infrastructure. For instance, a cable operator that diversifies as a broadband provider can use the same customer data network, the same customer call centers and local offices, the same billing and customer accounting systems, and the same customer service infrastructure to support all its products and services.[6]

Strategic Fit and Economies of Scope

Strategic fit in the value chain activities of a diversified corporation's different businesses opens up opportunities for economies of scope—a concept distinct from *economies of scale.* Economies of *scale* are cost savings that accrue directly from a larger operation; for example, unit costs may be lower in a large plant than in a small plant. **Economies of scope,** however, stem directly from cost-saving strategic fit along the value chains of related businesses. Such economies are open only to a multibusiness enterprise and are the result of a related diversification strategy that allows sibling businesses to share technology, perform R&D together, use common manufacturing

> **CORE CONCEPT**
> **Economies of scope** are cost reductions stemming from strategic fit along the value chains of related businesses (thereby, a larger scope of operations), whereas *economies of scale* accrue from a larger operation.

or distribution facilities, share a common sales force or distributor/dealer network, and/or share the same administrative infrastructure. *The greater the cross-business economies associated with cost-saving strategic fit, the greater the potential for a related diversification strategy to yield a competitive advantage based on lower costs than rivals.*

The Ability of Related Diversification to Deliver Competitive Advantage and Gains in Shareholder Value

Economies of scope and the other strategic-fit benefits provide a dependable basis for earning higher profits and returns than what a diversified company's businesses could earn as stand-alone enterprises. Converting the competitive advantage potential into greater profitability is what fuels $1 + 1 = 3$ gains in shareholder value—the necessary outcome for satisfying the *better-off test*. There are three things to bear in mind here: (1) Capturing cross-business strategic fit via related diversification builds shareholder value in ways that shareholders cannot replicate by simply owning a diversified portfolio of stocks; (2) the capture of cross-business strategic-fit benefits is possible only through related diversification; and (3) the benefits of cross-business strategic fit are not automatically realized—*the benefits materialize only after management has successfully pursued internal actions to capture them.*[7]

DIVERSIFYING INTO UNRELATED BUSINESSES

LO3

Become aware of the merits and risks of corporate strategies keyed to unrelated diversification.

An unrelated diversification strategy discounts the importance of pursuing cross-business strategic fit and, instead, focuses squarely on entering and operating businesses in industries that allow the company as a whole to increase its earnings. Companies that pursue a strategy of unrelated diversification generally exhibit a willingness to diversify into *any industry* where senior managers see opportunity to realize improved financial results. Such companies are frequently labeled *conglomerates* because their business interests range broadly across diverse industries.

Companies that pursue unrelated diversification nearly always enter new businesses by acquiring an established company rather than by internal development. The premise of acquisition-minded corporations is that growth by acquisition can deliver enhanced shareholder value through upward-trending corporate revenues and earnings and a stock price that *on average* rises enough year after year to amply reward and please shareholders. Three types of acquisition candidates are usually of particular interest: (1) businesses that have bright growth prospects but are short on investment capital, (2) undervalued companies that can be acquired at a bargain price, and (3) struggling companies whose operations can be turned around with the aid of the parent company's financial resources and managerial know-how.

Building Shareholder Value Through Unrelated Diversification

Given the absence of cross-business strategic fit with which to capture added competitive advantage, the task of building shareholder value via unrelated diversification ultimately hinges on the ability of the parent company to improve its businesses via other means. To succeed with a corporate strategy keyed to unrelated diversification, corporate executives must:

- Do a superior job of identifying and acquiring new businesses that can produce consistently good earnings and returns on investment.

- Do an excellent job of negotiating favorable acquisition prices.

- Do such a good job *overseeing* and *parenting* the firm's businesses that they perform at a higher level than they would otherwise be able to do through their own efforts alone. The parenting activities of corporate executives can take the form of providing expert problem-solving skills, creative strategy suggestions, and first-rate advice and guidance on how to improve competitiveness and financial performance to the heads of the various business subsidiaries.[8]

The Pitfalls of Unrelated Diversification

Unrelated diversification strategies have two important negatives that undercut the pluses: very demanding managerial requirements and limited competitive advantage potential.

Demanding Managerial Requirements   Successfully managing a set of fundamentally different businesses operating in fundamentally different industry and competitive environments is an exceptionally difficult proposition for corporate-level managers. The greater the number of businesses a company is in and the more diverse they are, the more difficult it is for corporate managers to:

1. Stay abreast of what's happening in each industry and each subsidiary.
2. Pick business-unit heads having the requisite combination of managerial skills and know-how to drive gains in performance.
3. Tell the difference between those strategic proposals of business-unit managers that are prudent and those that are risky or unlikely to succeed.
4. Know what to do if a business unit stumbles and its results suddenly head downhill.[9]

As a rule, the more unrelated businesses that a company has diversified into, the more corporate executives are forced to "manage by the numbers"— that is, keep a close track on the financial and operating results of each subsidiary and assume that the heads of the various subsidiaries have most everything under control so long as the latest key financial and operating measures look good. Managing by the numbers works if the heads of the various business units are quite capable and consistently meet their numbers. But problems arise when things start to go awry and corporate management has to get deeply involved in turning around a business it does not know much about.

> Unrelated diversification requires that corporate executives rely on the skills and expertise of business-level managers to build competitive advantage and boost the performance of individual businesses.

Limited Competitive Advantage Potential The second big negative associated with unrelated diversification is that such a strategy *offers limited potential for competitive advantage beyond what each individual business can generate on its own.* Unlike a related diversification strategy, there is no cross-business strategic fit to draw on for reducing costs; transferring capabilities, skills, and technology; or leveraging use of a powerful brand name and thereby adding to the competitive advantage possessed by individual businesses. *Without the competitive advantage potential of strategic fit, consolidated performance of an unrelated group of businesses is unlikely to be better than the sum of what the individual business units could achieve independently in most instances.*

Misguided Reasons for Pursuing Unrelated Diversification

Competently overseeing a set of widely diverse businesses can turn out to be much harder than it sounds. In practice, comparatively few companies have proved that they have top management capabilities that are up to the task. Far more corporate executives have failed than been successful at delivering consistently good financial results with an unrelated diversification strategy.[10] Odds are that the result of unrelated diversification will be $1 + 1 = 2$ or less. In addition, management sometimes undertakes a strategy of unrelated diversification for the wrong reasons.

- *Risk reduction.* Managers sometimes pursue unrelated diversification to reduce risk by spreading the company's investments over a set of diverse industries. But this cannot create long-term shareholder value alone since the company's shareholders can more efficiently reduce their exposure to risk by investing in a diversified portfolio of stocks and bonds.
- *Growth.* While unrelated diversification may enable a company to achieve rapid or continuous growth in revenues, only profitable growth can bring about increases in shareholder value and justify a strategy of unrelated diversification.
- *Earnings stabilization.* In a broadly diversified company, there's a chance that market downtrends in some of the company's businesses will be partially offset by cyclical upswings in its other businesses, thus producing somewhat less earnings volatility. In actual practice, however, there's no convincing evidence that the consolidated profits of firms with unrelated diversification strategies are more stable than the profits of firms with related diversification strategies.
- *Managerial motives.* Unrelated diversification can provide benefits to managers such as higher compensation, which tends to increase with firm size and degree of diversification. Diversification for this reason alone is far more likely to reduce shareholder value than to increase it.

CORPORATE STRATEGIES COMBINING RELATED AND UNRELATED DIVERSIFICATION

There's nothing to preclude a company from diversifying into both related and unrelated businesses. Indeed, the business makeup of diversified companies varies considerably. Some diversified companies are really *dominant-business enterprises*—one major "core" business accounts for 50 to 80 percent of total revenues and a collection of small related or unrelated businesses accounts for the remainder. Some diversified companies are *narrowly diversified* around a few (two to five) related or unrelated businesses. Others are *broadly diversified* around a wide-ranging collection of related businesses, unrelated businesses, or a mixture of both. And a number of multibusiness enterprises have diversified into *several unrelated groups of related businesses.* There's ample room for companies to customize their diversification strategies to incorporate elements of both related and unrelated diversification.

EVALUATING THE STRATEGY OF A DIVERSIFIED COMPANY

Strategic analysis of diversified companies builds on the methodology used for single-business companies discussed in Chapters 3 and 4 but utilizes tools that streamline the overall process. The procedure for evaluating the pluses and minuses of a diversified company's strategy and deciding what actions to take to improve the company's performance involves six steps:

▶**LO4**

Gain command of the analytical tools for evaluating a company's diversification strategy.

1. Assessing the attractiveness of the industries the company has diversified into.

2. Assessing the competitive strength of the company's business units.

3. Evaluating the extent of cross-business strategic fit along the value chains of the company's various business units.

4. Checking whether the firm's resources fit the requirements of its present business lineup.

5. Ranking the performance prospects of the businesses from best to worst and determining a priority for allocating resources.

6. Crafting new strategic moves to improve overall corporate performance.

The core concepts and analytical techniques underlying each of these steps are discussed further in this section of the chapter.

Step 1: Evaluating Industry Attractiveness

A principal consideration in evaluating the caliber of a diversified company's strategy is the attractiveness of the industries in which it has business operations. The more attractive the industries (both individually and as a group) a diversified company is in, the better its prospects for good long-term performance. A simple and reliable analytical tool for gauging industry attractiveness involves calculating quantitative industry attractiveness scores based upon the following measures.

- *Market size and projected growth rate.* Big industries are more attractive than small industries, and fast-growing industries tend to be more attractive than slow-growing industries, other things being equal.

- *The intensity of competition.* Industries where competitive pressures are relatively weak are more attractive than industries with strong competitive pressures.

- *Emerging opportunities and threats.* Industries with promising opportunities and minimal threats on the near horizon are more attractive than industries with modest opportunities and imposing threats.

- *The presence of cross-industry strategic fit.* The more the industry's value chain and resource requirements match up well with the value chain activities of other industries in which the company has operations, the more attractive the industry is to a firm pursuing related diversification. However, cross-industry strategic fit may be of no consequence to a company committed to a strategy of unrelated diversification.

- *Resource requirements.* Industries having resource requirements within the company's reach are more attractive than industries where capital and other resource requirements could strain corporate financial resources and organizational capabilities.

- *Seasonal and cyclical factors.* Industries where buyer demand is relatively steady year-round and not unduly vulnerable to economic ups and downs tend to be more attractive than industries with wide seasonal or cyclical swings in buyer demand.

- *Social, political, regulatory, and environmental factors.* Industries with significant problems in such areas as consumer health, safety, or environmental pollution or that are subject to intense regulation are less attractive than industries where such problems are not burning issues.

- *Industry profitability.* Industries with healthy profit margins are generally more attractive than industries where profits have historically been low or unstable.

- *Industry uncertainty and business risk.* Industries with less uncertainty on the horizon and lower overall business risk are more attractive than industries whose prospects for one reason or another are quite uncertain.

Each attractiveness measure should be assigned a weight reflecting its relative importance in determining an industry's attractiveness; it is weak methodology to assume that the various attractiveness measures are equally important. The intensity of competition in an industry should nearly always carry a high weight (say, 0.20 to 0.30). Strategic-fit considerations should be assigned a high weight in the case of companies with related diversification strategies; but for companies with an unrelated diversification strategy, strategic fit with other industries may be given a low weight or even dropped from the list of attractiveness measures. Seasonal and cyclical factors generally are assigned a low weight (or maybe even eliminated from the analysis) unless a company has diversified into industries strongly characterized by seasonal demand and/or heavy vulnerability to cyclical upswings and downswings. The importance weights must add up to 1.0.

Next, each industry is rated on each of the chosen industry attractiveness measures, using a rating scale of 1 to 10 (where 10 signifies *high* attractiveness and 1 signifies *low* attractiveness). Weighted attractiveness scores are then calculated by multiplying the industry's rating on each measure by the corresponding weight. For example, a rating of 8 times a weight of 0.25 gives a weighted attractiveness score of 2.00. The sum of the weighted scores for all

TABLE 8.1

Calculating Weighted Industry Attractiveness Scores					

Rating scale: 1 = Very unattractive to company; 10 = Very attractive to company

Industry Attractiveness Measure	Importance Weight	Industry A Rating/Score	Industry B Rating/Score	Industry C Rating/Score	Industry D Rating/Score
Market size and projected growth rate	0.10	8/0.80	5/0.50	2/0.20	3/0.30
Intensity of competition	0.25	8/2.00	7/1.75	3/0.75	2/0.50
Emerging opportunities and threats	0.10	2/0.20	9/0.90	4/0.40	5/0.50
Cross-industry strategic fit	0.20	8/1.60	4/0.80	8/1.60	2/0.40
Resource requirements	0.10	9/0.90	7/0.70	5/0.50	5/0.50
Seasonal and cyclical influences	0.05	9/0.45	8/0.40	10/0.50	5/0.25
Societal, political, regulatory, and environmental factors	0.05	10/0.50	7/0.35	7/0.35	3/0.15
Industry profitability	0.10	5/0.50	10/1.00	3/0.30	3/0.30
Industry uncertainty and business risk	0.05	5/0.25	7/0.35	10/0.50	1/0.05
Sum of the assigned weights	1.00				
Overall weighted industry attractiveness scores		**7.20**	**6.75**	**5.10**	**2.95**

the attractiveness measures provides an overall industry attractiveness score. This procedure is illustrated in Table 8.1.

Calculating Industry Attractiveness Scores   There are two necessary conditions for producing valid industry attractiveness scores using this method. One is deciding on appropriate weights for the industry attractiveness measures. This is not always easy because different analysts have different views about which weights are most appropriate. Also, different weightings may be appropriate for different companies—based on their strategies, performance targets, and financial circumstances. For instance, placing a low weight on financial resource requirements may be justifiable for a cash-rich company, whereas a high weight may be more appropriate for a financially strapped company.

The second requirement for creating accurate attractiveness scores is to have sufficient knowledge to rate the industry on each attractiveness measure. It's usually rather easy to locate statistical data needed to compare industries on market size, growth rate, seasonal and cyclical influences, and industry profitability. Cross-industry fit and resource requirements are also fairly easy to judge. But the attractiveness measure that is toughest to rate is that of intensity of competition. It is not always easy to conclude whether competition in one industry is stronger or weaker than in another industry. In the event that the available information is too skimpy to confidently assign a rating value to an industry on a particular attractiveness measure, then it is usually best to use a score of 5, which avoids biasing the overall attractiveness score either up or down.

Despite the hurdles, calculating industry attractiveness scores is a systematic and reasonably reliable method for ranking a diversified company's industries from most to least attractive.

Step 2: Evaluating Business-Unit Competitive Strength

The second step in evaluating a diversified company is to determine how strongly positioned its business units are in their respective industries. Doing an appraisal of each business unit's strength and competitive position in its industry not only reveals its chances for industry success but also provides a basis for ranking the units from competitively strongest to weakest. Quantitative measures of each business unit's competitive strength can be calculated using a procedure similar to that for measuring industry attractiveness. The following factors may be used in quantifying the competitive strengths of a diversified company's business subsidiaries:

- *Relative market share.* A business unit's *relative market share* is defined as the ratio of its market share to the market share held by the largest rival firm in the industry, with market share measured in unit volume, not dollars. For instance, if business A has a market-leading share of 40 percent and its largest rival has 30 percent, A's relative market share is 1.33. If business B has a 15 percent market share and B's largest rival has 30 percent, B's relative market share is 0.5.

- *Costs relative to competitors' costs.* There's reason to expect that business units with higher relative market shares have lower unit costs than competitors with lower relative market shares because of the possibility of scale economies and experience or learning curve effects. Another indicator of low cost can be a business unit's supply chain management capabilities.

- *Products or services that satisfy buyer expectations.* A company's competitiveness depends in part on being able to offer buyers appealing features, performance, reliability, and service attributes.

- *Ability to benefit from strategic fit with sibling businesses.* Strategic fit with other businesses within the company enhance a business unit's competitive strength and may provide a competitive edge.

- *Number and caliber of strategic alliances and collaborative partnerships.* Well-functioning alliances and partnerships may be a source of potential competitive advantage and thus add to a business's competitive strength.

- *Brand image and reputation.* A strong brand name is a valuable competitive asset in most industries.

- *Competitively valuable capabilities.* All industries contain a variety of important competitive capabilities related to product innovation, production capabilities, distribution capabilities, or marketing prowess.

- *Profitability relative to competitors.* Above-average returns on investment and large profit margins relative to rivals are usually accurate indicators of competitive advantage.

After settling on a set of competitive strength measures that are well matched to the circumstances of the various business units, weights indicating each measure's importance need to be assigned. As in the assignment of weights to industry attractiveness measures, the importance weights must add up to 1.0. Each business unit is then rated on each of the chosen strength measures, using a rating scale of 1 to 10 (where 10 signifies competitive *strength* and a rating of 1 signifies competitive *weakness*). If the available information is too skimpy to confidently assign a rating value to a business unit on a particular strength measure, then it is usually best to use a score of 5. Weighted strength ratings are calculated by multiplying the business unit's rating on each strength measure by the assigned weight. For example, a strength score of 6 times a weight of 0.15 gives a weighted strength rating of 0.90. The sum of weighted ratings across all the strength measures provides a quantitative measure of a business unit's overall market strength and competitive standing. Table 8.2 provides sample calculations of competitive strength ratings for four businesses.

Using a Nine-Cell Matrix to Evaluate the Strength of a Diversified Company's Business Lineup   The industry attractiveness and business strength scores can be used to portray the strategic positions of each business in a diversified company. Industry attractiveness is plotted on the vertical axis and competitive strength on the horizontal axis. A nine-cell grid

▶ TABLE 8.2

Calculating Weighted Competitive Strength Scores for a Diversified Company's Business Units					

Rating scale: 1 = Very weak; 10 = Very strong

Competitive Strength Measure	Importance Weight	Business A In Industry A Rating/Score	Business B In Industry B Rating/Score	Business C In Industry C Rating/Score	Business D In Industry D Rating/Score
Relative market share	0.15	10/1.50	1/0.15	6/0.90	2/0.30
Costs relative to competitors' costs	0.20	7/1.40	2/0.40	5/1.00	3/0.60
Ability to match or beat rivals on key product attributes	0.05	9/0.45	4/0.20	8/0.40	4/0.20
Ability to benefit from strategic fit with sister businesses	0.20	8/1.60	4/0.80	4/0.80	2/0.60
Bargaining leverage with suppliers/ buyers; caliber of alliances	0.05	9/0.45	3/0.15	6/0.30	2/0.10
Brand image and reputation	0.10	9/0.90	2/0.20	7/0.70	5/0.50
Competitively valuable capabilities	0.15	7/1.05	2/0.30	5/0.75	3/0.45
Profitability relative to competitors	0.10	5/0.50	1/0.10	4/0.40	4/0.40
Sum of the assigned weights	1.00				
Overall weighted competitive strength scores		**7.85**	**2.30**	**5.25**	**3.15**

emerges from dividing the vertical axis into three regions (high, medium, and low attractiveness) and the horizontal axis into three regions (strong, average, and weak competitive strength). As shown in Figure 8.3, high attractiveness is associated with scores of 6.7 or greater on a rating scale of 1 to 10, medium attractiveness to scores of 3.3 to 6.7, and low attractiveness to scores below 3.3. Likewise, high competitive strength is defined as a score greater than 6.7, average strength as scores of 3.3 to 6.7, and low strength as scores below 3.3. *Each business unit is plotted on the nine-cell matrix according to its overall attractiveness and strength scores, and then shown as a "bubble." The size of each bubble is*

▶FIGURE 8.3 **A Nine-Cell Industry Attractiveness–Competitive Strength Matrix**

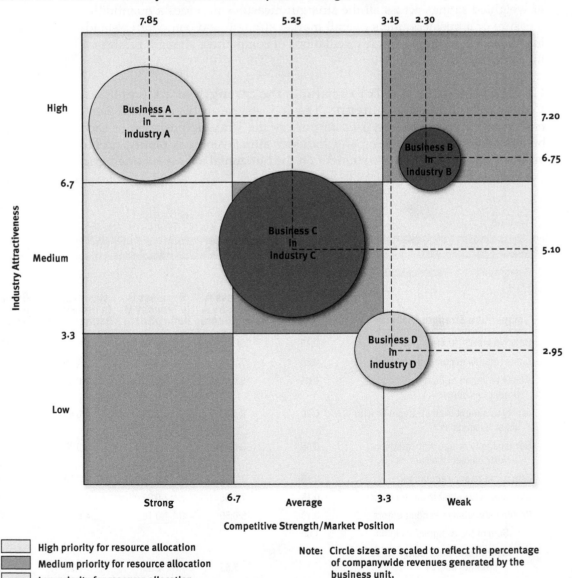

scaled to what percentage of revenues the business generates relative to total corporate revenues. The bubbles in Figure 8.3 were located on the grid using the four industry attractiveness scores from Table 8.1 and the strength scores for the four business units in Table 8.2.

The locations of the business units on the attractiveness–strength matrix provide valuable guidance in deploying corporate resources. In general, *a diversified company's best prospects for good overall performance involve concentrating corporate resources on business units having the greatest competitive strength and industry attractiveness.* Businesses plotted in the three cells in the upper left portion of the attractiveness–strength matrix have both favorable industry attractiveness and competitive strength and should receive a high investment priority. Business units plotted in these three cells (such as business A in Figure 8.3) are referred to as "grow and build" businesses because of their capability to drive future increases in shareholder value.

Next in priority come businesses positioned in the three diagonal cells stretching from the lower left to the upper right (businesses B and C in Figure 8.3). Such businesses usually merit medium or intermediate priority in the parent's resource allocation ranking. However, some businesses in the medium-priority diagonal cells may have brighter or dimmer prospects than others. For example, a small business in the upper right cell of the matrix (like business B), despite being in a highly attractive industry, may occupy too weak a competitive position in its industry to justify the investment and resources needed to turn it into a strong market contender. If, however, a business in the upper right cell has attractive opportunities for rapid growth and a good potential for winning a much stronger market position over time, management may designate it as a grow and build business—the strategic objective here would be to move the business leftward in the attractiveness–strength matrix over time.

Businesses in the three cells in the lower right corner of the matrix (business D in Figure 8.3) typically are weak performers and have the lowest claim on corporate resources. Such businesses are typically good candidates for being divested or else managed in a manner calculated to squeeze out the maximum cash flows from operations. The cash flows from low-performing/low-potential businesses can then be diverted to financing expansion of business units with greater market opportunities. In exceptional cases where a business located in the three lower right cells is nonetheless fairly profitable or has the potential for good earnings and return on investment, the business merits retention and the allocation of sufficient resources to achieve better performance.

The nine-cell attractiveness–strength matrix provides clear, strong logic for why a diversified company needs to consider both industry attractiveness and business strength in allocating resources and investment capital to its different businesses. A good case can be made for concentrating resources in those businesses that enjoy higher degrees of attractiveness and competitive strength, being very selective in making investments in businesses with intermediate positions on the grid, and withdrawing resources from businesses that are lower in attractiveness and strength unless they offer exceptional profit or cash flow potential.

Step 3: Determining the Competitive Value of Strategic Fit in Multibusiness Companies

The potential for competitively important strategic fit is central to making conclusions about the effectiveness of a company's related diversification strategy. This step can be bypassed for diversified companies whose businesses are all unrelated (because, by design, no cross-business strategic fit is present). Checking the competitive advantage potential of cross-business strategic fit involves evaluating how much benefit a diversified company can gain from value chain matchups that present:

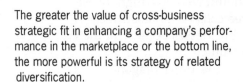

The greater the value of cross-business strategic fit in enhancing a company's performance in the marketplace or the bottom line, the more powerful is its strategy of related diversification.

1. Opportunities to combine the performance of certain activities, thereby reducing costs and capturing economies of scope.

2. Opportunities to transfer skills, technology, or intellectual capital from one business to another.

3. Opportunities to share use of a well-respected brand name across multiple product and/or service categories.

But more than just strategic fit identification is needed. The real test is what competitive value can be generated from this fit. To what extent can cost savings be realized? How much competitive value will come from cross-business transfer of skills, technology, or intellectual capital? Will transferring a potent brand name to the products of sibling businesses grow sales significantly? Absent significant strategic fit and dedicated company efforts to capture the benefits, one has to be skeptical about the potential for a diversified company's businesses to perform better together than apart.

Step 4: Evaluating Resource Fit

The businesses in a diversified company's lineup need to exhibit good resource fit. **Resource fit** exists when (1) businesses, individually, strengthen a company's overall mix of resources and capabilities and (2) a company has sufficient resources that add customer value to support its entire group of businesses without spreading itself too thin.

CORE CONCEPT

A diversified company exhibits **resource fit** when its businesses add to a company's overall mix of resources and capabilities and when the parent company has sufficient resources to support its entire group of businesses without spreading itself too thin.

CORE CONCEPT

A strong **internal capital market** allows a diversified company to add value by shifting capital from business units generating *free cash flow* to those needing additional capital to expand and realize their growth potential.

Financial Resource Fit One important dimension of resource fit concerns whether a diversified company can generate the internal cash flows sufficient to fund the capital requirements of its businesses, pay its dividends, meet its debt obligations, and otherwise remain financially healthy. While additional capital can usually be raised in financial markets, it is also important for a diversified firm to have a healthy **internal capital market** that can support the financial requirements of its business lineup. The greater the extent to which a diversified company is able to fund investment in its businesses through internally generated free cash flows rather than from equity issues or borrowing, the more powerful its financial resource fit and the less dependent the firm is on external financial resources.

A *portfolio approach* to ensuring financial fit among the firm's businesses is based on the fact that different businesses have different cash flow and investment characteristics. For example, business units in rapidly growing industries are often **cash hogs**—so labeled because the cash flows they generate from internal operations aren't big enough to fund their expansion. To keep pace with rising buyer demand, rapid-growth businesses frequently need sizable annual capital infusions—for new facilities and equipment, for technology improvements, and for additional working capital to support inventory expansion. Because a cash hog's financial resources must be provided by the corporate parent, corporate managers have to decide whether it makes good financial and strategic sense to keep pouring new money into a cash hog business.

> **CORE CONCEPT**
>
> A **cash hog** generates operating cash flows that are too small to fully fund its operations and growth; a cash hog must receive cash infusions from outside sources to cover its working capital and investment requirements.

In contrast, business units with leading market positions in mature industries may be **cash cows**—businesses that generate substantial cash surpluses over what is needed to adequately fund their operations. Market leaders in slow-growth industries often generate sizable positive cash flows *over and above what is needed for growth and reinvestment* because the slow-growth nature of their industry often entails relatively modest annual investment requirements. Cash cows, though not always attractive from a growth standpoint, are valuable businesses from a financial resource perspective. The surplus cash flows they generate can be used to pay corporate dividends, finance acquisitions, and provide funds for investing in the company's promising cash hogs. It makes good financial and strategic sense for diversified companies to keep cash cows in healthy condition, fortifying and defending their market position to preserve their cash-generating capability over the long term and thereby have an ongoing source of financial resources to deploy elsewhere.

> **CORE CONCEPT**
>
> A **cash cow** generates operating cash flows over and above its internal requirements, thereby providing financial resources that may be used to invest in cash hogs, finance new acquisitions, fund share buyback programs, or pay dividends.

A diversified company has good financial resource fit when the excess cash generated by its cash cow businesses is sufficient to fund the investment requirements of promising cash hog businesses. Ideally, investing in promising cash hog businesses over time results in growing the hogs into self-supporting *star businesses* that have strong or market-leading competitive positions in attractive, high-growth markets and high levels of profitability. Star businesses are often the cash cows of the future—when the markets of star businesses begin to mature and their growth slows, their competitive strength should produce self-generated cash flows more than sufficient to cover their investment needs. The "success sequence" is thus cash hog to young star (but perhaps still a cash hog) to self-supporting star to cash cow.

If, however, a cash hog has questionable promise (either because of low industry attractiveness or a weak competitive position), then it becomes a logical candidate for divestiture. Aggressively investing in a cash hog with an uncertain future seldom makes sense because it requires the corporate parent to keep pumping more capital into the business with only a dim hope of turning the cash hog into a future star. Such businesses are a financial drain and fail the resource fit test because they strain the corporate parent's ability to adequately fund its other businesses. Divesting a less attractive cash hog business is usually the best alternative unless (1) it has highly valuable strategic fit with other business units or (2) the capital infusions needed from the corporate parent are modest relative to the funds available, and (3) there's a decent chance of growing the business into a solid bottom-line contributor.

Aside from cash flow considerations, two other factors to consider in assessing the financial resource fit for businesses in a diversified firm's portfolio are:

- *Do individual businesses adequately contribute to achieving companywide performance targets?* A business exhibits poor financial fit if it soaks up a disproportionate share of the company's financial resources, while making subpar or insignificant contributions to the bottom line. Too many underperforming businesses reduce the company's overall performance and ultimately limit growth in shareholder value.

- *Does the corporation have adequate financial strength to fund its different businesses and maintain a healthy credit rating?* A diversified company's strategy fails the resource fit test when the resource needs of its portfolio unduly stretch the company's financial health and threaten to impair its credit rating. General Motors, Time Warner, and Royal Ahold, for example, found themselves so financially overextended that they had to sell some of their business units to raise the money to pay down burdensome debt obligations and continue to fund essential capital expenditures for the remaining businesses.

Examining a Diversified Company's Nonfinancial Resource Fit   Diversified companies must also ensure that the nonfinancial resource needs of its portfolio of businesses are met by its corporate capabilities. Just as a diversified company must avoid allowing an excessive number of cash hungry businesses to jeopardize its financial stability, it should also avoid adding to the business lineup in ways that overly stretch such nonfinancial resources as managerial talent, technology and information systems, and marketing support.

- *Does the company have or can it develop the specific resources and competitive capabilities needed to be successful in each of its businesses?*[11] Sometimes the resources a company has accumulated in its core business prove to be a poor match with the competitive capabilities needed to succeed in businesses into which it has diversified. For instance, BTR, a multibusiness company in Great Britain, discovered that the company's resources and managerial skills were quite well suited for parenting industrial manufacturing businesses but not for parenting its

 Resource fit extends beyond financial resources to include a good fit between the company's resources and core competencies and the key success factors of each industry it has diversified into.

distribution businesses (National Tyre Services and Texas-based Summers Group). As a result, BTR decided to divest its distribution businesses and focus exclusively on diversifying around small industrial manufacturing.

- *Are the company's resources being stretched too thinly by the resource requirements of one or more of its businesses?* A diversified company has to guard against overtaxing its resources, a condition that can arise when (1) it goes on an acquisition spree and management is called upon to assimilate and oversee many new businesses very quickly or (2) when it lacks sufficient resource depth to do a creditable job of transferring skills and competencies from one of its businesses to another.

Step 5: Ranking Business Units and Setting a Priority for Resource Allocation

Once a diversified company's businesses have been evaluated from the standpoints of industry attractiveness, competitive strength, strategic fit, and resource fit, the next step is to use this information to rank the performance prospects of the businesses from best to worst. Such rankings help top-level executives assign each business a priority for corporate resource support and new capital investment.

The locations of the different businesses in the nine-cell industry attractiveness/competitive strength matrix provide a solid basis for identifying high-opportunity businesses and low-opportunity businesses. Normally, competitively strong businesses in attractive industries have significantly better performance prospects than competitively weak businesses in unattractive industries. Also, normally, the revenue and earnings outlook for businesses in fast-growing businesses is better than for businesses in slow-growing businesses. As a rule, *business subsidiaries with the brightest profit and growth prospects, attractive positions in the nine-cell matrix, and solid strategic and resource fit should receive top priority for allocation of corporate resources.* However, in ranking the prospects of the different businesses from best to worst, it is usually wise to also consider each business's past performance as concerns sales growth, profit growth, contribution to company earnings, return on capital invested in the business, and cash flow from operations. While past performance is not always a reliable predictor of future performance, it does signal whether a business already has good to excellent performance or has problems to overcome.

Allocating Financial Resources   Figure 8.4 shows the chief strategic and financial options for allocating a diversified company's financial resources. Divesting businesses with the weakest future prospects and businesses that lack adequate strategic fit and/or resource fit is one of the best ways of generating additional funds for redeployment to businesses with better opportunities and better strategic and resource fit. Free cash flows from cash cow businesses also add to the pool of funds that can be usefully redeployed. *Ideally,* a diversified company will have sufficient financial resources to strengthen or grow its existing businesses, make any new acquisitions that are desirable, fund other promising business opportunities, pay off existing

▶FIGURE 8.4 **The Chief Strategic and Financial Options for Allocating a Diversified Company's Financial Resources**

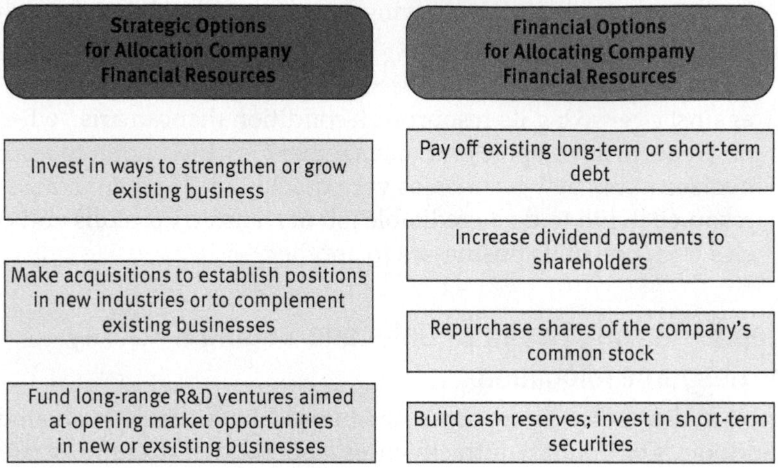

debt, and periodically increase dividend payments to shareholders and/or repurchase shares of stock. But, as a practical matter, a company's financial resources are limited. Thus, for top executives to make the best use of the available funds, they must steer resources to those businesses with the best opportunities and performance prospects and allocate little if any resources to businesses with marginal or dim prospects—this is why ranking the performance prospects of the various businesses from best to worst is so crucial. Strategic uses of corporate financial resources (see Figure 8.4) should usually take precedence unless there is a compelling reason to strengthen the firm's balance sheet or better reward shareholders.

Step 6: Crafting New Strategic Moves to Improve the Overall Corporate Performance

The conclusions flowing from the five preceding analytical steps set the agenda for crafting strategic moves to improve a diversified company's overall performance. The strategic options boil down to four broad categories of actions:

1. Sticking closely with the existing business lineup and pursuing the opportunities these businesses present.
2. Broadening the company's business scope by making new acquisitions in new industries.
3. Divesting some businesses and retrenching to a narrower base of business operations.
4. Restructuring the company's business lineup and putting a whole new face on the company's business makeup.

Sticking Closely with the Existing Business Lineup The option of sticking with the current business lineup makes sense when the company's present businesses offer attractive growth opportunities and can be counted

LO5

Understand a diversified company's four main corporate strategy options for solidifying its diversification strategy and improving company performance.

on to generate good earnings and cash flows. As long as the company's set of existing businesses puts it in a good position for the future and these businesses have good strategic and/or resource fit, then rocking the boat with major changes in the company's business mix is usually unnecessary. Corporate executives can concentrate their attention on getting the best performance from each of the businesses, steering corporate resources into those areas of greatest potential and profitability. However, in the event that corporate executives are not entirely satisfied with the opportunities they see in the company's present set of businesses, they can opt for any of the three strategic alternatives listed in the following sections.

Broadening the Diversification Base   Diversified companies sometimes find it desirable to add to the diversification base for any one of the same reasons a single business company might pursue initial diversification. Sluggish growth in revenues or profits, vulnerability to seasonality or recessionary influences, potential for transferring resources and capabilities to other related businesses, or unfavorable driving forces facing core businesses are all reasons management of a diversified company might choose to broaden diversification. An additional, and often very important, motivating factor for adding new businesses is to complement and strengthen the market position and competitive capabilities of one or more of its present businesses. Procter & Gamble's acquisition of Gillette strengthened and extended P&G's reach into personal care and household products—Gillette's businesses included Oral-B toothbrushes, Gillette razors and razor blades, Duracell batteries, Braun shavers and small appliances (coffeemakers, mixers, hair dryers, and electric toothbrushes), and toiletries (Right Guard, Foamy, Soft & Dry, White Rain, and Dry Idea).

Divesting Some Businesses and Retrenching to a Narrower Diversification Base   A number of diversified firms have had difficulty managing a diverse group of businesses and have elected to get out of some of them. Retrenching to a narrower diversification base is usually undertaken when top management concludes that its diversification strategy has ranged too far afield and that the company can improve long-term performance by concentrating on building stronger positions in a smaller number of core businesses

> Focusing corporate resources on a few core and mostly related businesses avoids the mistake of diversifying so broadly that resources and management attention are stretched too thin.

and industries. Hewlett-Packard spun off its testing and measurement businesses into a stand-alone company called Agilent Technologies so that it could better concentrate on its PC, workstation, server, printer and peripherals, and electronics businesses.

But there are other important reasons for divesting one or more of a company's present businesses. Sometimes divesting a business has to be considered because market conditions in a once-attractive industry have badly deteriorated. A business can become a prime candidate for divestiture because it lacks adequate strategic or resource fit, because it is a cash hog with questionable long-term potential, or because it is weakly positioned in its industry with little prospect of earning a decent return on investment. Sometimes a company acquires businesses that, down the road, just do not work out as expected even though management has tried all it can think of to make them profitable. Other business units, despite adequate financial performance, may not mesh as well with the rest of the firm as was originally thought. For instance, PepsiCo divested its group of fast-food restaurant businesses to focus its resources on its core soft drink and snack foods businesses, where their resources and capabilities could add more value.

Evidence indicates that pruning businesses and narrowing a firm's diversification base improves corporate performance.[12] Corporate parents often end up selling businesses too late and at too low a price, sacrificing shareholder value.[13] A useful guide to determine whether or when to divest a business subsidiary is to ask, "If we were not in this business today, would we want to get into it now?"[14] When the answer is no or probably not, divestiture should be considered. Another signal that a business should become a divestiture candidate is whether it is worth more to another company than to the present parent; in such cases, shareholders would be well served if the company were to sell the business and collect a premium price from the buyer for whom the business is a valuable fit.[15]

Selling a business outright to another company is far and away the most frequently used option for divesting a business. But sometimes a business selected for divestiture has ample resources to compete successfully on its own. In such cases, a corporate parent may elect to spin the unwanted business off as a financially and managerially independent company, either by selling shares to the investing public via an initial public offering or by distributing shares in the new company to existing shareholders of the corporate parent.

Broadly Restructuring the Business Lineup Through a Mix of Divestitures and New Acquisitions

Corporate restructuring strategies involve divesting some businesses and acquiring others so as to put a new face on the company's business lineup. Performing radical surgery on a company's group of businesses is an appealing corporate strategy when its financial performance is squeezed or eroded by:

CORE CONCEPT

Corporate restructuring involves radically altering the business lineup by divesting businesses that lack strategic fit or are poor performers and acquiring new businesses that offer better promise for enhancing shareholder value.

- Too many businesses in slow-growth, declining, low-margin, or otherwise unattractive industries.
- Too many competitively weak businesses.
- An excessive debt burden with interest costs that eat deeply into profitability.
- Ill-chosen acquisitions that haven't lived up to expectations.

Candidates for divestiture in a corporate restructuring effort typically include not only weak or up-and-down performers or those in unattractive industries but also business units that lack strategic fit with the businesses to be retained, businesses that are cash hogs or that lack other types of resource fit, and businesses incompatible with the company's revised diversification

---

 CONCEPTS & CONNECTIONS 8.1

VF'S CORPORATE RESTRUCTURING STRATEGY THAT MADE IT THE STAR OF THE APPAREL INDUSTRY

VF Corporation's corporate restructuring that included a mix of divestitures and acquisitions has provided its shareholders with returns that are more than five times greater than shareholder returns provided by competing apparel manufacturers. In fact, VF delivered a total shareholder return of 21 percent between 2000 and 2010, and its 2010 revenues of $7.7 billion made it number 310 on *Fortune*'s list of the 500 largest U.S. companies. The company's corporate restructuring began in 2000 when it divested its slow-growing businesses including its namesake Vanity Fair brand of lingerie and sleepwear. The company's $136 million acquisition of North Face in 2000 was the first in a series of many acquisitions of "lifestyle brands" that connected with the way people lived, worked, and played. Since the acquisition and turnaround of North Face, VF has spent nearly $5 billion to acquire 19 additional businesses, including about $2 billion in 2011 to acquire Timberland. New apparel brands acquired by VF Corporation include Timberland, Vans skateboard shoes, Nautica, John Varvatos, and 7 For All Mankind sportswear, Reef surf wear, and Lucy athletic wear. The company also acquired a variety of apparel companies specializing in apparel segments such as uniforms for professional baseball and football teams and law enforcement.

VF Corporation's acquisitions came after years of researching each company and developing a relationship with an acquisition candidate's chief managers before closing the deal. The company made a practice of leaving management of acquired companies in place, while bringing in new managers only when necessary talent and skills were lacking. In addition, companies acquired by VF were allowed to keep long-standing traditions that shaped culture and spurred creativity. For example, the Vans headquarters in Cypress, California, retained its half-pipe and concrete floor so that its employees could skateboard to and from meetings.

In 2010, VF Corporation was among the most profitable apparel firms in the industry with net earnings of $571 million. The company expected new acquisitions that would push the company's revenues to $8.5 billion in 2011.

Sources: Suzanne Kapner, "How a 100-Year-Old Apparel Firm Changed Course," *Fortune*, April 9, 2008, online edition; and www.vf.com, accessed July 26, 2011.

---

strategy (even though they may be profitable or in an attractive industry). As businesses are divested, corporate restructuring generally involves aligning the remaining business units into groups with the best strategic fit and then redeploying the cash flows from the divested business to either pay down debt or make new acquisitions.

Over the past decade, corporate restructuring has become a popular strategy at many diversified companies, especially those that had diversified broadly into many different industries and lines of business. In 2004, GE's CEO Jeffrey Immelt led GE's withdrawal from the insurance business by divesting several companies and spinning off others. He further restructured GE's business lineup with other major initiatives including (1) spending $10 billion to acquire British-based Amersham and extend GE's Medical Systems business into diagnostic pharmaceuticals and biosciences, thereby creating a $15 billion business designated as GE Healthcare and (2) acquiring the entertainment assets of debt-ridden French media conglomerate Vivendi Universal Entertainment and integrating its operations into GE's NBC division, thereby creating a broad-based $13 billion media business positioned to compete against Walt Disney, Time Warner, Fox, and Viacom. In 2009, GE agreed to sell a 51 percent stake in NBC Universal to Comcast for about $30 billion. Immelt suggested that the divestiture of its media business unit would allow the company to redeploy resources into its energy business. In 2011, the company spent approximately $8 billion to acquire Converteam, a French company that specialized in wind turbines and two oil-industry companies, John Wood Group and Dresser. Concepts & Connections 8.1 discusses how VF Corporation shareholders have benefited through the company's large-scale restructuring program.

KEY POINTS

1. The purpose of diversification is to build shareholder value. Diversification builds shareholder value when a diversified group of businesses can perform better under the auspices of a single corporate parent than they would as independent, stand-alone businesses—the goal is to achieve not just a $1 + 1 = 2$ result but rather to realize important $1 + 1 = 3$ performance benefits. Whether getting into a new business has potential to enhance shareholder value hinges on whether a company's entry into that business can pass the attractiveness test, the cost-of-entry test, and the better-off test.

2. Entry into new businesses can take any of three forms: acquisition, internal development, or joint venture/strategic partnership. Each has its pros and cons, but acquisition usually provides quickest entry into a new entry; internal development takes the longest to produce home-run results; and joint venture/strategic partnership tends to be the least durable.

3. There are two fundamental approaches to diversification—into related businesses and into unrelated businesses. The rationale for *related* diversification is based on cross-business *strategic fit:* Diversify into businesses with strategic fit along their respective value chains, capitalize on strategic fit relationships to gain competitive advantage, and then use competitive advantage to achieve the desired $1 + 1 = 3$ impact on shareholder value.

4. *Unrelated diversification* strategies surrender the competitive advantage potential of strategic fit. Given the absence of cross-business strategic fit, the task of building shareholder value through a strategy of unrelated diversification hinges on the ability of the parent company to: (1) do a superior job of identifying and acquiring new businesses that can produce consistently good earnings and returns on investment; (2) do an excellent job of negotiating favorable acquisition prices; and (3) do such a good job of overseeing and parenting the collection of businesses that they perform at a higher level than they would on their own efforts. The greater the number of businesses a company has diversified into and the more diverse these businesses are, the harder it is for corporate executives to select capable managers to run each business, know when the major strategic proposals of business units are sound, or decide on a wise course of recovery when a business unit stumbles.

5. Evaluating a company's diversification strategy is a six-step process:

   • Step 1: *Evaluate the long-term attractiveness of the industries into which the firm has diversified.* Determining industry attractiveness involves developing a list of industry attractiveness measures, each of which might have a different importance weight.

- Step 2: *Evaluate the relative competitive strength of each of the company's business units.* The purpose of rating each business's competitive strength is to gain clear understanding of which businesses are strong contenders in their industries, which are weak contenders, and the underlying reasons for their strength or weakness. The conclusions about industry attractiveness can be joined with the conclusions about competitive strength by drawing an industry attractiveness–competitive strength matrix that helps identify the prospects of each business and what priority each business should be given in allocating corporate resources and investment capital.

- Step 3: *Check for cross-business strategic fit.* A business is more attractive strategically when it has value chain relationships with sibling business units that offer the potential to (1) realize economies of scope or cost-saving efficiencies; (2) transfer technology, skills, know-how, or other resources and capabilities from one business to another; and/or (3) leverage use of a well-known and trusted brand name. Cross-business strategic fit represents a significant avenue for producing competitive advantage beyond what any one business can achieve on its own.

- Step 4: *Check whether the firm's resources fit the requirements of its present business lineup.* Resource fit exists when (1) businesses, individually, strengthen a company's overall mix of resources and capabilities and (2) a company has sufficient resources to support its entire group of businesses without spreading itself too thin. One important test of financial resource fit involves determining whether a company has ample cash cows and not too many cash hogs.

- Step 5: *Rank the performance prospects of the businesses from best to worst and determine what the corporate parent's priority should be in allocating resources to its various businesses.* The most important considerations in judging business-unit performance are sales growth, profit growth, contribution to company earnings, cash flow characteristics, and the return on capital invested in the business. Normally, strong business units in attractive industries should head the list for corporate resource support.

- Step 6: *Crafting new strategic moves to improve overall corporate performance.* This step entails using the results of the preceding analysis as the basis for selecting one of four different strategic paths for improving a diversified company's performance: *(a)* Stick closely with the existing business lineup and pursue opportunities presented by these businesses, *(b)* broaden the scope of diversification by entering additional industries, *(c)* retrench to a narrower scope of diversification by divesting poorly performing businesses, and *(d)* broadly restructure the business lineup with multiple divestitures and/or acquisitions.

➤➤➤ ASSURANCE OF LEARNING EXERCISES

1. See if you can identify the value chain relationships that make the businesses of the following companies related in competitively relevant ways. In particular, you should consider whether there are cross-business opportunities for *(a)* transferring competitively valuable resources, expertise, technological know-how and other capabilities, *(b)* cost sharing where value chain activities can be combined, and/or *(c)* leveraging use of a well-respected brand name.

LO1, LO2, LO3

www.mcgrawhillconnect.com

OSI Restaurant Partners

- Outback Steakhouse.
- Carrabba's Italian Grill.
- Roy's Restaurant (Hawaiian fusion cuisine).
- Bonefish Grill (Market-fresh fine seafood).
- Fleming's Prime Steakhouse & Wine Bar.
- Lee Roy Selmon's (Southern comfort food).
- Cheeseburger in Paradise.
- Blue Coral Seafood & Spirits (fine seafood).

L'Oréal

- Maybelline, Lancôme, Helena Rubenstein, Kiehl's, Garner, and Shu Uemura cosmetics.
- L'Oréal and Soft Sheen/Carson hair care products.
- Redken, Matrix, L'Oréal Professional, and Kerastase Paris professional hair care and skin care products.
- Ralph Lauren and Giorgio Armani fragrances.
- Biotherm skin care products.
- La Roche–Posay and Vichy Laboratories dermocosmetics.

Johnson & Johnson

- Baby products (powder, shampoo, oil, lotion).
- Band-Aids and other first-aid products.
- Women's health and personal care products (Stayfree, Carefree, Sure & Natural).
- Neutrogena and Aveeno skin care products.
- Nonprescription drugs (Tylenol, Motrin, Pepcid AC, Mylanta, Monistat).
- Prescription drugs.
- Prosthetic and other medical devices.
- Surgical and hospital products.
- Accuvue contact lenses.

LO1, LO2, LO3, LO4, LO5

2. Peruse the business group listings for United Technologies shown below and listed at its website (www.utc.com). How would you characterize the company's corporate strategy? Related diversification, unrelated diversification, or a combination related-unrelated diversification strategy? Explain your answer.

Carrier—the world's largest provider of air-conditioning, heating, and refrigeration solutions.

Hamilton Sundstrand—technologically advanced aerospace and industrial products.

Otis—the world's leading manufacturer, installer and maintainer of elevators, escalators and moving walkways.

Pratt & Whitney—designs, manufactures, services and supports aircraft engines, industrial gas turbines and space propulsion systems.

Sikorsky—a world leader in helicopter design, manufacture and service.